"Every Christian preacher must preach
Testament is made up of different genre.
own power and problems. Here are the musings of nineteen different scholars
who present the challenges and the benefits of these up-to-date ancient writings that should persuade a pastor to study the New Testament again for the
first time."

Haddon Robinson, Harold John Ockenga Professor of Preaching, Gordon-Conwell
Theological Seminary

"You will find in this collection of essays a treasure trove of convictions and
insights about preaching the New Testament that can nourish, challenge and
enrich any pastor's sermons. I read it eagerly and thankfully, in agreement and
disagreement, but with gratitude throughout."

Mark Labberton, Ogilvie Associate Professor of Preaching and director, Ogilvie Institute of
Preaching, Fuller Theological Seminary

"This is a first-rate set of essays from an international slate of contributors—
scholars and students of the New Testament who are also preachers themselves. In conversation with the best of evangelical scholarship, they boldly
address the challenges facing proclamation of the New Testament in a
postmodern context. At once intellectually profound and immediately practical, these studies offer a masterful combination of careful exegesis, incisive
theological reflection and balanced homiletical application for the life of the
church today."

Michael P. Knowles, George Franklin Hurlburt Professor of Preaching, McMaster Divinity
College, Hamilton, Ontario

PREACHING THE NEW TESTAMENT

Edited by IAN PAUL *&* DAVID WENHAM

IVP Academic

An imprint of InterVarsity Press
Downers Grove, Illinois

InterVarsity Press
P.O. Box 1400, Downers Grove, IL 60515-1426
Internet: www.ivpress.com
Email: email@ivpress.com

This collection © Inter-Varsity Press, 2013

InterVarsity Press® is the book-publishing division of InterVarsity Christian Fellowship/USA®, a movement of students and faculty active on campus at hundreds of universities, colleges and schools of nursing in the United States of America, and a member movement of the International Fellowship of Evangelical Students. For information about local and regional activities, write Public Relations Dept., InterVarsity Christian Fellowship/USA, 6400 Schroeder Rd., P.O. Box 7895, Madison, WI 53707-7895, or visit the IVCF website at www.intervarsity.org.

ISBN 978-0-8308-3990-2

Printed in the United States of America ∞

Library of Congress Cataloging-in-Publication Data
A catalog record for this book is available from the Library of Congress.

P	23	22	21	20	19	18	17	16	15	14	13	12	11	10	9	8	7	6	5	4	3	2	1
Y	33	32	31	30	29	28	27	26	25	24	23	22	21	20	19	18	17	16	15	14	13		

CONTENTS

CONTRIBUTORS

Charles A. Anderson is a pastor at The Crossing in Columbia, Missouri. He was previously Lecturer in Biblical Studies at Oak Hill College, London.

D. A. Carson is Research Professor at Trinity Evangelical Divinity School, Deerfield, Illinois.

R. T. France, who died in February 2012, was a former Principal and New Testament Tutor at Wycliffe Hall, Oxford.

Justin K. Hardin is Tutor in New Testament at Wycliffe Hall, Oxford, and is a member of the Faculty of Theology at the University of Oxford.

Mariam J. Kamell is Assistant Professor of New Testament at Regent College, Vancouver.

I. Howard Marshall is Professor Emeritus of New Testament at Aberdeen University.

Jason Maston is Tutor in New Testament at Highland Theological College, Dingwall.

John Nolland is visiting Professor in New Testament at Trinity College, Bristol, and Professor at Bristol University.

Peter Oakes is Greenwood Senior Lecturer in the New Testament at Manchester University.

William Olhausen is Rector of St Matthias Church, Killiney-Ballybrack, Republic of Ireland.

Ian Paul is Dean of Studies at St John's College, Nottingham.

Klyne Snodgrass is Professor of New Testament Studies at the North Park Theological Seminary, Chicago, Illinois.

Helge Stadelmann is Professor of Practical Theology at the Giessen School of Theology (FTH Giessen), Germany, and the Evangelische Theologische Faculteit Leuven, Belgium.

Christoph Stenschke is Professor of New Testament at Forum Wiedenest, Bergneustadt, and the University of South Africa.

Stephen Travis was Vice-Principal and Lecturer in New Testament Studies at St John's College, Nottingham.

David Wenham is Senior Lecturer in New Testament at Trinity College, Bristol.

Paul Weston is Tutor in Mission and Homiletics at Ridley Hall, Cambridge.

Stephen I. Wright is Director of Postgraduate Research and Tutor in Biblical Studies and Practical Theology at Spurgeon's College, London.

ABBREVIATIONS

AB	Anchor Bible
AcT	*Acta theologica*
AD	Anno Domini (after Christ)
AFCS	Acts in Its First Century Setting
AV	Authorized (King James) Version of the Bible
BBR	*Bulletin for Biblical Research*
BECNT	Baker Exegetical Commentary on the New Testament
Bib	*Biblica*
BR	*Biblical Research*
BST	The Bible Speaks Today
BZNW	Beihefte zur Zeitschrift für die neutestamentliche Wissenschaft
CBQ	*Catholic Biblical Quarterly*
CBR	*Currents in Biblical Research*
CJT	*Canadian Journal of Theology*
EJT	*European Journal of Theology*
esp.	especially
ET	English Translation
EvQ	*Evangelical Quarterly*
EvT	*Evangelische Theologie*
ExpTim	*Expository Times*

FRLANT	Forschungen zur Religion und Literatur des Alten und Neuen Testaments
HTR	*Harvard Theological Review*
IBC	Interpretation: A Bible Commentary for Teaching and Preaching
IBS	*Irish Biblical Studies*
ICC	International Critical Commentary
IVPNTC	Inter-Varsity Press New Testament Commentary
JBL	*Journal of Biblical Literature*
JSNT	*Journal for the Study of the New Testament*
JSNTSup	Journal for the Study of the New Testament, Supplement Series
LCL	Loeb Classical Library
LEC	Library of Early Christianity
LXX	Septuagint
NETR	*Near East School of Theology Theological Review*
NICNT	New International Commentary on the New Testament
NIDNTT	*New International Dictionary of New Testament Theology*, ed. C. Brown, 3 vols. (Exeter: Paternoster, 1975, 1976, 1978)
NIGTC	New International Greek Testament Commentary
NIV	New International Version of the Bible
NIVAC	New International Version Application Commentary
nos.	numbers
NovTSup	Novum Testamentum Supplements
NRSV	New Revised Standard Version of the Bible
NSBT	New Studies in Biblical Theology
NT	New Testament
NTAbh	Neutestamentliche Abhandlungen
NTG	New Testament Guides
NTS	*New Testament Studies*
OCD	*Oxford Classical Dictionary*, ed. S. Hornblower and A. Spawforth, *Oxford Classical Dictionary*, 3rd ed. (Oxford: Oxford University Press, 1996)
OT	Old Testament
par.	parallel(s)
PNTC	Pillar New Testament Commentary
RevExp	*Review and Expositor*
RSV	Revised Standard Version of the Bible
RV	Revised Version of the Bible
SNTSMS	Society for New Testament Studies Monograph Series
SP	Sacra pagina
SwJT	*South Western Journal of Theology*

Them	*Themelios*
TLZ	*Theologische Literatur Zeitung*
TNIV	Today's New International Version
TNTC	Tyndale New Testament Commentaries
tr.	translation, translated by
TynB	*Tyndale Bulletin*
WBC	Word Biblical Commentary
WUNT	Wissenschaftliche Untersuchungen zum Neuen Testament

INTRODUCTION

Ian Paul and David Wenham

Preaching matters. Paul Scott Wilson, in the first edition of his *The Practice of Preaching*, makes a bold claim:

> I believe that the sermon is not the dilution of theology; it is rather the completion of theology, made complete through Christ speaking it and constituting the church through it. We might even say that the church is most truly the church when it is preaching in worship, for it is through the Word and sacrament that salvation comes to the world, and it is through our lives being transformed in the cruciform image that our acts of justice, mercy, peace and love are begun once more in power.[1]

This implies that whatever we know about the New Testament, however much we have studied it, whatever truths we have mined there, have real value only as they are proclaimed so that the lives of others (and our lives with them) are transformed by this truth. Darrell Johnson makes a similarly bold claim. When God speaks, lives are changed. When we preach faithfully, we are participating in God's speech. So when we preach, we are participating in God's transformation of his world.[2]

---

1. Paul Scott Wilson, *The Practice of Preaching* (Nashville: Abingdon, 1995), p. 70.
2. Hence the subtitle of his book *The Glory of Preaching: Participating in God's Transformation of the World* (Downers Grove: IVP Academic, 2009).

But for those committed to the importance of Scripture in teaching and discipleship there arises a paradoxical question: Why preach at all? In his classic volume on preaching, John Stott sets out an argument for the importance of biblical preaching. It works through the statements God is light; God has acted; God has spoken; Scripture is God's word written; God still speaks through what he has spoken; God's word is powerful.[3] This still leaves a question: Why the need to preach? Why not simply read Scripture together, and allow it to have its powerful, transforming effect? After all, many in Christian history have been converted, challenged and changed by the simple reading of Scripture – and in many places Scripture itself makes the assumption that reading (or hearing) on its own will be sufficient. In fact, much of what forms our Scriptures was in the first place preaching or proclamation – from Moses, through the prophets, to Jesus and Paul.

Yet at a key point in the Old Testament there comes a change. In Nehemiah 8, following the rebuilding of the walls of Jerusalem, the people assemble to hear Ezra reading from the Book of Moses. What is particularly interesting is that there are Levites stationed around the platform, 'making it clear [or 'translating it'] and giving the meaning so that the people understood what was being read' (v. 8). So, for the first time, Scripture itself makes clear that reading Scripture alone is not enough. A gap has opened up between people and text, and it is a gap that needs bridging. The text of Nehemiah is not specific about what that gap is – a spiritual gap, opened up by the disobedience that brought exile? Is it a cultural gap, where the returning people are at a cultural distance from the people they are reading about? Is it one of language – does this text now need translation? Whatever the reason, the gap needs bridging; the message of the written word needs articulation in a spoken word if it is to become a living word to the people once again. We see the same moment of transition, from a self-explanatory text to one that needs interpretation, hinted at in Peter's description of Paul's teaching as 'hard to understand' and open to 'distortion' (2 Pet. 3:16).

So this book is about Christian preaching and in particular about preaching the New Testament.[4] It addresses the question of bridging the gap primarily from the end of the text, rather than from that of the listeners. How should we preach in a way that is faithful, and is not just a case of our hanging some

---

3. John R. W. Stott, *I Believe in Preaching* (London: Hodder & Stoughton, 1982), pp. 92–108.

4. On the OT see G. J. R. Kent, P. J. Kissling and L. A. Turner (eds.), *'He Began with Moses . . .': Preaching the Old Testament Today* (Nottingham: Inter-Varsity Press, 2010).

thoughts on to a biblical hook? We are not in this volume writing about preaching technique or how to be rhetorically effective, though that is not an unimportant question. Many scholars believe that the New Testament writers were very interested in conveying their message persuasively, and so we should do the same. This book is not about persuasive communication, but is a contribution from New Testament scholars who are also preachers, sharing some insights about how to interpret and communicate the New Testament today. It is not designed as a scholarly book for scholars either on hermeneutics or on the biblical writings themselves, but it is a book informed by scholarship and designed to be useful to preachers who are at the coalface of ministry.

It has been said that interpreting the Bible is like translating from one language to another. Good and effective translation can happen only if two things are true, namely that the translators know (1) the original language of what they are translating, and (2) the language into which they are translating. A failure at either end is serious, maybe even fatal, and we are all familiar with the multilingual instructions on a particular product that are humorously wrong, if nothing worse. Faithful interpretation of the Bible requires a similar combination of skills – skill in understanding the biblical text in its own context and horizon, and then skill in conveying the meaning of the text into our context and contexts.

And this is a challenging task. It is a challenge, both to the understanding and the imagination, to get into the original context and into the mind of the writer. Moving from one language and culture to another is hard enough in the same era – see the humorous instruction on the packet. Moving across centuries and back in history is much more difficult, and we cannot interrogate the original speaker or writer to ask, 'What did you mean?' At least the process of interrogation has to be much more indirect and is much more difficult. There are not only questions about the meaning of words, which anyway can mean many different things in different contexts, but also questions of genre, emphasis and culture. What is needed is a historically disciplined imagination. We need imagination to recognize that the situation of the writer and first readers was different from the situation we ourselves are in, and discipline to recognize the boundaries of possible meaning for that first audience.

At the dawn of the modern era, advocates of the historical-critical method believed that they could determine the objective meaning of the text with certainty. Now, at the dawn of the postmodern era, we are faced with the opposite challenge – the idea that there is no objectivity in meaning, and one interpretation is as good as another. This book is written with the conviction that neither is true. No one has infallible access to an objective, non-negotiable view of what a text means. But some views are more convincing than others, and it is possible to say things about a text with good reason and conviction. The chapters in this volume aim to set out those things, to do them with critical judgment but also with awareness of the writer's own situation. There is no infallible route to a perfectly objective interpretation, but Christians have historically and defensibly believed that God has revealed himself in history and that we do have access to that revelation, even granted our imperfect lenses and the inevitable provisionality of some of our judgments. This book makes no claims to infallibility, but it arises out of the conviction that there are useful things to say about right and wrong ways to interpret and apply the New Testament.

The book is not exhaustive, and some readers may be disappointed not to find neat answers to their particular questions, whether about specific texts (such as 1 Peter on preaching to the spirits in prison) or about bigger issues. For example, one contentious question concerns whether the healing ministry of Jesus, which he then shared with the disciples, is a ministry that we should expect to see reproduced in the church today. There is no easy answer to such questions, and this book will not give all the answers. But it does aim to offer a useful way into the question of preaching the New Testament, which will encourage followers of Jesus not just to follow his moral example, but to follow him in being effective teachers of God's kingdom, truth and way.

This volume came out of a meeting of the New Testament Group of the Tyndale Fellowship for Biblical and Theological Research held in July 2011. We are grateful not just to the authors but to participants at the conference and to all who have contributed through their comments and advice.

We are glad to have in this volume Dick France's chapter 'Preaching on the Infancy Narratives'. Dick died after an unexpected and short illness in February 2012 at the age of 73, and his chapter is probably the last thing he wrote for publication. Dick was a much-loved friend and colleague of many of the contributors to the volume, and was a model preacher and teacher of the New Testament. He wrestled seriously and expertly with the text and its meaning, as his many writings and commentaries attest, but he was also totally committed to communicating the message of the New Testament to today's world. At his funeral there were moving testimonies to his humble and faithful preaching and teaching ministry in the West of Wales where he lived before his death. We are dedicating this volume to his memory, with thankfulness for someone who followed Jesus in his life and teaching.

1. PREACHING THE GOSPELS

D. A. Carson

To write a brief chapter on how to preach the Gospels feels a bit like offering a how-to manual prescribing how to paint the ceiling of the Sistine Chapel by introducing paint-by-numbers.[1] It is not just that the real task has complexities that mock such reductionism; there is also the little matter of the unquantifiable gifts and calling of the preacher. Moreover, there is nothing to substitute for unction, for which careful instruction, no matter how important, is no substitute. So what follows makes no pretension of comprehensiveness. Rather, presupposing that readers already enjoy some background and experience in expository preaching, this chapter offers seven observations – bits of advice, really – in the hope of enriching the ministry of those who preach the Gospels.

Knowing what the Gospels are about

The Gospels are about Jesus. More particularly, they are about Jesus' coming, his earthly ministry (including his works and his words), all rushing towards

---

1. I prefer to say 'Preaching the Gospels' rather than 'Preaching from the Gospels' because the former focuses on what the content of the sermon should be while the latter opens up the possibility of using the Gospels as little more than a springboard.

the cross and resurrection. This seems so obvious it scarcely needs saying – yet it does need saying, and the preacher must remember it for at least four reasons.

First, it is now well known that first-century Christians did not speak of four Gospels – the Gospel of Matthew, the Gospel of Mark, and so on – but of one gospel, the gospel of Jesus Christ, *according to* Matthew, Mark, Luke and John. Not until the second century did 'gospel' become a label for a distinctive literary genre in the New Testament. That means that in the eyes of the human authors and first readers the Gospels had more in common than is commonly allowed today in some scholarly circles, where the emphasis is placed on differences and discontinuities. I will say more about their distinctive differences below, but it is premature to reflect at length on their differences until we grasp their fundamental commonality: they are all about the good news of Jesus Christ, and the preacher must not forget this point.

This reality simultaneously distinguishes the four canonical Gospels from second- and third-century Gospels, and focuses our attention on what is of primary importance. The so-called *Gospel of Thomas*, for instance, is not a Gospel in a first-century sense at all. It carries no narrative (apart from two or three tiny snippets), and it does not steer its readers towards the cross and resurrection. It is a sayings-source, almost certainly a secondary one. Only the first-century Gospels, that is, the canonical Gospels, have this 'one gospel' feature in common: the good news of Jesus, including his teaching and works of power, rushing towards his cross and resurrection. One remembers how the apostle Paul insists that the matters 'of first importance' centre on Jesus' death and resurrection (1 Cor. 15:3): in this he shares with first-century writers and readers the significance of our canonical Gospels. Those who preach these Gospels must never lose sight of this central affirmation.

Secondly, this suggests that approaches to preaching the Gospels that focus on, say, the teaching of Jesus abstracted from the cross and resurrection of Jesus, or the parables of Jesus taught in so open-ended a way that we overlook their place in the developing argument of books that are driving towards the cross and resurrection, are fundamentally reductionistic at best, and may be frankly misleading. I will enlarge on this point from a slightly different angle below. The converse is also true: attempts to expound the cross and resurrection in each of the Gospels without unpacking how this climactic theme pulls together all the preceding material, including teaching about the kingdom (especially in the Synoptics) and eternal life (especially in John), are not listening with sufficient attentiveness to the massive Christocentricity of these documents.

Thirdly, if the focus is on the good news of Jesus Christ, then the Gospels are not *primarily* about the nature of discipleship, the profiles of true believers or how to engage in evangelism. True, each of the four Gospels addresses themes such as these, but they are always derivative themes tied to who Jesus is and why he came. For the preacher this means that if a sermon series on any one of the canonical Gospels spends much more time on some facet of discipleship than on the person and work of Christ, the priorities laid down by these four books have become skewed. To allude once again to Paul: the apostle confesses that he determined to do nothing but preach Christ crucified – and, rightly understood, that is precisely what these four books do.

Fourthly, the Gospels show how the coming-to-faith of the apostles and others is *different* from any coming-to-faith today. We preachers frequently draw lines to show the commonalities and to stimulate application, and certainly there are some lessons we can learn from, say, the belief, unbelief or restoration of the apostle Peter, the doubt of Thomas, the successes and failures of the apostles' first attempts at public ministry – all lessons readily and happily applied today. But we dare not overlook that at Caesarea Philippi (Mark 8 par. Matt. 16), where Peter makes his great Christological confession, what he means by confessing Jesus as the promised Messiah is not exactly what any Christian means today. True, Jesus assures Peter that his insight is the fruit of divine revelation: while others have doubts, Peter is convinced that Jesus really is the promised Christ. But no Christian today can think of Christ without including in the mental picture his death and resurrection. By contrast, the ensuing verses demonstrate rather dramatically that Peter had no category whatsoever for a crucified Christ. In other words, Peter's coming to what we might call full Christian faith depended in part on the passage of time until the next major salvation-historical appointment, the death and resurrection of the Son of God. However much we insist that the apostles should have grasped this point sooner than they did, the records show that they did not – and in this respect their coming-to-faith is different from ours. When people come to faith today, they may have to wait quite a long time until they understand the nature of the gospel, or overcome their doubts, or their sin becomes ugly enough in their eyes to draw them towards repentance, but they do *not* have to wait on God's timing for the advent of the next great redemptive-historical event.

Another way of making the same point is to say that the Gospel writers are less interested in the psychological profile of how people come to faith than in unpacking who Jesus is – in particular, how we got from there to here, from perceptions of divine mercy and salvation under the old covenant to perceptions of divine mercy and salvation under the new, from Old

Testament promises of a coming redeemer to the insistence that Jesus fulfils those promises, however badly even his own followers understood them until Jesus himself drew the strands together that showed him to be, simultaneously, the promised Davidic Son of God and the Passover Lamb (John), the Conquering King and the Suffering Servant (Matthew). This drumming theme – how we got from there to here – lies behind much of the apostles' jerky coming-to-faith, a coming-to-faith that could not be complete until Jesus' cross and resurrection (and, one might argue, until the coming of the Spirit, especially, though not exclusively, in Luke-Acts and John). Yet another way of making the same point is the way the Gospel writers use an array of devices to alert readers to the fact that the people in the story they are telling have not yet arrived at full Christian understanding. Matthew, for instance, reminds his readers that the person John the Baptist is doubting is in fact the Messiah (Matt. 11:2 – he normally simply uses 'Jesus').[2] In John's Gospel people frequently speak better than they know, and John points it out in order to make clear what is *really* going on, even if the people in the narrative do not yet perceive it: the best known instance, though certainly not the only one, is of course Caiaphas (John 11:49–52).

All of this means that the focus is on Jesus himself, and especially how he is the goal – or, if we change the image, the fulcrum – of God's redemptive purposes. The partial or even failed understandings of the participants in the narrative function to point to him, not to provide a profile of a generic coming-to-faith.

In short, if we preach the Gospels faithfully, we will focus supremely on preaching Jesus Christ.

Recognizing the kind of writing

The substantial literature that debates what kind of genre a canonical Gospel is – akin to an ancient biography, perhaps, or *sui generis* – is sometimes in danger of overlooking how many genres are found *within* each Gospel: narrative, genealogy, proverb, discourse, parable, apocalyptic, and more. The preacher will be careful not to treat each of these exactly the same way, for each has its own way of conveying information and making its rhetorical appeal. Beyond

---

2. See D. A. Carson, 'Christological Ambiguities in Matthew', in Harold H. Rowdon (ed.), *Christ the Lord: Studies in Christology* (Festschrift for Donald Guthrie; Leicester: Inter-Varsity Press, 1982), pp. 97–114.

distinctions in literary genre, the Gospels deploy a wide variety of rhetorical devices. Matthew and John, for instance, frequently use irony, Mark and Luke much less so.

The important thing for preachers to remember as they unpack such devices or carefully negotiate a distinctive literary genre is that they must not only wear their learning lightly, but ensure that their sermon does not so draw attention to the genre or the literary device that attention is drawn away from Christ and the focus of the particular unit, with the result that they elicit more admiration for the cleverness of the author (or, God help us, the preacher) than for what the biblical text actually says. Just as an effective literary device or a distinctive genre does its best work without drawing attention to itself, so the preacher who unpacks the text will aim to preserve the same priorities.

Looking at the longer units

Gifted expositors are capable of working through Gospels at a slow pace, line by line, in much the same way that they handle, say, Romans. When they succeed in this approach, they are often dealing with discourse material (e.g. the Sermon on the Mount). For most of us, however, the Gospels afford a fine opportunity to choose longer units of text than the half-verse – and this for at least three reasons.

First, many of the natural longer units within Gospel texts cry out to be treated as a whole. The obvious example is parables, but they could rapidly be followed by miracle stories, resurrection accounts and blocks of controversies. It is *possible* to pick such units apart and devote several sermons to each, but for most of us it is questionable whether it is *wise* to do so.

Secondly, a great deal is to be said for showing how strings of pericopae flow together. For example, although it would be entirely appropriate to devote a single sermon to Matthew 8:1–4, it may help people understand their Bibles if they hear a sermon on Matthew 8:1–17. In the preceding verses, Matthew 7 closes with an emphasis on Jesus' authority in his teaching; in 8:1–13 we find a corresponding emphasis on Jesus' authority in several decisive deeds and utterances. In particular: (1) The authority of Jesus to heal and transform is implicit in his person and mission (8:1–3). (2) The authority of Jesus, formally submissive to the law of Moses, in fact both transcends and fulfils it (8:4). (3) The authority of Jesus is so sweeping that when he speaks, God speaks (8:5–9). (4) The authority of Jesus is a great comfort to the eyes of faith and a great terror to the merely religious (8:10–13). (5) The authority of Jesus is a function of his work on the cross (8:14–17).[3] This outline could easily be introduced or concluded with further thematic ties to Jesus' authority elsewhere in Matthew (e.g. the closing Great Commission, 28:18–20). In the past I have preached five individual sermons on the block of material from Matthew 24:36 to Matthew 25:46, but I have also covered all of this material in one sermon, under the rubric 'How to wait for Jesus' return'.[4]

Thirdly, the Gospel of John is a special case. It has a great deal of discourse material in it, so preachers who enjoy moving through such material slowly have often turned to this Gospel and proceeded slowly. Nevertheless, the Gospel of John operates with fewer themes than do the Synoptics, with the result that many preachers begin to tackle the book, intending to cover all twenty-one chapters, and peter out after a while, because they find themselves repeating themselves and saying things similar to what they have said in preceding sermons. For instance, the apparent theological 'point' of many sections is encouragement to believe. One way to address this challenge is to expound longer units and focus on what each unit says *about Jesus Christ*, with the intent of encouraging people to believe. The rich diversity comes from the way this Gospel unpacks Jesus, even if its application tends to be narrower (or perhaps more pointedly focused) than what one finds in the Synoptics (e.g. John has little of the ethical breadth of the Sermon on the Mount).

Living inside a Gospel

In line with the way one ought to prepare to preach *any* book of the Bible, the preacher needs to live inside a Gospel for a while before trying to preach any part of it. Reading it through at a single sitting, several times, is a great way to begin; for those who have the training, working carefully through the text in Greek during preceding months will prove personally rewarding and homiletically enriching. For although it is true that in some ways the four Gospels tell the one, same, story (as we have seen), yet each covers the material from a distinctive angle, with distinctive emphases.

This is the place to reflect a little on the place of Gospel harmonies. So

---

3. The outline derives from the first chapter of D. A. Carson, *When Jesus Confronts the World: An Exposition of Matthew 8–10* (Leicester: Inter-Varsity Press, 1987).

4. E.g. D. A. Carson, 'Waiting for the Kingdom, Waiting for the King', *The Gospel Witness* 67 (1988), pp. 277–286 <http://s3.amazonaws.com/tgc-documents/carson/1988_waiting_for_kingdom_King.pdf>, accessed 28 June 2012.

far as our records go, harmonies have been around since the second century, when Tatian produced his work for Syriac-speaking churches. Numerous harmonies are available today, in both English and Greek. They can be very helpful to the preacher trying to make sense of how various units in the four Gospels fit together *historically* (e.g. How do the first five chapters of John relate to the Synoptics, which include none of that material? What materials, like the feeding of the five thousand, are found in all four Gospels? Is it possible and wise to order the resurrection appearances?). Calvin's justly famous exposition of the Gospels is essentially an exposition of a harmony. Yet there is an important drawback to this approach. When the Gospels were first written, they were circulated as independent books, and read and preached as independent books. The last evangelist to write (probably John) did not say to himself, 'I'm now going to produce a supplement in order to enrich the preaching of harmonies.' He wrote a *book* that he wanted to be read and taught in the circles he envisaged. This is not to deny the insight of Bauckham and others who have strongly argued that the Gospels were intended to be read by *all* Christians, not some hermetically sealed-off community.[5] Rather, even if we accept this thesis without demurral, the fact remains that each evangelist wrote his own book. Each of the four canonical Gospels makes its own contribution to the canon, to the Word of God written, and the preacher's *first* job is to be faithful to what has been written, not simply to his own harmony of what has been written.[6] Of course, one must also add that some critics use this insight to drive as many wedges as possible among the Gospels (one thinks of a Bart Ehrman), but more sober scholarship much prefers to think in terms of complementary visions. Still, if one works only with a harmony, one is likely to overlook the distinctive contributions and emphases of each book – addressing wealth in Luke, profound reflections on believing and eternal life in John, and so forth.

So live inside the book you are expounding. It is helpful to read commentaries and biblical theologies, of course, but above all read and reread the book. Observe the distinctive emphases bound up with vocabulary choices, themes and development of the plotline. It is the tracing out of the plotline in each book that will spare the preacher from making ghastly mistakes generated by

---

5. Richard Bauckham (ed.), *The Gospels for All Christians: Rethinking the Gospel Audiences* (Grand Rapids: Eerdmans, 1998).

6. At the popular level, preachers could usefully peruse T. D. Alexander, *Discovering Jesus: Why Four Gospels to Portray One Person?* (Wheaton: Crossway; Nottingham: Inter-Varsity Press, 2010).

focusing so narrowly on the text at hand that he cannot see its place in the flow. For example, it is well known that Luke describes Jesus resolutely setting out for Jerusalem and the cross from 9:51 on: the so-called Lucan travel narrative shapes how one ought to read the account all the way to chapter 19. Luke regularly groups blocks of material in various topical ways, but the marker in 9:51 warns us that in Luke's mind the trajectory towards the cross carries huge significance. Among other things, that means that any interpreter should be asking what each pericope contributes to the journey to Jerusalem, and, conversely, what Jesus' commitment to take the road to Jerusalem says about the meaning of each pericope. Read the parable of the good Samaritan (10:25–37) in splendid isolation, and you may be tempted to imagine that Jesus is teaching that the manner in which we inherit eternal life in line with the achievement of obedience envisaged by the lawyer – loving God with heart and soul and strength and mind, and one's neighbour as oneself – is precisely by behaving like the Samaritan. If things are as cut and dried as that, why is Jesus resolutely heading for the cross? How does the parable of the Good Samaritan tie itself to the pericopae that immediately precede and succeed it? That Jesus demands such behaviour is clear ('Go and do likewise', 10:37); yet the way it is configured in the flow of the narrative demands a more sensitive reading than that suggested by merit theology.

Close reading of a Gospel – indeed, of any book – will allow the interpreter to discover structures that have interpretative importance, along with relatively minor themes that may also have interpretative significance – structures and themes that will add depth and zest to many sermons. For example, if we remain for a moment with the parable of the Good Samaritan (Luke 10:25–37), the unit unfolds in two dialogues with the same structure. In the first dialogue (10:25–29) (1) the lawyer asks a question (v. 25), (2) Jesus responds by asking his own question (v. 26),[7] (3) the lawyer answers Jesus' question (v. 27), and only then (4) does Jesus answer the lawyer's question (v. 28). The pattern is then repeated in the second dialogue: (1) the lawyer asks his question (v. 29), then (2) Jesus poses his question (v. 36) – and what we call the parable of the good Samaritan is simply Jesus' set-up for his question.

---

7. Randy Newman, *Questioning Evangelism* (Grand Rapids: Kregel, 2004), draws attention to the many times in which Jesus answers a question with his own question, and infers lessons that would be useful to any preacher. Cf. also Stan Guthrie, *All That Jesus Asks: How His Questions Can Teach and Transform Us* (Grand Rapids: Baker, 2010); Robert H. Stein, *The Method and Message of Jesus' Teaching*, 2nd ed. (Louisville: Westminster John Knox, 1994).

That is the framework in which the parable must be understood. Only then (3) does the lawyer answer Jesus' question (v. 37a), followed (4) by Jesus' answer to the lawyer (v. 37b).

These observations drive us to observe a couple of minor themes. The question the lawyer raises in the first dialogue is introduced by Luke's acerbic comment that he 'stood up to test Jesus' (v. 25). That links up with many depictions of rising opposition to Jesus, including some where certain individuals are not asking their questions in order to gain wisdom but in the hope they might 'catch Jesus in something he said' (20:20). More interesting is Luke's comment regarding the lawyer's motives as he poses the first question in the *second* dialogue. 'But *he wanted to justify himself*', Luke comments, 'so he asked Jesus, "And who is my neighbour?"' (10:29). The minor theme of self-justification is not hard to find in Luke's Gospel. From reading elsewhere in the New Testament we learn that 'justification' frequently depicts *God's* declaring *sinners* to be just, on the basis of what he has done for them in Christ. On one axis, the opposite of such justification is *self*-justification, in which *sinners* declare *themselves* to be just. Transparently, that is what is going on in this passage (10:29). In chapter 16, where Jesus says many pointed things about money, Luke tells us, 'The Pharisees, who loved money, heard all this and were sneering at Jesus' (16:14). This prompts Jesus to tell them, 'You are the ones *who justify yourselves in the eyes of others*, but God knows your hearts' (16:15). In chapter 18 Jesus tells the parable of the Pharisee and the tax collector. Only the broken and contrite man 'went home *justified before God*' (18:14). The other man, busily thanking God that he is not like other men, is so busy justifying himself that he sees no need to be justified by God. Self-justification is a sufficiently important minor theme in Luke that it surfaces even when the vocabulary of justification is not deployed.

It would be easy to discuss many other themes that surface in one or more of the canonical Gospels:[8] they lie there waiting to be uncovered by patient reading and rereading of the biblical text. Once uncovered, they enrich our attempts to preach the Gospels responsibly and accurately. Instead of teasing out more structures and themes, however, to close this section I will draw attention to another phenomenon that emerges from close reading of the Gospels. I am referring to material that apparently clashes with what is found in other Gospels. The best known of these clashes occur between

---

8. See D. A. Carson and Douglas J. Moo, *An Introduction to the New Testament*, 2nd ed. (Grand Rapids: Zondervan; Leicester: Apollos 2005), pp. 162–165, 192–194, 219–221, 276–278. Consult also many of the NT theologies now available.

John and the Synoptics, but there are intra-Synoptic tensions as well. Of the large anomalies, probably none is better known than John's placement of the cleansing of the temple in John 2 rather than during Holy Week. But there are many subtler anomalies, illustrated, for example, by the debates surrounding John's calendar of events surrounding the cross. Does John have Jesus die on Passover? How can his dates be sorted out so as to make sense of the Synoptic witness? Theologically? By appealing to another calendar? Are there better interpretations of crucial passages, interpretations that apparently resolve the discrepancy?

For the purposes of this chapter, it is enough to suggest how a preacher ought to proceed when confronted by such passages.

First, read widely enough in the commentaries that you do not automatically gravitate to the first 'solution' you stumble across. Complex issues almost always admit several ways of approaching the problem.

Secondly, be prepared to offer a solution in terms of probabilities: for example, 'Of the various solutions that have been put forward, perhaps the most credible is . . .' – or something of that order. In other words, many problems in Gospel harmonization are not so much incapable of resolution, as prohibitive of reasonable certainty. It is not that there are no answers, but that there are too many possible answers and too little information to warrant a strong voice on any of them.

Thirdly, do not use up much sermon time dealing with such issues. You may have to do enough work on the problem that you are reasonably clear in your mind as to which solution is most plausible (or least implausible!), but that does not mean you necessarily have to drop all your information and reasoning into the minds of the members of the congregation. Most such questions are the sorts of things you can address adequately in thirty seconds. That you have done so will alert the handful of people in the congregation who are aware of the problem that you have done your homework, and if any of them are troubled (e.g. undergraduate students in biblical studies), they will then feel free to approach you afterward for further information and bibliography.

Fourthly, it is almost always wise in such discussions to avoid expressions that sound vaguely superior or self-promoting: for example, 'Although most scholars think such-and-such, I have come to the conclusion that this-and-that.'

Fifthly, the only occasions when at least *a little* more time in the sermon should be devoted to one of these perceived problems occur when (1) the way you address the problem has a direct bearing on the theological message you find in the passage, or (2) the manner in which you handle the text, complete with both knowledge and humility, becomes important as a way of modelling what it means to bow before Scripture with godly integrity.

Planning the series

One of the most difficult decisions to make is how long a series you are planning to undertake. At least five overlapping considerations play into such decisions.

First, the length of the passage you choose: the shorter the passage, the longer it takes to get through a block of material (an entire Gospel, for instance, or a sizable section within a Gospel, such as the Sermon on the Mount or the Farewell Discourse). If you preach on half a verse per Sunday, your series could last for years.

Secondly, the congregation: congregations are exceedingly variable, not only with respect to their average level of education and propensity to read, but, not less important, their mobility. A congregation in which half the congregation turns over every three or four years (as in some university towns) may suggest that the preacher should cover quite different kinds of biblical material during that span of time, which in turn may warrant shorter series.

Thirdly, competing pastoral needs: a congregation in which half a dozen people are diagnosed with terminal cancer in the space of a couple of months, or a congregation located in a community that has just endured a local disaster, may be better served by expository messages on passages that bring comfort, that wrestle with evil and disaster, that affirm God's goodness and sovereignty and elicit faith in the midst of tears, rather than passages that plough on sequentially regardless of what is happening. Urgent pastoral needs may cry out for shorter series. On the other hand, a singularly ill-taught church may be best helped by being taught how to *read* biblical books, how to understand them and apply them, and that is often best accomplished by demonstrating these skills in appropriate expository series.

Fourthly, congregational expectations (which may or may not align with pastoral assessments of congregational *needs*): especially in the early stages of one's ministry one must be aware of what the congregation has come to expect. These expectations may be godly or ungodly, well founded or ill founded, and of course with time they can be moulded and modified. Usually, however, it takes time to bring about the changes, and during the transition preachers must make choices that reflect their assessment of how much change is good for the congregation. For instance, a congregation that has never heard careful expository preaching may be well served with several relatively short series of expositions.

Fifthly, the gifts of the preacher: younger or less experienced preachers, just starting out, need to learn the discipline and power of expository preaching in their own experience, but usually do not yet enjoy the gifts that warrant long series, even though they sometimes think they do.

Obviously these five considerations interact with one another. Moreover, they are applicable to almost any biblical book one chooses to expound. How, then, are they particularly relevant to preaching the Gospels? Any New Testament book, of course, can be broken down into its constituent units. Thus a series could be based on, say, Romans 5 – 8 or Romans 9 – 11. Yet the Gospels are so structured, as we have already seen, with numerous literary genres (e.g. parables, beatitudes, discourses, miracle stories, apocalyptic) and well-defined sections, that they are particularly susceptible to being broken down into shorter series, or, alternatively, being expounded at length. One could imagine a series on Luke's parables, Matthew's Olivet Discourse, John's Farewell Discourse, and so forth. Moreover, because the Gospels treat all the turning points in Jesus' earthly ministry, it is possible to align one's treatment of the Gospels with the liturgical year: Advent, Christmas, Good Friday and Easter, and Pentecost.

Seeing biblical themes

The best expository preaching not only deals fairly and accurately with the text at hand, but frequently also draws attention to the inner-canonical tendons that hold the entire Bible together. Nowhere is such attention more important than in the Gospels.

This demands a bit of explanation. A handful of themes – perhaps twenty or so – run through almost the entire Bible. They include kingdom, temple, glory, covenant, priesthood, sacrifice, creation, Son of God, wisdom, marriage or adultery, life and death, rest and reconciliation. A much greater number of themes appear not at the beginning of the Bible, but only later in the Bible's storyline, and then become relatively important, even if they show up more sporadically than the most central themes. Many of these themes have been explored in specialist monographs of some sort, not least those monographs committed to biblical theology.[9] For example, it is easy to discern temple themes in the original creation and in the garden of Eden. Sacrifice, closely related to temple, continues throughout the patriarchal period (for instance, one thinks of Bethel, the house of God). With the giving of the law comes

---

9. E.g. NSBT <http://www.thegospelcoalition.org/resources/nsbt>, accessed 27 June 2012.

detailed instruction about the construction and service of the tabernacle, not least the relevance of the most holy place and the significance of the ark of the covenant, followed by detailed accounts of various sorts (e.g. crossing the Jordan with the ark, the theft of the ark by the Philistines). Once David is settled as king, he proposes to build a more permanent structure, a temple, but God in his sovereignty assigns the task to Solomon. The destruction of the temple aligns with the punishment of the kingdom of Judah – but even here Ezekiel makes it clear that Judah and Jerusalem are not destroyed owing to the superior military strength of Babylon's Nebuchadnezzar, the regional superpower, but because God himself has abandoned Jerusalem with judicial determination and righteous wrath, even while he determines to be the real 'sanctuary' for his exiled covenant people (Ezek. 8 – 11). There follows the return from exile, and in due course the construction of a new temple that endures, enriched and beautified by the Herods, until Jesus' day and beyond. Nevertheless, Jesus 'cleanses' that temple, declares that he himself is the temple of God (i.e. the great meeting place between God and his sinful people, John 2) and announces the destruction of the Jerusalem temple (Matt. 24 par. Mark 13). That destruction is carried out in AD 70, but about that same time Paul is urging his readers to think of the church as the temple of God, and even of the individual Christian's body as the temple of God. The last book of the New Testament envisages a new Jerusalem where there is no temple, 'because the Lord God Almighty and the Lamb are its temple' (Rev. 21:22). Indeed, the new Jerusalem has the dimensions of a perfect cube, corresponding to the shape of the most holy place: God's redeemed people are pictured as enjoying the immediate presence of God for ever.[10]

The same sort of summary could easily be set out for each of the other themes I have briefly listed. A moment's reflection discloses that knowledge of these tendons, these trajectories through the Scriptures, constitutes a major part of what enables us 'to put our Bibles together', to see how the Bible 'works'. The question to ask is this: When will Christians in our congregations learn these trajectories and therefore grow in their grasp of the Bible as a whole? One important way to meet this need is to resolve to lay out such trajectories when we come across some part of them in the course of our regular exposition.

To put this matter another way: expository preaching can be too narrowly

---

10. All of this has been set out with much more exegetical and theological rigour by G. K. Beale, *The Temple and the Church's Mission: A Biblical Theology of the Dwelling Place of God*, NSBT 17 (Leicester: Apollos; Downers Grove: InterVarsity Press, 2004).

exegetical. It can so focus on the immediately chosen text that we fail to make clear how our passage fits into its *canonical* context. But if when we butt up against one of these major (or relatively minor) biblical trajectories located in the passage we are preaching, we pause to sketch out the entire trajectory, we are not only situating our passage within the entire Bible, but are helping believers to put their Bibles together. To summarize such a trajectory need not take long: depending on the detail we include, it can be done in a minute or two, or in ten minutes. Nor should we resolve to do this *every* time we find such a trajectory in our text: that kind of repetition could become boring. So it must be done selectively, freshly – but it must be done.

The Gospels are particularly appropriate texts for this sort of treatment. For the Gospels, as we have seen, focus on Jesus, and tell believers 'how we got from there to here'. Many strands from the Old Testament come to a focal point in the Gospels, in Jesus Christ, in the kingdom he introduces, in the new covenant he seals with his blood, in the eternal life he bestows, in the revelation that reaches its culmination in him. Then, like light radiating outward from its focal point, these trajectories project forward in the rest of the New Testament documents.[11]

In other words, taking the time, in expounding the Gospels, to trace out, however briefly, some of these biblical trajectories not only helps believers put their Bibles together a little better, but makes the Gospels themselves come alive within the shape imposed by the canon.

Connecting preaching and theology

One more extension beyond an exclusive focus on the immediate text characterizes the best expository preaching. If the sixth observation underscores the importance of tracing the trajectories of Scripture, and thus of establishing the connection between expository preaching and biblical theology, this seventh and final observation underscores the importance of tracing parallel structures of thought within Scripture and in later Christian thought, and thus of establishing the connection between expository preaching and historical and systematic theology.

---

11. For appropriate trajectories *forward* from Jesus to Paul see esp. David Wenham, *Paul: Follower of Jesus or Founder of Christianity?* (Grand Rapids: Eerdmans, 1995); or, at a more popular level, idem, *Paul and Jesus: The True Story* (Grand Rapids: Eerdmans, 2002).

For example, you are expounding the Johannine Prologue, and come to John 1:14, 'The Word became flesh'. Obviously, that clause must be unpacked within the flow of 1:1–18. You might usefully survey the way 'word' or 'word of God' is used in Scripture, and indicate why John deploys it as a Christological title: the Word or the Word of the Lord or the Word of God is regularly associated with creation, revelation and redemption, so it is not surprising that John appropriates it as a Christological title. But you might also usefully tie this passage to others that affirm the incarnation (e.g. Luke 1 – 2; Heb. 2:5–18), and reflect on the exquisite precision of the clause that rules out such ancient and modern heresies as Nestorianism and Arianism. Such distinctions can be introduced in four or five minutes. They serve to remind believers that theological distinctions have been important throughout the history of the church: confessional orthodoxy reflects centuries of thought and debate, which ultimately hinge on accurately interpreting biblical texts. When we take this sort of step, then we begin to bridge the great hiatus that commonly exists between the structures of exegetical or expository thought on the one hand, and the structures of systematic and dogmatic confessionalism on the other.

It is easy to multiply examples of what might be attempted. One might reflect on the connections between the use of 'Son of God' in Mark and John and contemporary debates over the use of the term in trinitarian witness to Muslims; on the relevance of the Paraclete passages to the doctrine of the Holy Spirit; on Luke's treatment of wealth and poverty to the still more massive structures of thought pertaining to these themes found elsewhere in Scripture; on the links between parts of the passion narrative (e.g. Matt. 27:25–51a) to the doctrine of the atonement; and so on. You must of course be careful not to stray too far from the text, lest your sermon become just one topical lecture; equally, you must not pretend that everything in Scripture or in some later doctrinal formulation is to be read back into the text as if there were no dangers in anachronism. Nevertheless, to clarify the links between the biblical text and related themes in Scripture, and between the biblical text and post-canonical theological syntheses, is part of the happier face of the recent quest for 'theological interpretation of Scripture' – a movement that would find greater credibility if it were undertaken by those with sure exegetical discipline.[12]

---

12. Cf. D. A. Carson, 'Theological Interpretation of Scripture: Yes, But . . .', in R. Michael Allen (ed.), *Theological Commentary: Evangelical Perspectives* (Festschrift for Henri Blocher; London: T. & T. Clark, 2011), pp. 187–207.

It is time to wrap this up. If there is a common thread that binds these seven observations together, it is this: to preach the Gospels faithfully is to preach Jesus Christ – not only the historical Jesus in the days of his flesh (though never less than that), but the rich panoply of biblical themes that focus on him and the salvation he has secured for his people. Thus every well-ordered expository sermon from the Gospels should reiterate the invitation in the ancient hymn:

Venite adoramus,
Venite adoramus,
Venite adoramus, Dominum.[13]

© D. A. Carson, 2013

---

13. 'O come let us adore him, O come let us adore him, O come let us adore him, [Christ] the Lord!'

2. PREACHING ON THE INFANCY NARRATIVES

R. T. France

A number of special factors affect preaching on the 'infancy narratives' (Matt. 1 – 2 and Luke 1 – 2):

1. They comprise a unique complex of narrative events probably better known (or at least *thought* to be better known!) and loved than almost any other part of the New Testament.
2. Both Matthew and Luke, in their different styles, use these chapters to develop a sustained and far-reaching presentation of the significance of Jesus as the Messiah foretold in the Old Testament.
3. Preaching on these passages generally takes place at a season of the church year that brings its own special expectations, and the congregation is likely to include a good number who are not regular church attenders during the rest of the year.

The following chapter is structured around the first two of those observations, while always trying to bear the third in mind.

The Christmas story

Most people's awareness of the Christmas story is derived mainly from school nativity plays, in which Luke's tea-towelled shepherds rub shoulders with Matthew's magi (promoted to royal status), and a surly innkeeper and his wife are surrounded by infant angels with tinsel halos. Add to this cocktail an array of Christmas cards depicting a glowing stable surrounded by bleak midwinter snow and populated by a smiling ox and ass, and you have the ingredients for the satisfyingly feel-good *Schmaltzfest* that is the modern Christmas. And I enjoy it as much as anyone.

But the preacher is aware, even if the congregation is not, that the traditional scene faces challenges from two different (though unfortunately sometimes confused) scholarly directions. On the one hand, virtually every element in the biblical narratives is regarded by some scholars as myth rather than history, while on the other hand, some scholars seek to restore the historical character of the gospel stories by stripping them of centuries of exegetical misunderstanding and legendary elaboration. The preacher who invokes either (or both) of these scholarly tendencies in a Christmas sermon risks being regarded as at best a spoilsport, a rocker of a very popular boat and at worst as downright heretical. Let us look at each in turn.

Myth and history
Objections to the historical character of the infancy narratives tend to focus on four fronts, which can be only briefly outlined here.[1]

The supernatural character of the events
Most of the characters in the stories are reassuringly normal, but alongside Mary and Joseph, the shepherds and the magi we read also of a moving, directing star (Matthew), a chorus of angels (Luke) and a birth without a human father (Matthew and Luke). If it is concluded on philosophical or scientific grounds that these things could not have happened, the rest of the narrative is easily dismissed by association with such grounds. Such philosophical or scientific considerations apply also, of course, to a large part of the gospel

---

1. I have explored these issues in S. E. Porter and T. Holmen (eds.), *Handbook for the Study of the Historical Jesus* (Leiden: Brill, 2011), vol. 3, pp. 2362–2371, and more fully with regard to Matthew in R. T. France and D. Wenham (eds.), *Gospel Perspectives* (Sheffield: JSOT, 1981), vol. 2, pp. 239–266.

narratives as a whole, not least to the resurrection, which lies at the heart of the Christian gospel.

The relation to secular history

Most of the material in the infancy narratives exists in its own limited world and does not interact with secular history. But we do have an extensive history of the reign of Herod the Great from Josephus, and he says nothing either of the visit of the magi or of the killing of the children in Bethlehem. This is an argument from silence, of course, and even with access to the histories of Nicolaus of Damascus Josephus, writing a century later, need not have been privy to everything that happened during Herod's reign, especially if those events were of a limited, local character. What we do know of Herod from Josephus indicates a man who is unlikely to have baulked at the elimination of a few babies when he felt his throne to be under threat.

Luke has also provided a hostage to fortune in his account of the 'world-wide' census that brought Joseph and Mary to Bethlehem. Not only is such a census unrecorded for the period while Herod was still alive, but it is historically improbable in Judea before the imposition of direct Roman rule. There *was* a Roman census in Judea which fits Luke's account quite well, but that was in AD 6, ten years too late. Many suggestions continue to be made to salvage Luke's credibility, but none has carried general conviction. If Luke did make a mistake about the date of the census, the question remains whether this in itself affects the reliability of the events that he associates with it.

The differences between Matthew and Luke

The two evangelists tell different stories: Matthew focuses mainly on the experiences of Joseph, Luke, on those of Mary (together with a parallel motif, unknown to Matthew, of the birth of John the Baptist). So there is little scope for disagreement between them: they simply do not interact, beyond the basic essentials of a betrothed couple called Joseph (a descendant of David) and Mary, conception by the Holy Spirit without human intercourse, the angelic revelation of the name Jesus, the birth in Bethlehem in the reign of Herod, and the upbringing in Nazareth. But there are unexplained silences: Matthew seems not to know of any connection with Nazareth before the birth, while Luke's narrative leaves no space for the escape to Egypt and the return to Galilee after Herod's death. Clearly the two evangelists had different source material, and neither offers a complete chronological record of the events; but is it fair to look for such precision in storytelling of the period? The days of pedantic footnotes had not yet dawned.

The literary character of these chapters

In the second part of this chapter we will look at what Matthew and Luke are aiming to achieve in these opening chapters. It is immediately obvious that they are not simply reporting facts for their own sake, but rather weaving a rich tapestry of scriptural motifs and allusions in order to introduce Jesus as the Messiah of Israel's expectation. The remarkable series of psalmlike canticles in Luke 1 – 2 and the equally remarkable concentration of formula quotations in Matthew 1 – 2 are only the most prominent features of an underlying 'fulfilment' motif that colours even the details of several of the infancy stories. In Matthew in particular the very structure of 1:18 – 2:23, with each successive scene focused on its formula quotation, shows that the evangelist did not write these chapters out of pure narrative interest, but in order to demonstrate his central theme of the fulfilment of Scripture even in the earliest days of Jesus the Messiah.

So the suspicion arises for many scholars that the stories themselves owe their origin not to remembered events but to creative meditation on Scripture. Old Testament texts and motifs have become actualized into supposed events. If the Messiah is the son of David, he must have been born in David's town; if he is to lead the new exodus, his birth must echo that of Moses, with Herod taking the role of the biblical Pharaoh. Some scholars are happy therefore to dismiss the whole narrative content of these chapters as pious fiction; others allow that beneath the scriptural coating is a basic factual element, but one that is hard to disentangle from its devotional accretions.

Such judgments are not susceptible to definitive proof or disproof. But a couple of considerations may be set over against the cruder form of historical scepticism that sees the gospel events as spun out of the Old Testament texts they allegedly 'fulfil', so that for instance Matthew invented the flight to Egypt on the basis of Hosea 1:11 and the slaughter of the children on the basis of Jeremiah 31:15. First, it is hard to see why Matthew should have thought of those texts at all if he was looking for 'fulfilment' potential. Not many of Matthew's formula quotations involve what would normally be recognized as 'messianic texts', and of the five such quotations in chapters 1–2 only Micah 5:2 could be so described. So why did those obscure texts, which look to the past rather than to the future, need to be cited at all unless the tradition Matthew had received already contained the narrative details of exile in Egypt and the death of children? Secondly, what sort of apologetic is it that claims to find Old Testament texts 'fulfilled' in purely imaginary events, invented on the basis of those same texts?

Scholarly scepticism and preaching

The preacher with theological training and with access to commentaries will be aware of such objections to the Christmas story, but how far should they affect the sermon? I would guess that most people in most Christmas congregations would know little and care less about such issues. Their knowledge of the Christmas story, even if distorted by traditional elements outside the biblical narratives (see the section 'Back to the text' below), is of events generally assumed actually to have taken place in Nazareth and Bethlehem two thousand years ago, and they will expect the preacher to think so too. So can the whole academic debate responsibly be left at the bottom of the pulpit steps?

This must be a matter for judgment on the part of preachers, depending on how they assess the level of academic sophistication in their congregation. There may be a few who have actually read scholarly articles or commentaries that raise such issues. There will probably be more who are vaguely aware, perhaps through the sort of television programme frequently aired at religious festivals, that it is fashionable to express scepticism about the good old stories. If the preacher judges that such awareness may be sufficiently widespread to make it difficult for people to accept a straightforward exposition of the story at face value, then it would be irresponsible to pass over the problem in silence.

But that does not necessarily mean that a full-scale apologetic lecture should take the place of positive exposition. A few introductory remarks may suffice, perhaps supplemented by an invitation to take the academic issues up individually afterwards. In the preceding sections I have tried to indicate in the briefest outline the sort of approach that such introductory remarks might take. Such comments may be enough to show that the preacher is not unaware of the issues, without allowing them to hijack the primary intent of the sermon. If, as I suspect, most people expect a Christmas sermon to be not an academic lecture but a thought-provoking exploration and application of the traditional stories, is it fair to deny them that for the sake of the (possibly few) members of the congregation who would prefer an academic debate?

A similar dilemma faces the preacher at Easter, when there is probably more widespread awareness of scholarly disputes about what actually happened. But I would judge that at Christmas (especially if the occasion is a carol service or a nativity play) there is usually a higher proportion of 'fringe' attenders for whom the essential historicity of the Christmas story is not, and need not be, controversial.

Back to the text
The Christmas story most people 'know' is not simply that told by the evangelists, and may at times be in tension with what the Gospels actually say. It may not worry people too much to be told that there are no ox and ass in Luke's account, nor any snow on the ground, and they may even accept with

equanimity that Matthew's magi were not kings and may not even have been three. But threaten the stable and the inn, and you can expect trouble. After all, does it not say in so many words that there was no room for them in the inn, and that is why the baby was born in a stable?

Well, no – not quite! Many of us will by now be aware of the exegetical challenge Kenneth Bailey issued in the late 1970s to the traditional Western Christmas scene, and which since then has found increasing acceptance among exegetes.[2] In a nutshell, (1) the word Luke uses in 2:7 (*katalyma*) does not mean 'inn' (for which he uses *pandocheion*, Luke 10:34) but 'guest room' (as in Luke 22:11), and (2) in a typical Palestinian home the mangers were located not in a separate building but within the one-room house, where the animals were housed on a lower level than the family living area. The same arrangement was found until recently in a traditional Welsh 'long house'. So Joseph, arriving at his family home (and therefore naturally expecting to find accommodation with relatives), discovered that the separate guest room (on the roof, as in 2 Kgs 4:10?) was already occupied (by other visitors in town for the census?); instead they stayed with the family in the main living room; and when the baby was born, a manger on the edge of the living area provided a warm and comfortable makeshift cradle. It is Western unfamiliarity with Middle Eastern culture that has invented the unwelcoming 'inn' and the iso-lated, draughty 'stable'. Jesus' birth took place in the warm and welcoming (if crowded and smelly) atmosphere of a normal peasant home.

But to advocate this understanding is to pull the rug from under not only many familiar carols ('a lowly cattle shed'; 'a draughty stable with an open door') but also a favourite theme of Christmas preachers: the ostracism of the Son of God from human society, Jesus the refugee. This is subversive stuff. When I first started advocating Bailey's interpretation,[3] it was picked up by a Sunday newspaper and then reported in various radio programmes as a typical example of theological wrecking, on a par with the then notorious debunk-ing of the factuality of the resurrection by the Bishop of Durham! It proved

---

2. K. E. Bailey, 'The Manger and the Inn: The Cultural Background of Luke 2:7', *NETR* 2 (1979), pp. 33–44; repr. in *Evangelical Review of Theology* 4 (1980), pp. 201–217; idem, *Jesus Through Middle Eastern Eyes* (Downers Grove: Inter-Varsity Press; London: SPCK, 2008), pp. 25–37 (a shorter and less technical version). Cf. also H. Must, *NTS* 32 (1986), pp. 136–143; and brief comments by J. Nolland, *Luke 1–9:20*, WBC (Dallas: Word, 1989), pp. 105–106. Note the use of 'guest room' at Luke 2:7 in TNIV and NIV (2011 revision).

3. In a short article in *Third Way*, Dec. 1984, entitled 'No Room for the Inn?'

remarkably difficult for some people to distinguish between an attempt to peel away later accretions in order to reinstate what the text actually says and an assault on the historicity of events the text records.

But I have persisted in challenging the stable from time to time, in family service talks as well as in adult sermons, and have found that the reaction is much more positive than negative when the issue is suitably explained (especially here in Wales, where some people still remember the 'long houses'). A recent sermon along these lines in a church where I was a visitor produced a gratifying series of people coming to me afterwards and saying how much more sense Bailey's reading made. Several people there had experience of non-Western cultures, and saw that of course Cousin Joe from the north would never have been allowed to go to a commercial inn, even if Bethlehem had one (which is very questionable): it would have been an unforgivable insult to the extended family.

But is it worth disturbing people's inherited assumptions? In this case, I think so. The problem with the stable is that it distances Jesus from the rest of us. It puts even his birth in a unique setting, in some ways as remote from normal life as if he had been born in Caesar's palace. But the message of the incarnation is that Jesus is one of us. He came to be what we are, and it fits well with that theology that his birth in fact took place in a normal, crowded, warm, welcoming Palestinian home, just like many another Jewish boy of his time. It is as the Word become flesh and living among us that we have seen his glory.

One of my favourite themes for Christmas sermons is the paradoxical but wholesome blend within the Christmas story of the totally extraordinary (angelic revelation, messianic titles, supernatural conception) coming into the very ordinary, humdrum setting of shepherds, baby clothes and a Palestinian peasant home. There among the warmth and bustle of an ordinary family the true light began shining. Christmas is above all the time to celebrate the coming of Immanuel, 'God with us'. If Bailey's rebranding of the Bethlehem story helps us gain a deeper insight into that saving paradox, it should not be hidden away for fear of upsetting people's cherished misconceptions.

The fulfilment of Scripture

There is a significant mismatch between what most Christmas congregations expect to hear and what Matthew and Luke were primarily interested in conveying in their opening chapters. They did not write to tell the story of how Jesus was born. Indeed, Matthew hardly mentions Jesus' birth, but rather focuses on events that preceded and followed it, while Luke's account of Jesus' birth is a relatively brief, though central, part in a complex of stories about the families of Elizabeth and Mary. In their different ways both evangelists present us rather with an extended demonstration that the child born in Bethlehem is the Messiah of Old Testament expectation. Should this then also be the concern of the Christmas preacher, and if so how may it be conveyed today?

Matthew

The plan of the first two chapters of Matthew has been outlined in two different ways, which I believe are complementary rather than in conflict.

First, Krister Stendahl's chapter 'Quis et Unde?' (Who and Whence?) famously argued, on the basis of the content, that chapter 1 answers the question of identity, 'Who [is Jesus]?', and chapter 2, the question of geographical origin, 'Where [did Jesus come] from?'[4]

Secondly, in my commentary I divided these chapters, on the basis of their literary form, into two sections, 'The "Book of Origin" of the Messiah' (1:1–17) and 'A Demonstration that Jesus of Nazareth is the Messiah: Five Scriptural Proofs' (1:18 –2:23). The latter section consists of five episodes set before and after Jesus' birth, each of which is focused on a formula quotation.

The preacher who bases a sermon on an episode in Matthew's 'infancy narrative' should recognize that it is not a free-standing story but part of a carefully constructed complex, and that its purpose in Matthew's plan was to demonstrate the scriptural credentials of Jesus as Messiah. In practice such a sermon is likely to be on either Joseph's dilemma (1:18–25) or the visit of the magi (2:1–11); I do not recall hearing (or preaching) many sermons on the escape to Egypt, Herod's slaughter of the children or the settlement in Nazareth.

But do congregations today either need or want to be convinced from Scripture that Jesus is the Messiah promised to the Jews? And even if they do, how receptive are most modern Gentile congregations likely to be to the extremely creative (some would say fanciful) deductions that Matthew makes (or rather is supposed by commentators to have made) from his odd selection of texts? The formula quotations of chapters 1–2 are a happy hunting ground for the exegetical commentator, and call forth an extraordinary range of sug-

---

4. K. Stendahl, 'Quis et Unde? An Analysis of Matthew 1–2', in W. Eltester (ed.), *Judentum, Urchristentum, Kirche* (Berlin: Töpelmann, 1960), pp. 94–105; repr. in G. N. Stanton, *The Interpretation of Matthew* (London: SPCK, 1995), pp. 69–80.

gested scriptural connections, with each commentator vying with the next in the rabbinic subtlety deployed. But is this what our Christmas congregations have come for?

So perhaps it is not surprising that Luke, with his greater human interest and more accessible style of storytelling, is the more popular quarry for texts for Christmas sermons (together, of course, with the prologue of John, the familiar Christmas reading in which 'St John unfolds the great mystery of the incarnation'). But I would be sorry to see Matthew abandoned as 'too difficult' or too culturally remote.

I do not think I have ever preached an actual sermon on Matthew's genealogy, but I have found great interest when it is explained as not simply a list of names but a radical theological statement. Its royal focus is easily grasped, especially when the significance of the two turning points of the 3 × 14 structure (David and the exile, the beginning and end of monarchy) is explained. And while not everyone today is convinced by the numerological significance of the coming of the seventh seven, people can still grasp something of Matthew's excitement as he discovers the whole pattern of Old Testament history now arriving at its intended climax in the new Son of David. But I suppose most expository attention these days is given to what is for Matthew a very minor part of the genealogy: the presence of the four women in 1:3–6. Their non-Jewish ethnicity and dubious marital status are commonly used as the basis for meditation on God's unexpected choices, sometimes in explicit relation to the decidedly unconventional means of Jesus' own arrival. In my experience Michael Goulder's notorious poem on the subject can be guaranteed to evoke strong reactions (usually, but not always, favourable) from a congregation.[5]

It is failure to appreciate the significance of the genealogy in Matthew's project that has led to the story of Joseph's dilemma (1:18–25) often being thoughtlessly labelled as an account of the birth of Jesus. It is nothing of the sort. The genealogy has left a major apologetic problem. Joseph is a descendant of David, a legitimate heir to the kingship, but, as 1:16 has made explicitly clear, *Jesus is not his son*. It is only as Joseph, Son of David (1:20), submits to divine pressure to adopt and name Jesus as his official son that his genealogy becomes the genealogy *of Jesus* too. The whole story depends on Joseph's not being the biological father of Jesus, and it is this that is the focus of the much-debated quotation from Isaiah 7:14 which provides Matthew with the theologically significant title Immanuel. Most congregations are unlikely to be

---

5. M. D. Goulder, *Midrash and Lection in Matthew* (London: SPCK, 1974), p. 232.

very interested in the debates over Matthew's handling of the Isaiah prophecy, but the virgin birth is a central, and controversial, part of the Christmas story, and the preacher might well use this short pericope as a basis for exploring it. The more fully Matthew's scriptural and apologetic agenda is appreciated, the more obvious it becomes that he and Luke have introduced this theme into their infancy narratives in quite different ways and therefore probably also from independent sources, a point not without its importance for Christian apologetics.

Space does not allow me to explore in detail the homiletical possibilities arising from Matthew's other most memorable story, that of the magi, with its rich scriptural resonances, especially through the Son of David typology which links this story to that of the visit of the Queen of Sheba, and through the echoes of the stories of the birth of Moses and the hostility of Pharaoh. Typology is probably not high on most people's interpretative agenda, but here is a familiar pericope in which it is close to the surface, and therefore an opportunity for the preacher to introduce people to what was certainly a major element in the New Testament (and especially Matthean) presentation of Jesus as the fulfilment of Israel's hope.

Luke

Luke's infancy chapters are not only significantly longer than Matthew's, but also present a much more varied range of narrative moments, with a more developed characterization and human interest that make them more immediately attractive to the preacher. And then there are the wonderful Lucan canticles, which stand in a class of their own. Space does not allow us to go through the pericopes seriatim, so a few sample soundings must suffice. I will confine myself to the sections that deal with Mary and Jesus rather than the parallel story of Elizabeth and John, since the latter, though obviously of great importance to Luke and therefore to exegetes of Luke, is not so likely to be the focus of our Christmas preaching.

The annunciation to Mary (Luke 1:26–38)
Classical Christian art and frequent repetition at Services of Nine Lessons and Carols have made this one of the most familiar stories of the infancy cycle. Luke places heavy emphasis on the miraculous conception without human sexual intercourse. This pericope and Matthew 1:18–25 are the only places in the New Testament where that issue is directly addressed, and the preacher can hardly avoid making this a central theme of the sermon, with all the apologetic issues it raises in the light of modern scientific understanding and also in relation to the nature of the incarnation (how human is a man without

a human father?). But Luke shows no embarrassment on either front, and a sermon that is to do justice to Luke's concerns will focus primarily on the positive contribution the virgin conception makes to his presentation of the uniqueness of Jesus. The pericope includes a succession of titles or descriptions of Jesus that encapsulate this emphasis: the name Jesus, 'Son of the Most High', 'the throne of his father David', 'his kingdom will never end', 'holy one', 'the Son of God'. The preacher on this pericope faces a Christological embarras de richesses (superfluity of good things).

But it is also a story about Mary, and Christmas is the time of year when one can most naturally focus on Mary herself without provoking controversy over the claims and counter-claims of Catholic and Protestant concerning her status in Christian worship and salvation. God's surprising choice of a young village girl, and her response to both the honour and the peril of her calling, allow the preacher to explore her role as a model of faith and obedience in extreme circumstances, a worthy recipient of the congratulation (*makarismos*) that will be pronounced concerning her (vv. 45, 48).

The Magnificat (Luke 1:39–56)

The canticles of Luke's infancy chapters are unique and wonderful, both as poetry and as spiritual meditation. This has made it all too easy to take them out of their context and turn them into free-standing psalms, and they will be familiar as such especially to many whose background is in Catholic or Anglican worship. And of course they richly repay study and exposition on that basis. The Magnificat in particular is one of the most powerful expressions in Scripture of God's 'bias to the poor' and of the subversive principles of his kingdom in which the first are last and the last first.

But it can also be a liberating experience for a congregation who have long been familiar with the Magnificat as a sublime piece of liturgy to be reminded that Luke introduces it as the personal response of a village girl to the overwhelming grace of God in her own life and calling, to be made to read it through her eyes and to reflect on how its universal principles were to apply to her future experience and to the mission of her promised son. The preacher may usefully explore the numerous echoes of the song of Hannah (1 Sam. 2:1–10) and of other Old Testament poetic passages as a way of entering into the mind of Mary at the moment when God turned her life upside down.[6]

---

6. There is textual evidence for a tradition in some parts of the early church that the Magnificat was the song not of Mary but of Elizabeth, and some modern scholars have defended that reading; see R. E. Brown, *The Birth of the Messiah* (New York:

The birth of Jesus (Luke 2:1–7)
See the brief comments and suggestions in the section 'Back to the text'
above; space allows no more.

Simeon and the Nunc Dimittis (Luke 2:22–35)
Here we have moved beyond Christmas, but remain within the infancy narratives. Those churches that preserve the ancient feast of Candlemas on 2
February provide the preacher with a welcome opportunity to reflect on the
Janus character of the feast, looking back to Christmas in Simeon's hymn of
praise for the coming of the long-awaited Messiah, but also looking forward
to Good Friday in his warning to Mary of the heart-piercing sorrows to come.
It is a bitter-sweet festival, a stark reminder of the paradox that lies at the heart
of the 'salvation' Simeon hailed.

In the atmosphere of Old Testament piety that surrounds this episode it is
important to note in the Nunc Dimittis the theme of 'light for the Gentiles',
an aspect of Old Testament expectation (Gen. 12:3; Isa. 49:6; etc.) apparently
not widely recognized in contemporary Judaism, but which is to become
one of the key features of Luke's development of his central theme of 'salvation' (as of course it was also in Matthew's story of the magi). Predominantly
Gentile modern Christian congregations may need to be reminded of the
importance of this aspect of our Jewish heritage.

Doubleday; London: Geoffrey Chapman, 1977), pp. 334–336. The majority remain
convinced that Luke attributed it to Mary.

3. PREACHING *JESUS'* PARABLES

Klyne Snodgrass

Everyone loves Jesus' parables – or at least *some* of them. The parables of the prodigal, the good Samaritan and the sower are preached on repeatedly, but many of the other parables do not receive much attention and are confusing to many people.[1] The problem, of course, is that many people have already heard sermons on the most famous parables and know what the preacher will say before the words are formed, which is deadly. People justifiably go to sleep. All the parables deserve to be heard, yet we live in a world where some people, indeed many, have not heard any of these stories. How can we communicate with both groups?

The importance of parables both as a message and a means of communication is clear. About one-third of Jesus' teaching in the Synoptic Gospels is in parables, so they are crucial if we are to understand Jesus and his message.[2]

---

1. The common lectionary includes most parables but not parallels and not the parables of the leaven or of the faithful and unfaithful servant. No doubt the latter is omitted because of its harshness. The harsh statement on the purpose of parables in Mark 4:10–12 is also omitted. For treatment of this and other issues see my *Stories with Intent: A Comprehensive Guide to the Parables of Jesus* (Grand Rapids: Eerdmans, 2008).

2. Most works on the historical Jesus, however, give minimal attention to the

They are fictional stories picturing truth, or, as sometimes expressed, 'imaginary gardens with real toads'. Their power to attract and communicate is evident. Parables are *concrete* and *personal*. They enliven speech, create interest, give focus, make understanding possible and produce insight. They provide a window on life, by implication an important window or they would not be told. They are participatory, for they draw us into something particular and concrete, usually into a narrative world, but people must choose to enter that narrative world, even if they do so unaware or at their own peril. People are drawn to participate in an imaginary world and to make decisions that confront their own world and life. A good parable then creates distance, provokes and appeals. The parable distances one temporarily from one's own context, provokes to decision or insight and appeals for the decision or insight to be applied to life. To communicate the power of the parables I suggest the following.

Use concrete and personal language

Notice how politicians nearly always speak about specific people and concrete cases when highlighting a problem or success. People do not care about generalities. We use abstract thought for convenience, but learning takes place most easily with the concrete, particular and personal. Wendell Berry commented, 'Abstraction is the enemy, *wherever* it is found,' and added 'The Devil's work is abstraction.'[3] Abstraction is viewed so negatively because it is lifeless, general, unrelated to us in its current form, and sometimes even dangerous because of its generalizations and depersonalization. The abstract is not without value. We learn in the concrete, but we store in the abstract. We could not possibly store all concrete particularities, so we generalize and store abstract ideas. The problem is that we then try to teach in the abstract with loss of the personal and still wonder why people do not get it. People need the conviction of good ideas, but they also need the insight provided by particular stories and analogies. Preaching the parables gives people the advantage and power of the concrete in a way that abstract language never can. Preaching

---

parables, and books on parables often give inadequate attention to the historical Jesus.

3. 'Out of Your Car, Off Your Horse', in *Sex, Economics, Freedom, or Community: Eight Essays* (New York: Pantheon, 1993), p. 23 (his italics); and 'The Gift of Good Land', in *The Gift of Good Land: Further Essays, Cultural and Agricultural* (San Francisco: North Point, 1981), p. 278.

needs to be concrete and personal. Good preaching of parables should engage as much as Jesus' parables did, should recreate the same dynamic, response and insight as Jesus' parables, even though in a different context with *some* different needs.

Study the advantages of indirect communication

Parables are so effective because they are indirect communication, a point emphasized by Fred Craddock, following Søren Kierkegaard.[4] Children's sermons are a form of indirection. Everyone is aware how much adults enjoy and benefit from children's sermons, often more than from the 'adult' sermon. Since sermons for children are not to or for adults and are concrete rather than abstract, adults leave their defences down and the message has impact. Direct communication often meets resistance, especially if people think they already know the subject. Indirect communication enables, even forces, people to view some other person and subject from a new angle of vision, an angle not their own. Parables then are like Trojan horses.[5] Defences go down, and objectivity and fairness are enabled, which if taken seriously require people to respond *personally*, not in the abstract. Most parables are personal: they tell of another person and call hearers to stand in that person's place and *be* a person. Parables invoke participation.

Søren Kierkegaard made masterful use of parables in confronting the Danish church in just this way to urge one to be an individual, not part of the crowd. His explanation of indirect communication is insightful. He argued all communication of knowledge is direct communication, whereas communication of capability, which persuades people to be and do something, especially that which is ethical, is indirect communication.[6] Capability is what preaching seeks to effect.

---

4. See Fred Craddock, *Overhearing the Gospel* (Nashville: Abingdon, 1978), pp. 79–140.

5. Clarence Jordan and Bill Lane Doulos, *Cotton Patch Parables of Liberation* (Scottsdale: Herald, 1976), pp. 38–43.

6. *Søren Kierkegaard's Journals and Papers*, ed. and tr. Howard V. Hong and Edna H. Hong, 6 vols. (Bloomington: Indiana University Press, 1967), vol. 1, p. 273, 282–319. He argued that an illusion can never be destroyed directly and that only by indirect means can illusion be radically removed. See his *The Point of View for My Work as an Author: A Report to History and Related Writings*, tr. Walter Lowrie (London: Oxford University Press, 1939), p. 24.

The indirection of parables breaks through our numbness and lack of perception. The problem for frequent churchgoers though is that familiarity has made them numb even to the parables. How can we restore the freshness of the parables? The solution is not in making up some novel interpretation that does not fit with Jesus or breathe the air of first-century Palestine, but in creating some diversion to keep people from thinking they are going down an old path. Two avenues are effective for such diversion. The first is to use further indirection by creating a new parable. Creating new parables that mirror the dynamics and intent of Jesus' parables in a modern context – without being so obvious that they fail – is not easy, but it is a very effective way to preach parables. Preachers need to be, or need to learn to be, capable with both concrete and indirect communication to engage people with theological ideas. Imagination and discernment are crucial, and both can be trained. The second avenue is defamiliarization (or disorientation). If people are numb because of familiarity, preaching can break through by dealing with problems in the text that most people ignore, by giving facts not usually known, or by emphasizing how different Jesus' context was from ours, such as with attitudes towards Pharisees. For example, the parable of the unforgiving servant raises questions whether forgiveness can be rescinded and about the nature of judgment, and it uses almost unthinkable hyperbole with the amount of the first debt. Further, it raises deeply practical and at times problematic issues about the relation of justice, grace, forgiveness, responsibility and judgment. Some feminists recoil from this parable, fearing that abusers might get off easily. How can we do justice to the magnanimous grace of God, the necessity of human forgiveness mirroring God's forgiveness, even in the evil and messiness of life, and the warning of judgment for the failure to forgive? We live in the tensions of life. Of course, like all parables, this one is a *partial* picture, not a full theology. Forgiveness is required of Christians but so also are the realities of naming evil and holding people responsible for evil. Forgiveness deals with the heart of the offended, but it does not mean the offender is not held accountable.

Commit to seeing both the text and people

The pastor must be one who has the ability really to see and hear the text of Scripture, to see and hear parishioners and their world, discern what is needed and be creative enough to know how people must be approached if the parable and the gospel are to be understood. It is about caring enough to take the time to understand people and their needs and actually desiring to communicate, not just talk. Those who say *listening is the first task of preaching* are correct, both with regard to Scripture and to people. This involves the ability to set ideas and realities in relation, to juxtapose, to draw analogies and to set contrasts. Contrasts are frequent in parables and are an especially effective way to make a point.

Parables urge actually seeing people. One of the most stunning examples is the little parable of the two debtors and its encasing narrative (Luke 7:36–50). After Simon the Pharisee gave the obvious answer to Jesus' question about which debtor loved more, the text says Jesus *turned to the woman* and *asked Simon*, 'Do you see this woman?' Simon had been looking at her the whole meal, but he had not *seen* her, which is an ailment from which we all suffer.

Keep the parables as *Jesus'* parables

We are not concerned merely with parables; the focus is *Jesus'* parables. I know what people mean by 'preaching the parables', but if it is not too pedantic and if my work *Stories with Intent* has any validity,[7] we do not preach the parables. Like the early church in the book of Acts, we preach Jesus and the kingdom, and parables are a particularly effective medium both for understanding and communicating Jesus' message. Unlike much that occurs in the name of parable interpretation, the parables cannot legitimately be separated from their author. They are *Jesus'* parables. They presuppose and support a theology, that encased in Jesus' teaching. They are not the theology by themselves, nor is it legitimate to derive another theology other than that of Jesus, at least if we claim to be preaching *his* parables. To shift the focus of the parables away from Jesus' context opens the door to manipulation for illegitimate ideological and theological concerns. This is a major problem; and if one doubts that, one should read what books from all sides have done to the parables.[8]

It is one thing to insist on the first-century Palestinian context of Jesus' parables and quite another to do justice to the redactional shaping of the evangelists, the contexts in which they have placed parables and the way they introduced them. We would be foolish to ignore the help such editorial activity offers and foolish not to assess carefully the effect of the redactional shaping and the contextual placement, particularly where *possible* parallels

---

7. See n. 1.
8. Reconstructions of parables are never convincing enough or authoritative enough to serve as a foundation for the life of the church.

appear in different contexts. One cannot preach effectively on the parables without noting the differences in the accounts and without determining the significance of the implicit commentary created by the redactional shaping.

A corollary of the insistence that parables should not be separated from Jesus and his first-century context is that any suggested teaching of a parable must be demonstrable from Jesus' non-parabolic teaching. The teaching in parables and that in non-parabolic material are two rails going in the same direction. Jesus did not have one message in the parable genre and another in other forms. We need the cross-check and commentary that each provides for the other. Any suggested interpretation of the *teaching* in a parable that cannot be demonstrated from non-parabolic material is surely suspect.[9]

A further help in treating the parables in Jesus' context is to ask what question the parable is addressing. *Discerning the implied question* Jesus addressed is a signpost towards valid interpretation. For example, surely several parables – the weeds and the wheat, the growing seed, the mustard seed, and the leaven – address the implied question of how the kingdom can be present if evil is still here and if very little evidence of the kingdom is observable.

Observe literary characteristics

Observe the literary characteristics both within a parable and within the redactional shaping and arrangement of the evangelists. No one will grasp the focus of Luke's parable of the banquet (14:15–24) who does not see Luke's grouping of several texts on meals, how he develops his explanation of discipleship and how he repeatedly uses the word *kaleō* (call, invite) twelve times in chapter 14,[10] which requires a reconsideration of the nature of Israel's election in the light of Jesus' coming.

Special attention should be given to key turning points in parables, particularly poignant expressions, contrasts, questions, the rule of end stress, and reversal of expectation. This entails more than seeing the facts of the narrative; it involves seeing the power and contour of the text. Key turning

---

9. Ernest Van Eck ('Review of *Stories with Intent*', *Review of Biblical Literature* 10 [2008], pp. 1–6) attempted to argue against this principle by saying the parables have violence that is contrary to Jesus' teaching of non-retaliation. He makes the mistake of confusing elements of genre, the violence in the parables, for the *teaching* of the parable. The parables do not teach violence, and no one ever thought they did.

10. Including *antikaleō* in v. 12.

points indicate a movement towards resolution or success (or failure). Luke 15:17 uses poignant words about the prodigal by saying, 'He came to himself,' which is the beginning of the resolution and substance for deep thought. The parable of the Pharisee and tax collector (Luke 18:9–14) contrasts two men at prayer and has that poignant prayer – in the shadow of the temple and possibly during the morning or evening sacrifice – 'Be gracious/propitiated [*hilasthēti*] to me, the sinner.'[11] In a reversal of expectations the known sinner, not the presumedly righteous man, is acquitted.

One aspect of literary concern has to do with time. Parable time is not real time, most evident perhaps with Matthew's parable of the wedding feast, where the meal is kept ready until after a war. It *does not work* to lay real time on parable time, as is evident when people become concerned that the invitation to the poor in Luke's parable of the banquet (14:21) is extended only after the rich have refused, or when Luke's two invitations are explained as the ongoing mission to Jews and to Gentiles or to the early and later Gentile mission. They are parables, not chronological or literalistic mirrors of reality or whole theologies.

Another literary aspect is that sometimes reality intrudes into a parable. When a master says, 'Enter into the joy of your master' (Matt. 25:21), the parable world has given way to the reality depicted. Parables sometimes do this, and it is not by default the work of the evangelist. A most obvious example from the Old Testament is Ezekiel 23:1–49, which describes the whoredom of two sisters, but already in verse 4 and at several places the reader knows the two sisters are Samaria and Jerusalem. Reality shines through the parabolic form when the prophet confronts emphatically or when the parable teller has no need to guard indirection, as is the case in parables directed to disciples.

Shun both allegorizing and dogmas that parables have only one point

The crucial issue in parable interpretation is and always has been how much of a parable corresponds to something else, that is, how many 'points' a parable has. Historically the church allegorized virtually every feature of a parable, usually in directions that have no relation to Jesus' teaching, and consequently Adolf Jülicher threw out all allegorizing, insisted that parables have only one point of comparison between image and reality, and thought the point of a

---

11. All translations from the Bible in this chapter are my own.

parable may be expressed as a general religious principle.[12] Jülicher's dictum about one point has often been asserted by people who have no concept of its origin. It took almost a century for the complaints against Jülicher to gain traction, but his views are largely rejected today. The idea that parables have only one central truth is like the use of training wheels to wean people off allegorizing.

The concern in parable interpretation though should *not* be on the questions 'What does this element stand for?' or 'How many correspondences are there?' even though correspondences may exist and may be identified. Parables are analogies, and the longer ones could not do their task without correspondences. Correspondences help determine the reference of the analogy, but they may be *inexact and partial* to maintain the cover of indirection.[13] The concern is the analogy, not the correspondences. Each parable must be approached in its own right, and I do not think formulas can be set that determine how many points a parable has. A parable may have as many points as it needs. The real issue is *how the analogy functions*, but parables are *not* one-for-one analogies, as if reality and image were connected by an equal sign. They picture actual realities *partly*, but are intended to make people think and question, and they do so often through hyperbole, surprise and *inexactness*. People want each parable to be a complete theology. *They never are.* As with metaphor generally, there is always an 'is' and an 'is not' with parables.

So, how much of a parable is important? All of it. Nothing is in a parable for no reason, but that does not mean each element has allegorical significance. We need greater literary sensitivity than that. Some elements in longer parables have correspondence and some do not, but they still have resonances. They set off bells that allude to Scripture texts, such as the harvest and sickle in the parable of the growing seed (Mark 4:26–29), imagery drawn from Joel 3:13 that resonates of God's judgment. Some of the elements in parables are there to heighten narrative tension, and some may have minor roles in the narrative with no theological relevance. Asking what has *prominence* in the story and remembering the *rule of end stress*[14] are ways to keep from being sidetracked. The parable of the vineyard workers in Matthew 20 is instructive. It has only two main characters – the owner and the first group hired. What of

---

12. Adolf Jülicher, *Die Gleichnisreden Jesu*, 2 vols. (Freiburg i. B.: Akademische Verlagsbuchhandlung von J. C. B. Mohr, 1888, 1889).

13. Note the inexactness of the correspondences in Nathan's parable to David in 2 Sam. 12:1–7. Bathsheba is not the one who dies.

14. That the important part is at the end.

the other hirings or the steward? They have no theological relevance. The five hirings heighten narrative tension. The last hiring is needed for the contrast with the first, but the parable would be much less effective with only the first and last. The mention of the steward allows the owner's directions to pay the last hired first and creates distance between the first hired and the owner to give space for the grumbling. Obviously issues of redactional shaping must be considered too.

Study parables that have the same form to see how various kinds of parables function

Not all parables look or act the same. Grouping parables according to form provides insight, not least in determining how much of a parable has significance. Some reject any idea of classification of parables, saying that we should just call them all parables as the New Testament does.[15] Any classification system is an imposition, yes, and no first-century reader classified parables or would have understood our classification systems. However, the New Testament uses *parabolē* for forms we would not, such as the proverb in Luke 4:23 or the riddle in Mark 3:23, so we do classify one way or another, even if it is only for distinguishing such uses or distinguishing between short and long parables. If certain parables are alike in form, it is myopic not to analyse the various forms and learn how they function. The only valid questions are whether a classification system is something we lay on parables or something learned from them and whether the system is flexible enough or a procrustean bed to which parables must conform.

I did not intend to create a classification system for parables, but late in my work felt constrained to because other systems were not sufficient and much was to be learned by doing so. Parables are indirect communication, most *doubly* indirect but some *singly* indirect. Double-indirect parables divert one's attention from oneself *and* from the subject of concern. They are about someone or something else *and* some other topic other than the one under discussion so that defences go down.[16] For example, the parable of the two builders is about someone else *and* another subject, building, while the concern is really about wise living in response to Jesus' message. Single-indirect parables

---

15. E.g. R. Zimmerman, 'How to Understand the Parables of Jesus: A Paradigm Shift in Parable Exegesis', *AcT* 29.1 (2009), pp. 157–182, esp. 167–169.

16. For broader treatment see Snodgrass, *Stories with Intent*, pp. 9–17.

are about another person, not the hearer, but *are about the topic* at hand. They are singly indirect. The rich fool is an obvious example;[17] it is about another person but about money, the subject of concern.

Under double-indirect parables I distinguish similitudes (extended analogies *without a plot*), interrogative parables (those beginning with 'Who from you?', a question often lost in translations to the detriment of understanding), narrative parables (extended analogies *with a plot*) and a particular kind of narrative parable, the juridical parable that forces one to decide against oneself (like Nathan's parable to David). A further category, based on logic, is evident in 'how much more' parables that can be either singly or doubly indirect.

While classification may appear at first unimportant for preaching, actually such awareness contributes crucial insights. This is most obvious with the interrogative parables. All these parables beginning 'Who from you?' (including Jewish and Greek examples) expect the *negative* answer 'No one.' For example, 'What man from you having a hundred sheep and having lost one will not leave the ninety-nine in the pasture and go for the lost until he finds it?' (Luke 15:4) means *no one* would neglect going after a lost sheep; it is what is expected for any rational person. Classification also helps with regard to the question of what elements have significance. Only the *important* people and elements of double-indirect parables have correspondence between image and reality. In a single-indirect parable like the rich fool the man and his barns do not stand for something else. In a similitude like the growing seed the farmer and the stages of growth do not stand for something else, and the attempts to decide whether the farmer stands for God, Jesus or the disciples in the analogy just do not work. The woman, the leaven and the loaves in the similitude of the leaven do not stand for anything. As with all parables, but especially the similitudes, *the analogy is about the whole process.* The present kingdom is like the process of a small, virtually unseen beginning, but the end will bring a full and pervasive result. In interrogative parables such as the friend at midnight, the two men, the family and the bread do not stand for something else, and no neighbour would refuse the request. The parable functions as a 'how much more' parable. If a friend will respond to a request even from a rude neighbour, how much more will God respond to our requests?

The double-indirect parables with a plot are usually longer, and the important elements *do* have significance. The analogy involved with the father, the

---

17. There are five single indirect parables, all in Luke, with the other four being the good Samaritan, the unjust steward, the rich man and Lazarus, and the Pharisee and the tax collector.

prodigal and the elder brother cannot work without correspondences with God, sinners and self-righteous people. Do the far country, the squandering, the robe, the calf, and so on have significance? They have significance, but they do not have correspondences to some theological reality. They have resonances that depict prodigality, restoration and celebration.

If a parable has several correspondences, does it still have only one meaning? The question is naive. Parables, like other literature, have communicative intent – our concern is the communicative intent of Jesus, but any writing has *layers* of significance and we would be remiss not to sense these. The issue with parables is always the *function of the analogy*. Preaching should focus on the function of the analogy and should seek to draw out the significance of that function for modern hearers. Within that function various theological aspects may be present and can be cross-checked with non-parabolic teaching. In other words, there may be numerous ways within the intent of an analogy by which a parable might be appropriated for a modern audience.

Focus on the theology of the parables

To speak of the theology of parables may raise questions. Some scholars in the past discouraged deriving theology from parables, saying that theology should instead be sourced from the letters of the New Testament. But if we are not to derive theology from the parables, why are we reading them? Also it has been popular to say that parables cannot be translated into abstract thought, so their stories may be discarded. Parables should not be reduced to abstract language and should certainly not be discarded, but they can be explained, as all the books on parables assume. The parables are there to give insight into God, the kingdom, the mission of Jesus to Israel and the nature of discipleship. Especially in preaching, the parables themselves remain the most effective way to convey the teaching in them. In some way and at some point the sermon should focus on retelling the parable, preserving as far as possible the dynamics and details of the original.

Doing theology from the parables requires knowing the limits of the analogy. The goal is always the function of the analogy, and the key is knowing when to *stop* interpreting. As with metaphor, parable interpretation is about understanding both the limits and the significance of the analogy.

With reference to theology, we must not forget that parables mean other than what they say. They are not about farming techniques, seeds or interesting people of the past. They point beyond themselves to another reality, the teaching of Jesus. One must discern that to which they point and its significance. That is why one is challenged to hear and discern their intent with expressions such as 'If anyone has ears to hear, let that person hear' (Mark 4:9). The only way to discern their intent is from understanding the context from which they emerge and to which they belong, the teaching of an eschatological restoration Prophet named Jesus. One can put them in another context, as many do, but they will no longer be the parables of Jesus. Jesus' parables and virtually all those in the Old Testament are prophetic instruments. Parables are a rhetorical strategy prophets used to confront, to instruct and to persuade – in Kierkegaard's words, to deceive people into the truth.[18]

Focus on the identity displayed or called for in the parable

I am convinced that hermeneutics must focus on identity as an important goal of interpretation. Scripture seeks to tell us who we are, and the parables portray the identity of God, of the kingdom and of various kinds of people. That makes up much of their theology. For example, the parable of the prodigal, in addition to providing a powerful description of one aspect of God's identity, is a discourse on identity. The leaving and squandering of the prodigal place him at odds with all his true identity stands for. They are an attempt to 'unson' himself,[19] but 'he came to himself', to a realization of an identity he dared not claim. He attempted to persuade the father to allow him to be someone else, a slave, but the father insisted he was a son, an identity restored and celebrated. A similar dynamic takes place with the elder brother, and identity is a factor in some way in most parables.

Do not run from the difficulties

We must not run *from* the difficulties, but run *to* them, for therein lies the opportunity for insight and growth. Some themes of the parables make people uncomfortable, especially judgment and the demand for obedience, but parables are prophetic instruments, and no prophet, especially Jesus, had a mission to make his hearers comfortable or lax in regard to obedience. Judgment and obedience cannot legitimately be ignored, even though people

---

18. *Søren Kierkegaard's Journals and Papers*, vol. 1, p. 288.

19. Miroslav Volf's expression; see his *Exclusion and Embrace: A Theological Exploration of Identity, Otherness, and Reconciliation* (Nashville: Abingdon, 1996), p. 158.

try desperately to do so.[20] On the contrary, they are essential aspects of Jesus' message and of Christian faith. But how will we deal with the violent language of some parables?

Let the Bible be an ancient book

Sometimes parables are as messy as life itself. They mirror the evil in the world and use that evil for the purpose of warning. We cannot sanitize the parables, even when they confront our polite sensibilities, but nor can we read the parables as first-century Semites did – unless we have theological amnesia. We will read and should read as twenty-first-century people; we can do no other. We read conscious of two millennia of world and church history, of evil, failure, holocausts, and even progress. We read hopefully as twenty-first-century people aware of and grieving over history and aware that these first-century parables were not told to us and do not address our agendas, but that they are relevant to us and instructive for us in understanding Jesus' intent and its relevance for our lives. We dare not force Jesus' parables to mirror our context or read them as if they are theological pictures addressed to our context. The parables are theological tools providing a vision of the kingdom – a kingdom of celebration, compassion, of wise living and of the restoration of Israel – and enabling our discussions of the dynamics of forgiveness, the nature of evil, and other issues.

The violent language in some parables *does not teach or condone* violence. It mirrors the seriousness of God's judgment. Dealing with this language will mean understanding it as *parabolic* language rather than in some literalistic fashion. God does not have torturers or dichotomize people, as Matthew 18:34–35 and 24:51 might suggest, and the language of torment for the rich man in Luke 16 is not a depiction of actual circumstances. Such language, like much of Jesus' other teaching, is hyperbole (such as pulling an eye out or cutting off an arm) and is intended to shock and move people to action. The non-parabolic teaching of Jesus provides a good check against taking the hyperbole literally.

---

20. Note how often Robert Capon ends up arguing parables mean the opposite of what they say; e.g. his 'dog biscuit' approach to the parable of the wheat and weeds. Jesus was throwing a dog biscuit to the disciples, condescending to their craving, but he did not really believe in the judgment comments he made. See his *Parables of the Kingdom* (Grand Rapids: Zondervan, 1985), pp. 127–131.

Aim for response

The parables are intended to cause hearing, to enable seeing and to elicit response. They challenge people actually to hear and respond. As with the parable of the sower, mere hearing is not enough; the only valid response is productive living. Preaching parables accordingly should always be a call to respond and act. But what moves people to respond? *Proximity produces impact.* Hearers must be brought close to both the speaker and the scriptural teaching; otherwise there will be no response. Proximity is established through identification of the speaker with the hearers so the hearers feel the speaker is one with them, understands and shares common ground. Proximity is also established through insight and solutions offered for perceived problems. It is also established by the hearer being ushered into a narrative world, the very work that parables do.

Obviously there are other avenues for preaching on parables, such as setting parables in relation to other biblical texts. What is clear though is that parables can be one of the most effective avenues for preaching, but here as elsewhere creativity, sensitivity and attention to the task are required. Let the one with ears hear.

© Klyne Snodgrass, 2013

4. PREACHING THE MIRACLES OF JESUS

Stephen I. Wright

The miracles in Jesus' ministry pose peculiar challenges for the preacher. Neither their original significance nor the use to which we should put the stories now is as unambiguous as sometimes thought. So I need to clarify both these areas before offering some pointers and an example concerning how we might approach the task of preaching Jesus' powerful works today.

The significance of the miracles in the Gospels

The Gospels use no single word for 'miracle'. Acts 2:22 uses three words to summarize Jesus' acts: 'deeds of power' (*dynameis*), 'wonders' (*terata*) and 'signs' (*semeia*). *Dynameis* emphasizes their divine origin: it is by the 'Spirit' or 'finger' of God that Jesus casts out demons (Matt. 12:28 par. Luke 11:20). *Terata* is vaguer, indicating any awesome, unexplained phenomenon. This is consonant with the use of the root *thaumazō* (I amaze) in the Synoptic Gospels to denote the awestruck response to Jesus' mighty acts (see Matt. 9:33; 21:20; Mark 5:20; Luke 11:14).[1] *Sēmeion* indicates a *significant* event or portent. The pagan attitude

---

1. For discussion of occurrences of this root in the LXX and NT see 'Miracle, Wonder, Sign', in *NIDNTT*, vol. 2, pp. 620–635, here pp. 621–626.

was to fear such things as harbingers of evil. For Jews, however, 'signs' always pointed ultimately to God: his creative power, his righteous judgment, his generous mercy. There is no 'world of signification' outside God's providence. All three words reinforce the sense that Jesus' works did not interrupt the divine order, but displayed it in a remarkable way.

John's Gospel regularly uses the third word, *sēmeia*, for Jesus' miracles. This is because John looks at them from the viewpoint of those who recognized them as pointers to Jesus' identity (2:11), and has an eye to their value in eliciting faith among his hearers or readers (20:30–31). This is all a part of John's dramatization of the story of Jesus as a story of his glorious light's dividing people into those who believe in him as God's Son and those who do not (3:18–21). The Synoptics, however, reserve this word mainly for the 'signs' sought by the hard-hearted (e.g. Matt. 16:4; Luke 23:8; cf. Luke 16:31), the deceptive 'signs' of false prophets (Matt. 24:24 par. Mark 13:22) and portents or 'signs' of the end (Matt. 24:30; Luke 21:11, 25). The preacher does well to bear in mind this ambivalence of usage. Jesus' works are indeed profoundly meaningful, pointing not only to the presence of God's kingdom, but also to the identity of the one proclaiming and enacting it. But their meaning was not obvious to all.

The Gospels view Jesus' works as a sign of the actual arrival of God's kingdom (Matt. 12:28 par. Luke 11:20), the re-establishment of his rightful rule over creation. This entailed a spiritual victory over the powers that held humans captive, demonstrated most graphically in Jesus' exorcisms. It is noteworthy that '[t]he possessed are helpless, not evil. In exorcism stories Jesus confronts evil powers, not evil people.'[2] Along with the resuscitations, the exorcisms demonstrate that no human condition is too 'far gone' for God through Jesus to deal with. The beautiful picture of the man called Legion sitting 'clothed and in his right mind' after Jesus had cast the demons out of him (Mark 5:15) encapsulates the wholeness of human dignity to which he had been restored.[3]

With varying degrees of emphasis, Jesus' miracles display the power of God to heal all aspects of the human person: body, mind, emotions, spirit. Many of the accounts refer to conditions we would today call disabilities rather than diseases. Jesus healed those who were paralysed, blind, deaf and dumb. This raises particularly sensitive and controversial issues for the preacher, which we will return to below.

---

2. Mike Graves, *The Sermon as Symphony: Preaching the Literary Forms of the New Testament* (Valley Forge: Judson, 1997), p. 108.

3. Bible quotations in this chapter are from the NRSV.

These were not just deeds done for individuals, however: they enabled the restoration of those individuals to the life of the community. Disease was frequently associated with impurity. Jesus breaks the taboos, for example by touching those with leprosy (Mark 1:41) and thus allowing the sufferer to gain official admittance to society again after his exclusion (Mark 1:44). In fact, Jeffrey John suggests that

> the healing miracles seem to have been selected by the evangelists to show Jesus healing at least one of every category of persons who, according to the purity laws of Jesus' society, were specifically excluded and labelled unclean, or who were set at varying degrees of distance from worship in the inner temple.[4]

The miracles, like Jesus' table fellowship with the excluded, were signs of community renewal.

The fact that the miracles aroused controversy points to a political dimension as well. Other exorcisms were also happening (Matt. 12:27): Jesus aroused interest not through the display of spiritual power per se, but because his remarkable works went along with a wider pattern of activities for which he sought no official authorization. His contravention of the Sabbath regulations, for example, would naturally arouse the suspicion and fear of officialdom (Mark 3:6), who accused him of being possessed himself (Mark 3:22). The issue is the source of his power, and it seems that Luke, at least, saw the conflict as a replay of that between Moses and the magicians of Egypt (Luke's phrase 'finger of God' in 11:20 evokes Exod. 8:19). The liberation of God's people is preceded by extraordinary displays of power met with blank resistance by those in authority. It is thus entirely plausible that though Jesus deliberately eschewed taking political power for himself through the performance of mighty works (Matt. 4:1–11; John 6:15), these works would have contributed to the opposition that led to his death. Power cannot be hidden, and when its exercise upsets vested interests, those interests will seek to extinguish it by whatever means.

The so-called nature miracles demonstrate the work of God on an even wider canvas. For a few focused moments we are allowed to glimpse a future in which the disorders of nature itself are overcome through God's rule. Like the other miracles, they do not introduce a permanently transformed state; rather, they point ahead to one. But nor do they have merely other-worldly significance. Perhaps the most striking example of this is the wedding at Cana

---

4. Jeffrey John, *The Meaning in the Miracles* (Norwich: Canterbury, 2001), p. 10.

(John 2:1–11), a story on one level simply about the overcoming of social embarrassment and shame. It illustrates as well as any of the miracles the invasion of the ordinary by the extraordinary, the mundane by the glorious, the tedious by the awesome, which attends the presence of Jesus.

In Jesus' works God's kingdom is re-established as he ordained it: *mediated through humanity* (Gen. 1:27–28). It was not simply God's power in Jesus, but God's power *in Jesus precisely as a human being* that defeated evil. Thus Jesus comes as the heir of Adam to fulfil Adam's task. But he comes specifically within the family of Israel, as Messiah. This 'anointed one' was sometimes expected to have healing powers, as is seen in the Dead Sea Scrolls (4Q521). When Bartimaeus cries out, 'Son of David, have mercy on me!' (Mark 10:48), he is reflecting the expectation that the messianic king will heal. There is also a link between the role of prophet (like kings, 'anointed ones') and a ministry of healing, as seen in the stories of Elijah and Elisha (1 Kgs 17 – 2 Kgs 5). No doubt the identification of Jesus as Messiah on the basis of his mighty works was neither straightforward nor unambiguous from the point of view of his contemporaries; the question of John the Baptist about whether Jesus is 'the one who is to come' indicates as much (Luke 7:19). Jesus does not answer this, but he does point John to the remarkable events occurring around him, which fulfil the vision of Isaiah 35:5–6 (Luke 7:22).

Moreover, in contrast to the kind of kingdom expectations aroused (and probably entertained) by John, Jesus saw the conflict as essentially spiritual, to be engaged in a non-violent way. He is the shoot from Jesse's branch, the one on whom the Spirit of the Lord rests, who 'shall strike the earth with the rod of his mouth' and 'shall kill the wicked' not with the sword but merely with a word, 'the breath of his lips' (Isa. 11:4; cf. Matt. 12:28).[5]

Jesus' works do not herald an immediate consummation of that kingdom. There is suffering for Jesus, his forerunner and his followers. The miracles express the 'now' of the kingdom but their environment shows us that it is also 'not yet'. The fact that the 'now' is not limited to Jesus' own ministry, however, is demonstrated by the miracles done through the apostles in Acts (e.g. 5:12), for which they were prepared during Jesus' ministry (e.g. Luke 10:17). Certainly Paul regarded signs and wonders, 'deed' as well as 'word',

---

5. See Anthony Le Donne, *Historical Jesus: What Can We Know and How Can We Know It?* (Grand Rapids: Eerdmans, 2011), pp. 88–89. On Jesus' own messianic consciousness as a miracle-worker see the careful conclusions in Graham H. Twelftree, *Jesus the Miracle Worker: A Historical and Theological Study* (Downers Grove: InterVarsity Press, 1999), pp. 275–277.

as integral to his mission among the Gentiles (Rom. 15:18–19). At the same time, the concentration of these early Christian miracles around the figures of the apostles may suggest that their primary function was to attest apostolic authenticity, rather than to continue as essential validations in all generations of the church's witness.

How, though, should we speak today of these remarkable events? Careful attention to the Gospels cannot give us a complete answer to this. We must place the miracles in a wider framework through which we can discern the theological significance of our own time, as well as that of Jesus.

Theological interpretation of the miracles

Communicating the significance of Jesus' miracles today brings the difficulties of contemporary theological appropriation of the New Testament into particularly sharp relief.

In the modern era the miracle stories have been used as part of the attempt to discredit historic Christianity as based on fanciful legend. Defences against this charge often appear, with hindsight, to cede too much ground to the opposition. For example, the argument of William Paley (1743–1805) that the miracles are 'proofs' of Christ's divinity not only remains unconvincing to rationalists who deny the possibility of miracles a priori, but it also misses the nature of the gospel evidence outlined above: that (1) the miracles were seen as signs of the coming kingdom of Yahweh, and of Jesus as the inaugurator of it, rather than of Jesus' 'divinity' in the abstract,[6] and (2) as pointers rather than knock-down 'proofs'.[7]

A common nineteenth-century approach was to 'save' the theological value of the miracles for the modern world by rationalizing them, that is, to

---

6. See the discussion in N. T. Wright, 'Whence and Whither Historical Jesus Studies in the Life of the Church', in Nicholas Perrin and Richard B. Hays (eds.), *Jesus, Paul and the People of God: A Theological Dialogue with N. T. Wright* (London: SPCK, 2011), pp. 115–158, here p. 134.

7. See Reginald H. Fuller, *Interpreting the Miracles* (London: SCM, 1963), pp. 11, 14–15. Christians may sometimes have been led astray by the AV's translation 'infallible proofs' for the Greek *tekmēria* in Acts 1:3 (RV and RSV dropped the 'infallible'; NRSV and NIV replaced it with 'convincing'). We should not impose Enlightenment assumptions about the nature and conditions of 'proof' upon a first-century concept.

show that they in fact accorded with a scientific understanding of natural pro-cesses.[8] David Friedrich Strauss introduced the idea that the miracle stories express theological conviction dressed in the typically 'mythological' language of a primitive culture.[9] Other 'liberal' scholars saw miracles merely as exam-ples of humanitarianism.[10] All such readings drastically underplay the concern of the Gospels with the genuinely material nature of these remarkable acts as they were attested, as well as the importance of materiality within that culture's world view. To some extent this applies also to the sensitive work of a late twentieth-century writer, Kathy Black.[11] She displays keen awareness of the social meanings of sickness and disability in both the setting of Jesus and the Western world today. However, her attention to the powerful way in which Jesus restored outcasts to society leads her to underplay the physicality and eschatological significance of the events.

In his book influenced by Rudolf Bultmann's emphasis on the Gospels' exist-ential challenge, Reginald Fuller describes the Gospel miracles not as 'tales of what happened in far-off Palestine two thousand years ago, but proclamations of the works of Christ today'.[12] Fuller understands these works as 'the preach-ing of the word and the ministry of the sacraments'.[13] This view, too, fails to do justice to the witness of the texts. Even more sceptical scholars acknowledge that the Gospels in some way refer 'back' to historical events, rather than just 'forward' to the church's preaching. Moreover, the theologically vital testimony to God's working in history is undercut if the miracle stories are taken simply as pointing to the present, excluding (or at least marginalizing) what happened in the past. The uniqueness of Jesus is sacrificed to his ongoing work, which itself starts to appear strangely emaciated. Fuller's approach ends up both flat-tening our perception of the stories' essence and diminishing our expectation of what contemporary 'works of Christ' might look like.

---

8. See Albert Schweitzer, *The Quest of the Historical Jesus*, tr. W. Montgomery, J. R. Coates, Susan Cupitt and John Bowden (London: SCM, 2000), pp. 43, 51.

9. David Friedrich Strauss, *The Life of Jesus Critically Examined*, tr. George Eliot and ed. Peter C. Hodgson, 4th ed. (Philadelphia: Fortress, 1972; repr. Ramsey, N. J.: Sigler, 1994). Strauss's introduction deals with the concept of 'myth', while ch. 9 deals with the miracles.

10. Fuller, *Interpreting the Miracles*, pp. 13–14.

11. Kathy Black, *A Healing Homiletic: Preaching and Disability* (Nashville: Abingdon, 1996).

12. Fuller, *Interpreting the Miracles*, p. 114.

13. Ibid., p. 116.

In the half-century since Fuller's book appeared, a much greater openness to the inexplicable has been noticeable in Western societies, where many are disenchanted with modernity's hard edges and open to all kinds of 'spirituality', more or less benign. Moreover, such societies also interpenetrate far more with those of the Majority World which have not inherited Enlightenment scepticism about the miraculous. However one interprets the language of the demonic (and it is interesting that even in the New Testament there is divergence of usage: in contrast to the Synoptics, John does not use it all), the phenomenon of possession, of one's personality being 'taken over' completely, is medically attested.[14] And across the spectrum of church life varieties of healing ministry have been rediscovered. All this helps to belie Bultmann's notorious dictum that it is impossible for people used to modern technology and medicine 'to believe in the New Testament world of spirits and miracles'.[15]

We cannot simply forget about the challenges to belief in miracles that arose in the Enlightenment and afterwards. Claims to have witnessed out-of-the-ordinary events are rightly subjected to scrutiny in our own age, as in any other. But to be open to new discovery is as much a part of the scientific process as it is of Christian discipleship. It is this mixed milieu of openness and criticism within which the gospel is proclaimed today, and this calls for preachers who are open without being credulous, and critical without being sceptical.

Four theological tendencies in our own time shape the task of the preacher of miracles. The 'restorationist' theology of some charismatic circles measures the spirituality of the contemporary church against that of Acts, looking for similar 'signs and wonders', and sometimes believing that Christians today are called to replicate the ministry of Jesus himself. In opposition to this, the Reformed 'cessationist' position asserts that miracles ceased once the age of the first Christians was over and the scriptural canon had come into being.[16]

Both positions are unconvincing. The Gospel miracles are indeed striking in their concentration and quality, as is appropriate to the uniqueness of Jesus and his mission. Nevertheless, the Gospels clearly show that Jesus expected

---

14. See Eric Eve, *The Healer from Nazareth: Jesus' Miracles in Historical Context* (London: SPCK, 2009), pp. 63–69.

15. Rudolf Bultmann, 'New Testament and Mythology', in Hans Werner Bartsch (ed.), *Kerygma and Myth* (New York: Harper & Row, 1961), pp. 1–44, here p. 5.

16. This position is sometimes based on (in my view) unfounded eisegesis of 1 Cor. 13:10: 'when the perfect comes [i.e. on this reading, the canon of Scripture!] the imperfect [i.e. spiritual gifts, miracles, etc.] will pass away'.

the disciples to continue his mission (e.g. John 20:21), which implies that we cannot regard his miracles as totally *sui generis*. But the debate propels us to a deeper understanding of how God works today,[17] and one helpful way forward is a third theological tendency, that of modern Roman Catholic theology inspired particularly by Karl Rahner. This encourages us to discern the signs of God's continued working in his world. The Christian should be able to recognize, and wonder at, the hand of the Creator in all sorts of occurrences and phenomena. Some of these we might label 'miraculous', some not, but it is useful to recall the frequent Johannine use of the broad term 'works' (*erga*) for Jesus' deeds (e.g. John 14:10–12): to focus on the spectacular is to focus too narrowly.

Thus Mary Katherine Hilkert, a Catholic homiletician, encourages preachers not only to name the world's sin and its need for redemption, but also to point to the marks of God's grace within it.[18] The works of Jesus remain unique, yet they also point forward, by family resemblance, to the continued signs of God's kingdom coming. They help us to interpret such events wherever they may occur. By 'family resemblance' here I do not mean their dramatic nature (though dramatic things still happen!), but rather the genuine signals of renewal and restoration – personal, communal and creational – that they emit. Through bringing together the deeds of Jesus and contemporary events – large or small – the preacher not only underlines the continuing redemptive significance of history, but also encourages hearers to receive and bear witness to God's repeated tokens of grace.

A fourth theological trend is narrative theology, which has argued that we cannot strip Scripture of its narrative quality, turning it into either rational proposition or existential challenge, without loss. In particular, such theology summons us to maintain the integrity of our Christian speech, telling the story we have received, without emaciating it through translation into alien terms such as those of rationalist philosophy. It implies that there is no need to 'explain away' the miracles or even 'explain' them, beyond setting them in the context within which we have received them (i.e. that of the biblical canon, classic creeds and church tradition).

---

17. The issue is treated helpfully by Keith Warrington in *Jesus the Healer: Paradigm or Unique Phenomenon?* (Carlisle: Paternoster, 2000), though I find his conclusion that Jesus' healing ministry was simply meant to teach lessons about himself as the bringer of the kingdom somewhat reductive.

18. Mary Katherine Hilkert, *Naming Grace: Preaching and the Sacramental Imagination* (New York: Continuum, 2003).

This approach does not spurn reason; it simply recognizes that the bounds of rationality stretch further than modernity has often acknowledged. We need not go so far as some narrative theologians in speaking only of 'the world of the text', and not the 'real world' behind it. But it now appears far more difficult to separate 'the world of the text' from the 'real world' than was thought half a century ago. Here developments in Gospel studies meet up with developments in theology. Richard Bauckham, for example, argues that it is impossible to separate 'testimony' such as that of the Gospels from bare, 'non-attested' facts.[19] James Dunn emphasizes the dependence of the Gospel stories on the 'impact' and memory of Jesus,[20] while Anthony Le Donne shows how important it is for students of Jesus and the Gospels to appreciate that narrative lenses shape all our perceptions, memories and historiography.[21]

In the light of these current debates, in the next section I will offer three pointers towards an appropriate preaching of Jesus' miracles today.[22]

Homiletical strategies

A canonical approach

Jesus' miracles were not the sudden intrusion of a previously passive God into his world. Scripture points to a still-active Creator whose wonderful works are *always* to be proclaimed to the ends of the earth. Indeed, the word 'miracle' often carries the dualistic Enlightenment implication of a stark separation between 'natural' and 'supernatural' spheres, and may thus be positively misleading.[23] Too often Christians have found themselves on the back foot defending the possibility of something happening outside the 'natural order', when a constant biblically informed celebration of God's amazing works within his world would have enabled a wholly less anxious and more positive approach to speaking of Jesus' miracles.

---

19. Richard Bauckham, *Jesus and the Eyewitnesses: The Gospels as Eyewitness Testimony* (Grand Rapids: Eerdmans, 2006), pp. 472–508.

20. James D. G. Dunn, *Jesus Remembered* (Grand Rapids: Eerdmans, 2003).

21. Le Donne, *Historical Jesus*.

22. My booklet *Reading Gospel Stories in Today's World*, Grove Biblical Series 56 (Cambridge: Grove, 2010), uses the miracles as a case study in contemporary practical use of Scripture.

23. See J. E. Colwell, 'Supernatural', in Sinclair B. Ferguson and David F. Wright (eds.), *New Dictionary of Theology* (Leicester: Inter-Varsity Press, 1988), p. 669.

Nowhere is the truth of God's continuing wonderful works celebrated more exuberantly than in the Psalms. The psalmist proclaims that the inhabitants of the world will be awed by 'the wonders from your signs' (*ta terata apo tōn sēmeiōn*, LXX Ps. 64:9). *Thaumasia* (the same root as *thaumazō*, found in the Gospels for people's amazement at Jesus' works: see above) is used in the LXX for God's marvellous deeds in creation and history (e.g. LXX Pss 9:2; 25:7; 70:17; 85:10).[24] We may also note Psalm 107, which recounts a series of circumstances in which God's people have found themselves in severe trouble, cried to him and known his redemption: hunger and thirst (vv. 4–9), enslavement and imprisonment (vv. 10–16), sickness related to sin (vv. 17–22) and storm at sea (vv. 23–32). All these things happened, and still happen, in the 'normal' course of history, geography and human life. But for the psalmist that course is never merely 'normal'. These are some of Yahweh's 'wonderful works to humankind', expressions of his 'steadfast love' (vv. 8, 15, 21, 31). It is not hard to see the foreshadowing here of things Jesus did, narrated in Mark 2 – 8. As the Evangelists surely recognized, Jesus does what Yahweh does. The mighty works of Jesus are startling in their immediacy and unique in their significance, but they are not a different class of events.

Thus unless the preacher is to operate within the 'functional atheism' that has been said to characterize much of Western society (including, at times, elements of church life), the extolling of God's mighty works, in the past and in the present, should be as natural as the scriptural air we breathe, with the works of Jesus the jewel in their crown.

A narrative approach

A narrative approach should fruitfully shape our preaching on two levels.

First, it will enable us to do justice to the works of Jesus both in their uniqueness and in their relationship to our contemporary world, as we place both within the 'grand narrative' of God. If the life, death and resurrection of Jesus are understood as the decisive turning point of history, this implies *both* (1) that the events of his ministry are not endlessly repeatable, *and* (2) that the world did not just revert to its previous state after his disappearance. The world has turned a corner; the new creation has begun; we anticipate its completion.

In such a perspective we recognize that the rule of Christ is now being shared by his people as they are renewed in the image of God (Col. 3:10). In this grand narrative the miracles are not mere metaphors or symbols of

---

24. See n. 1 above.

a 'spiritual' renewal. They are actual advances in the conflict with the evil that dehumanizes humans and despoils the earth, harbingers of the decisive victory of the resurrection. In the light of this triumph we discern the restoration of humans, their communities and natural environment as genuinely analogous to the miracles, and interpret these current events as signs of the kingdom yet to be consummated.

Black rightly highlights the danger of a purely 'metaphorical' understanding of the miracle stories, which may appear to reduce the significance (say) of physical blindness by interpreting instances of it in the Gospels in purely 'spiritual' (and negative) terms.[25] However, she herself undervalues the physicality of Jesus' healings in order to emphasize their social meaning of including disabled people as full members of the community. But we should not yield up the physical significance of Jesus' works for a communal one, any more than for a spiritual one. These are false antitheses. The Gospels and contemporary psychology are at one in affirming how deeply interrelated body, mind, emotions, spirit, community and environment are. Jesus' death and resurrection mark a crucial transition in the grand narrative, to be sure, but it is simply a transition from a *locally exercised* holistic ministry to a *worldwide* holistic ministry exercised by his followers in his name and the Spirit's power.[26] The continuity of the language of 'salvation' between the ministry of Jesus and the theology of the early church attests this.[27]

Secondly, preachers can learn from the evangelists how to narrate the individual stories. Thus we can avoid overdetermining their possible resonance and impact, leaving the outcome in the hands of God. As noted by Antoinette Clark Wire, 'miracles stories are affirmative statements, not questions or commands. These stories are good news, the kind of news which must be experienced.'[28] A narrative form of preaching can enable the extremes of need

---

25. Black, *Healing Homiletic*, pp. 54–56. See also the discussion of different models of preaching the gospel healing stories, interacting with Black, in Christopher Gower, *Speaking of Healing* (London: SPCK, 2003), pp. 47–59.

26. See the helpful interpretation of the saying about 'greater works' (John 14:12) along these lines in Warrington, *Jesus the Healer*, pp. 147–150.

27. Jesus says to individuals whom he has healed, 'your faith has saved you' (e.g. Mark 5:34). Seyoon Kim rightly argues that the 'salvation' associated with Jesus' kingdom proclamation allows no reductionism into purely this-worldly or other-worldly terms: 'Salvation and Suffering According to Jesus', *EvQ* 68.3 (1996), pp. 195–207, esp. p. 203.

28. Antoinette Clark Wire, 'The Structure of the Gospel Miracle Stories and Their

and the joy of deliverance to come alive in the imagination of our hearers. It is a fitting vehicle for communicating faith in the fact that God is indeed at work to re-establish his rule, without either making crass promises about expecting exactly the same sorts of 'works' today, or resignedly denying that we can discern his present working at all. In attending to the details of the stories we can recapture something of their raw testimony, allow their rich symbolism to emerge in a natural manner and raise the Christological questions in the way the texts themselves raise them.

Proclaiming the mystery

Thus a final pointer towards good preaching of the miracle stories might be 'proclaiming the mystery'. They cannot be made to yield either simple 'proof' of Christian claims, or the possibility of rationalization, without losing that numinous quality which infuses them. We are not privy to the mechanics of Jesus' feeding a hungry crowd with five loaves and two fish: but we can, like the evangelists, recall the event with wonder.

In his chapter in this volume on preaching the parables, Klyne Snodgrass rightly stresses the need to recapture their indirectness for our hearers. Something very similar may apply to the miracles. Craig Blomberg points out that in Mark the parables and miracles are met with similar misunderstanding by the disciples – to the extent that the same quotation from Isaiah 6:9–10, about seeing, and not seeing, is used in relation to both (4:12; 8:17–18).[29] But he also argues that '[j]ust as parables both concealed and revealed, Jesus' miracles, especially those over powers of the natural world, not only triggered misunderstanding but also revealed the in-breaking of the power of God's reign.'[30] It is appropriate then that the miracle stories, like the parables, are preached in such a way as to catch their provocative, unsettling tone, rather than taming them or making them 'obvious'.

Neither Jesus' parables nor his miracles were deliberately befuddling, but more than ordinary insight was needed to penetrate to the heart of both. They did not compel faith in Jesus, but aimed to elicit that which was there. Today

---

Tellers', *Semeia* 11 (1978), pp. 83–113, here 109, as cited in Graves, *Sermon as Symphony*, p. 113.

29. Craig L. Blomberg, 'The Miracles as Parables', in David Wenham and Craig L. Blomberg (eds.), *The Miracles of Jesus*, Gospel Perspectives 6 (Sheffield: JSOT, 1986), pp. 327–359, here pp. 328–329. See also the discussion of the connection between the parable of the sower and the feeding miracles in Eve, *Healer from Nazareth*, p. 108.

30. Blomberg, 'Miracles as Parables', p. 329.

also it is not the preacher's task to be deliberately obscure, but nor is it our task to compel faith. If telling the miracle stories evokes the kind of awed question in our hearers as that expressed by the disciples after the storm was stilled (Mark 4:41), will we not have done our job? 'Who then is this, that even the wind and the sea obey him?'

An example

The American Methodist Eugene Lowry preached a sermon on Mark 5:1–20 entitled 'Cries from the Graveyard'.[31] It begins thus:

> It was an ordinary little gentile village by the lake's edge . . .
> indistinguishable from a dozen other little gentile villages, perhaps. . . .
> except for at least one thing.
> If you were to spend the night there, it's quite possible you would lose some sleep.
> You would be awakened in the middle of the night with some awful cries and moans from some undisclosed source . . .
> cries that sounded half human, half like a wild animal.[32]

Immediately Lowry takes us into the scene. As he develops the story, he skilfully intertwines it with contemporary material in such a way as to allow us to feel both the uncanny force of the unique, original event and its uncomfortable resonances today.

He makes no attempt to demythologize, denigrate or rationalize the element of the demonic. Note how carefully he narrates the witness of the text:

> He was beside himself,
> not in control of his faculties.
> In fact, folks said that he had unclean spirits.
> He had a demon.[33]

But he also acknowledges the difficulty many have with this language, and uses the contemporary medical terminology of 'viruses' as an analogy to show

---

31. Reproduced with commentary in Graves, *Sermon as Symphony*, pp. 118–131, as part of his helpful chapter on preaching the miracles.
32. Ibid., p. 118.
33. Ibid.

that the reality presented here is not, in fact, as alien to us as we might think: 'What we mean when we speak of viruses, is that something has hold of us – quite beyond our control.'[34]

The sermon respects the affirmative form of the story and highlights the intertwining of spiritual, social and physical in Jesus' ministry. The real sting comes when Lowry comments on the local people's response to the miracle: not celebrating, but asking Jesus to leave. What seems initially surprising is shown to be normal behaviour: these were the owners of the drowned pigs, and 'Any time any person or group gets a freedom they never had before, somebody else loses some pigs.'[35] Lowry goes on to tell the story of how thousands of Native Americans were forced off land wanted by white people. He recalls driving through reservations in Oklahoma in his childhood, seeing Native Americans 'mute . . . detached . . . sitting with a distant look in their eyes', and remarks, 'It was like a graveyard . . . it *was* a graveyard . . . of smashed hopes, stolen dreams and broken promises.'[36] He continues:

> They had met their match, all right . . . that once proud Cherokee Nation.
> They had run up against some white folks who owned all the pigs.
> And now upon reflection I can't help but wonder . . .
> Did we chain them up on the reservation because they had a demon . . .
> or did they get the demon because we tied them up on the reservation?[37]

The sermon concludes, like the story, with the challenge to the man to go back and 'tell his friends'. Lowry points out that he did not yet have any – he would make them by sharing the message of liberation. With the minimum of explicit 'application' the hearers are left in no doubt that they too 'have some deciding to do'.[38]

© Stephen I. Wright, 2013

---

34. Ibid., p. 122.
35. Ibid., p. 125.
36. Ibid., p. 127 (his italics).
37. Ibid., p. 128.
38. Ibid., p. 129.

5. PREACHING THE SERMON ON THE MOUNT

David Wenham

Introduction: the primacy and difficulty of the Sermon

The Sermon on the Mount is top-priority teaching. Matthew and Luke make this clear both by recording it as Jesus' first sermon, and also by its forceful ending, with the parable of the builders emphasizing the need to hear and do 'these words of mine' (Matt. 7:24–27).[1]

Its importance has been recognized throughout church history, from the

---

1. The Lucan Sermon on the plain seems to be a version of the same sermon, beginning as it does with 'Blessed are you who are poor' and ending with the parable of the wise and foolish builders (6:17–26). I do not intend to discuss the relevant critical issues in this chapter. (But see some of my reflections in my chapter 'The Rock on Which to Build: Some Mainly Pauline Observations About the Sermon on the Mount', in D. M. Gurtner and J. Nolland [eds.], *Built upon the Rock: Studies in the Gospel of Matthew* [Grand Rapids: Eerdmans, 2007], pp. 187–206.) In this chapter I will mainly work with Matthew's form of the Sermon, though the points made will largely be applicable to Luke's form. The word 'sermon' is not ideal as a description of Jesus' address to his disciples, given the typical churchy connotations of the English word. But we will for convenience stick with the word.

time of the New Testament onwards.[2] This is hardly surprising, given the church's belief in Jesus as God's word incarnate and as the one who had 'the words of eternal life' (John 6:68). The Sermon on the Mount has been seen as eternally important. And its relevance is clear when we remind ourselves that the main part of the Sermon is about (1) relationships (including questions of marriage and sex, but also things such as swearing and attitudes to enemies), (2) religion, including prayer, (3) material needs and material wealth.

But despite its importance biblically and historically, modern preachers sometimes find the Sermon quite difficult,[3] for three reasons at least.

First, the Sermon is seen as presenting a legalistic works-based righteousness. Thus in Matthew 5:17–20 Jesus positively affirms the law, even down to the jot or tittle, and denounces those who fail to uphold it. Then Jesus says bluntly, 'unless your righteousness surpasses that of the Pharisees and the teachers of the law, you will certainly not enter the kingdom of heaven'. The rest of the Sermon is no better, with its strong emphasis on ethical behaviour and on that being a criterion of judgment; so the parable at the end of the Sermon is all about hearing *and doing,* and is preceded by Jesus' solemn warnings that saying 'Lord, Lord' and even doing mighty works in his name will not save. 'Then I will tell them plainly, "I never knew you. Away from me, you workers of law-lessness [literal tr.]!"', *anomia* in the Greek (7:21–23). It all sounds like works religion and far from the gospel of grace, and it seems the antithesis of Paul's assertion of freedom from the law.

This is problematic for those brought up on a Reformation emphasis on justification by faith not works, but also for those influenced by postmodern-ism and modern pluralism, for whom authoritative laying down of the law is abhorrent. It is also difficult for those with a high view of Scripture, since it

---

2. Witness the echoes of the sermon in the NT letters; for example, in the ethical teaching in Rom. 12 – 15; see Michael Thompson's *Clothed with Christ* (Sheffield: JSOT, 1994); also Christopher L. Carter, *The Great Sermon Tradition in Fiscal Framework in 1 Corinthians* (Cambridge: Cambridge University Press, 2009). On James and 1 Peter see chapters by P. Davids and G. Maier in D. Wenham, *Gospel Perspectives 5* (Sheffield: JSOT, 1984). On later church history see J. P. Greenman, T. Larsen and S. R. Spencer (eds.), *The Sermon on the Mount Through the Centuries* (Grand Rapids: Brazos, 2007).

3. On modern neglect of the Sermon see Glen Stassen and David Gushee's forceful comments in *Kingdom Ethics* (Downers Grove: InterVarsity Press, 2003), p. 11; also David Buttrick, *Speaking Jesus: Homiletic Theology and the Sermon on the Mount* (Louisville: Westminster John Knox, 2002), p. 4.

seems to point to a contradiction within the Bible, with Matthew opposing Paul.[4]

A second problem is the impossibility of the Sermon's demands. The preacher who says, 'anyone who looks at a woman lustfully has already committed adultery with her in his heart' (Matt. 5:28) and then 'You must be perfect' is liable to be laughed out of the pulpit – as someone living on a different and unreal planet. People have tried to help by suggesting that Jesus never intended to be offering a realistic way of life, but simply to be describing the perfect standards of God, thus making us realize our failure and need for his mercy and grace. In other words it is not practical ethics at all, but designed to drive us to our knees. But that view will not do: the Sermon is evidently a serious call to radical and practical discipleship – 'You are the salt of the earth . . . the light of the world . . .' (Matt. 5:13, 14) – and to take it as anything else is at best an ingenious evasion, and at worst to be like the man who built his house on sand by failing to listen to Jesus' words. Another scholarly proposal, namely that this is an interim ethic for those who expected the world to end very soon, similarly does not do justice to the text, and in any case fails to get the preacher off the hook, unless perhaps it justifies him or her in completely ignoring it.

A final area of difficulty has to do with interpreting some of the particular demands of the Sermon. Everyone recognizes that the Sermon offers some very radical ideas: 'do not take an oath', 'do not resist the one who is evil', 'give to the one who begs from you', 'love your enemies', 'do not lay up treasures on earth', 'judge not'. But how literally should these things be taken? The church throughout history has blatantly not followed the letter of Jesus' law: Christians have taken oaths, gone to war, laid up treasures on earth, and done a lot of judging. But can this be justified? Is it a case of Christians twisting Scripture to suit themselves? A significant number of Christians through the centuries have taken the teaching at its face value, for example espousing non-juring or pacifism, and have often suffered for their convictions.

The doubts in these three areas have undoubtedly deterred Christian preachers when it comes to the Sermon. We more readily run to the positive stories of grace in the Gospels, to parables like that of the prodigal son and to the Pauline gospel.

However, this need not and should not be so. This chapter will (1) look at the big questions about the interpretation (and so the preaching of the

---

4. D. Sim, *The Gospel of Matthew and Christian Judaism* (London: Continuum, 2000), pp. 207–211, argues for such an opposition.

sermon) I have identified; then (2) some relatively brief additional comments will be made about preaching the Sermon.

Some general observations about understanding the Sermon

The key to understanding the Sermon, as so often with understanding difficult issues in the Bible, lies in seeing things in context.

Three observations about the context
There is the context of Matthew's and Luke's Gospels as a whole
Although Matthew in his Gospel is interested in the Jewish law (and Judaism in general), in obedient living and divine judgment, his Gospel is far from grace-less. At the very start of the Gospel Jesus is named as the one who will save his people from their sins, and God's forgiveness is a theme that permeates the Gospel (1:21; 18:21–35). Jesus in Matthew, no less than in the other Gospels, is the one who brings the good news of the kingdom and healing; immediately before the Sermon on the Mount, the text from Isaiah is quoted about 'the people living in darkness have seen a great light' (4:16–25). Later in the Gospel there is the great invitation 'Come to me, all you who are weary and burdened . . . For my yoke is easy and my burden is light' (11:28–30), in contrast to the actions of the scribes and Pharisees (23:4). Jesus is the one who goes to the cross 'for the forgiveness of sins' (26:28; only in Matthew's account of the Last Supper), and whose death results in the tearing of the temple curtain and the raising of the dead (27:51–54). The Gospel is full of grace.

And, although Jesus came to fulfil the law, not to destroy it, he quotes Hosea on two different occasions: 'I desire mercy, not sacrifice' (9:13; 12:7), he justifies his disciples in their relaxed attitude to the Sabbath (12:1–14) and he speaks of the sons of the kingdom being free – in a passage that is intriguingly Pauline in its emphasis on freedom and not causing offence (17:24–27).

If Matthew's Gospel is full of grace through Jesus, Luke's is the more clearly so. It is not just the parable of the prodigal son, but passage after passage shows Jesus to be a friend of outsiders and sinners (ch. 15; 19:1–10; 23:40–43).

A second contextual clue has to do with the particular context in which Matthew was written
There is a whole range of scholarly views on the Gospel's origins: what seems clear is that Matthew was writing to people with a Jewish background and in the context of some conflict between Christians and the synagogue authorities.

One of the key Jewish objections to the new Christian movement seems to have been 'This Jesus movement makes claims to being true Judaism, but actually represents a serious undermining of Jewish law, traditions and identity.' Jesus himself was attacked for his liberalism towards the law, because of his mixing with sinners and his approach to the Sabbath; Jesus' followers, not least the turn-coat Paul, were seen as betraying the Jewish heritage, abandoning the Jewish law, dividing Jewish communities. And the accusation against Jesus and his followers was that they were lowering the standards of which the Jews were so proud and that were expressed in the received law of Moses. Reports of what was going on in some of the Christian churches, such as Corinth, would only have confirmed to the Jews that this was exactly what the new Christian movement was doing, including to former Jews who were embracing the new Messiah.

It is in that context that the Matthean emphasis on Jesus as fulfilling the law and bringing a higher righteousness makes sense. In Matthew 3:15 Jesus tells John the Baptist that it is appropriate for him 'to fulfil all righteousness', and in the Matthean Sermon on the Mount Jesus makes it very clear that he is not destroying the law or lowering standards, but 'fulfilling' it and bringing a higher, not a lower, ethic: the standard of the kingdom of God ('heaven' in Matthew) is perfection.

So Jesus in Matthew is not a Jewish legalist, even when he refers to the 'least of these commandments'; rather he is emphasizing that with his kingdom preaching he is not chipping away at the law, subtracting bits and lowering the standards. He is doing something much more radical: his teaching has God's authority and in a real sense supersedes the Old Testament law – 'you have heard that it was said . . . but I say to you'; he is bringing a new order, a new covenant, which is the fulfilment of the old, every bit of the old, but is much higher.

The third bit of context that is important is the context of the Sermon itself
Contrary to some impressions, the Sermon is shot through with grace. It begins in the Beatitudes on a strong note of grace: 'Blessed are the poor in spirit [Luke 'Blessed are the poor'], for theirs is the kingdom of heaven'. Matthew has nine beatitudes, the first eight being in the third person, 'they, theirs', and those eight have an almost poetic structure, the first and the last having the same refrain, 'for theirs is the kingdom of heaven', and the first four forming one stanza, the second four another.[5]

---

5. See C. H. Talbert's particularly helpful book *Reading the Sermon on the Mount* (Columbia: University of South Carolina Press, 2004), p. 49.

1 Blessed are the poor in spirit,
     for theirs is the kingdom of heaven.

2 Blessed are those who mourn,
     for they will be comforted.

3 Blessed are the meek,
     for they will inherit the earth.

4 Blessed are those who hunger and thirst for **righteousness**,
     for they will be filled.

5 Blessed are the merciful,
     for they will be shown mercy.

6 Blessed are the pure in heart,
     for they will see God.

7 Blessed are the peacemakers,
     for they will be called children of God.

8 Blessed are those who are persecuted because of **righteousness**,
     for theirs is the kingdom of heaven. (Matt. 5:3–10)

The first four beatitudes all speak of the 'happiness' of those in some sort of need: the kingdom is promised to them, and will bring them relief and 'happiness' indeed;[6] the second four speak of the kingdom's belonging to those whose lives are pure, loving and righteous. The shift of focus in the middle of the Beatitudes is striking, and it is as though an announcement of the grace of God to sinners comes first, and then comes a description of the transformed lives of the disciples who receive that grace.[7]

If the Sermon begins on a note of grace before moving on to a description of the transformed life Jesus' disciples are called to live, grace is not absent later from the Sermon. Conspicuously it is there in the Lord's Prayer and the petition 'forgive us our debts as we forgive those who are indebted to us'. Jesus presumes that his disciples will need to be forgiven, and to forgive others for their sins. And his prayer implicitly expresses the conviction that 'Our Father in heaven' will hear and answer such prayer.

---

6. The Greek word *makarios* so often translated 'blessed' in the English translations is better translated 'happy', though happy in the serious sense!

7. Luke's Beatitudes come into the first category. His version of the Beatitudes has been seen as more earthy or materialistic than Matthew's, which ties in with his interest in the real-life issues of wealth and poverty. But the message of grace is there equally.

There could seem to be a contradiction between the earlier challenge to perfection 'You must be . . .' and the recognition in the prayer that sins will continue and need forgiving. But the prayer itself suggests an answer to that problem.

The prayer of the Lord has seven petitions, not six as is often argued.[8] A literal translation highlights its form:

Father of us the one in the heavens,
(1) hallowed the name of you;
(2) come the kingdom of you;
(3) happen the will of you,
     as in heaven also on earth;
     (4) the bread of us for the coming day give us today,
(5) and forgive us the debts of us,
     as also we have forgiven the debtors of us;
(6) and do not bring us into temptation,
(7) but rescue us from the evil (one). (Matt. 9:9–13)

The prayer has three petitions, all asking in different ways for God's good and perfect will to be done 'on earth as in heaven', then a central petition asking for the Lord's provision of his children's material needs, and then three petitions addressing issues to do with sin, temptation and the devil's attacks. The emphasis on the negative realities in the lives of the disciples is striking, but this highlights the fact that Jesus' followers are in an 'already, not yet' situation: they are experiencing (and longing for more of) God's kingdom in their lives, but are also in an ongoing situation of conflict and struggle. They are to pray, because they need God's grace helping them to live kingdom lives and to do the will of God, but also forgiving them when they fail.

If the Lord's Prayer is about grace, so is the strong and powerful encouragement at the end of the Sermon to the disciples to 'Ask', 'seek' and 'knock' (7:7–11). They are to do that, because prayer is efficacious because of the graciousness of the heavenly Father, who loves to give 'good gifts' to those who ask him. The injunction to pray is not primarily demand, but encouragement and promise, given near the end of the Sermon, to disciples who are called to live the Sermon. They are to look to the heavenly Father, who cares for them practically, but will also help them to live as his children.

---

8. See my 'The Sevenfold Form of the Lord's Prayer in Matthew's Gospel', *ExpTim* 121.8 (2010), pp. 377–382.

The Sermon not impossible legalism, but about kingdom living

We are now in a position to go back to our opening questions about the Sermon's being legalistic and impossibly depressing. The Sermon is not a legalistic reinforcement of the Old Testament law, but is about living kingdom lives, like and with Jesus.

So after the Beatitudes, Jesus' opening challenge to his disciples is that they are to live as salt and light in the world. He does not say '*Try* to be light and salt' but 'You *are* salt and light,' so they are to act accordingly. The rest of the sermon can be seen as explaining some of what that means in practice. The call is to 'let your light shine before others, that they may see your good deeds and glorify your Father in heaven' (5:16).

That call can ring alarm bells with Christians. Is it recommending 'works-based' religion? And is it saying that flaunting good works is something justifiable, despite what Jesus says elsewhere in the sermon (6:1–18)? However, Jesus is certainly not saying 'draw attention to yourself', but rather 'live lives that speak of God to people'. And the word 'good' in the phrase 'good works' is *kalos*, which may appropriately be translated 'beautiful'; so Jesus is calling his disciples to beautiful living, living as children of the heavenly Father (as he emphasizes at various points in the Sermon), so that people can see that his disciples are living different and attractive lives.[9]

This is totally different from law-bound religion; though far from being destructive of the Old Testament law of God, it represents its 'fulfilment', as Jesus says in 5:17. He is in the business of bringing a far higher righteousness than that already quite high righteousness exemplified in the lives of the scribes and the Pharisees.

In Matthew's Gospel it is made clear at his baptism that Jesus himself is the model to 'fulfil all righteousness' (3:13–15). He goes on to overcome Satan's temptations, and then to come into Galilee, fulfilling the prophecy about the people who have 'seen a great light' (4:16). Then immediately in the next story Jesus calls his four disciples to come 'follow me', and they 'followed him' (4:18–22).

The scene is thus set for the Sermon to explain what following Jesus means. It means living like Jesus, as light in the world, living different lives, not superficially righteous but righteous from the heart, not compromising with evil (e.g. by use of oaths), not just loving those who will love us in return, but loving even enemies, like the heavenly Father. It means perfection.

---

9. The call to the disciples to live visibly different lives is an important one elsewhere in the NT; e.g. Mark 10:42; John 13:35; Phil. 2:14; 1 Pet. 3:1.

The call to perfection sounds hopeless and depressing when seen in one way. From another angle it is exactly what we would expect from Jesus: it is beautiful kingdom living. And to be called to perfection is not something negative. The young musician wants to be note-perfect, not just to get 60% of the notes right; the diver wants to do the perfect dive. So Jesus calls his disciples as God's children to be perfect. He knows they will fail; and there is mercy at that point, but that does not make a lower standard appropriate.

How to live this way
Kingdom living
But how can Jesus' disciples even begin to live that way? Matthew's Gospel emphatically does not suggest that moral effort is all that is needed. The call is in the context of following Jesus and in the context of God's kingly rule breaking in. Jesus' own kingdom ministry began with his baptism and endowment with the Spirit, and his kingdom work was 'by the Spirit of God' (12:28). It is clear that those who follow him have embraced his message and 'the kingdom of God has come upon' them. So they can begin to live it out, however falteringly. But what does this mean in practice?

Acknowledging that they are poor in spirit
The starting point is hearing the call of Jesus and responding. This involves recognizing one's own need – being poor in spirit, and recognizing the need for God's work. This starting point is Matthew 11:28, 'Come to me, all you who are weary and burdened, and I will give you rest.' Such coming to Jesus is becoming children of the heavenly Father.

Going with Jesus
If the beginning is coming, the next step is going with Jesus, following him and learning from him. For the disciples this was literal: they went with him, listened to him, watched him in action. For the readers of Matthew's Gospel there will not be physical following, but the promise of the Lord's presence is there in Matthew ('Immanuel', 1:23; 'I am with you always', 28:20). And the Gospel narrative itself is designed to give readers the experience of seeing and hearing Jesus, and thus growing as his disciples.[10]

---

10. Cf. John 20:29–31 on the evangelist's desire that people who do not see literally may still come to believe through his narrative. See also Heb. 12:2 on 'fixing our eyes on Jesus', and 1 Cor. 11:1 on imitating Jesus.

Prayer to the heavenly Father
And then there is prayer to the heavenly Father, prayer for his help, confidence in his willingness to give 'good gifts' (Matt. 7:11). In Luke that promise (not in his version of the Sermon) is that the Father will give 'the Holy Spirit' to those who ask (11:13). If this is the earliest interpretation of Jesus' 'good gifts', it surely expresses what Matthew implies: that living the Sermon is something the Holy Spirit enables.

So the Sermon is not legalistic or depressing, but a challenging and exciting picture of what God can do in the life of the disciple.

But how literal?

But is the Sermon to be taken completely literally? The answer must be no. Jesus uses vivid pictures to convey his message – hence the deliberately humorous picture of the man trying to get a speck out of his brother's eye (7:3–5), so also the joltingly strong words about chopping off the hand and plucking out the eye in relation to sexual sin (5:29–30). The Sermon as a whole is full of pictures and illustrations of what kingdom living will look like: signposts or 'verbal icons' into kingdom behaviour.[11] To interpret the signposts as laws takes away from the power of the Sermon, since Jesus is not giving regulations, so much as a way of life.

The danger in saying that it is not law or regulations is that this could evacuate the Sermon of its challenge. So I may effectively ignore its teaching on divorce, the use of oaths or love of enemies on the ground that it is not law but something more like inspiration or aspiration. But the Sermon is deliberately concrete and down to earth, and it is essential that the preacher does not replace what Jesus said with harmless generalizations about loving other people.

Practical conclusions for the preacher

If what I have suggested in the discussion so far is correct, what are the practical implications for today's preacher? Six things may briefly be noted.

Grace and relationship, not legalism
The Sermon can be heard as depressingly burdensome. It is essential to explain it in the context of grace, the kingdom of God and the power of the

---

11. So Talbert, *Reading*, p. 91.

Holy Spirit. Also in the context of relationship – with the heavenly Father, who (1) forgives, and (2) loves to hear and answer his children's prayer, with Jesus as Lord, the one who does not break a bruised reed (12:18; 11:28). It is not designed to produce a guilt trip, but is for those who hunger and thirst for righteousness.

Grace, not works

It is also important to preach the Sermon within a context of grace, because it can so easily be heard as teaching salvation by our own efforts. Few people think of themselves as perfect; many think they are good enough to reach the pass mark for the kingdom of heaven. Such thinking is miles away from the thinking of the Sermon, where the standard is higher than that of the scribes and Pharisees (who scored very high marks religiously) and where the calling is to perfection, not to some moderately righteous life. In this respect those who have seen the sermon as setting an impossible standard in order to drive us to our knees have a point. However, the sermon was not designed for this, but to describe the beautiful calling of discipleship, which God wills to produce within the hearts and lives of his people. It is his grace that makes it possible to start on the narrow road that leads to life, that helps us on that way and extends forgiveness when we fall.

Positive beauty

The Sermon can easily be heard as negative: do not do this and that – no treasures on earth, no lust, and so on. Even when it is positive, it can seem to be condemning. We must make clear how positive it is – the call to be salt and light, to extreme love, to lay up treasures in heaven, to prayer. Even the difficult parts are positive: being called to purity of heart – contrast our pornographic culture and our often-polluted minds – or to plain, honest speaking, or for a love that does not just reach friends and relatives, but that reaches out to enemies. It is a call away from grubby mediocrity and from superficial religiousness into something challenging and exciting, namely living as God wants human beings to be – this is true wisdom. The old song put it like this:

> Let the beauty of Jesus be seen in me,
> all his wondrous compassion and purity.
> O thou Spirit divine,
> all my nature refine,
> till the beauty of Jesus be seen in me.

John Stott's outstanding exposition of the Sermon on the Mount was originally entitled *Christian Counterculture*, and the Sermon is not a call to bourgeois
morality or boring religion, but to changed lives and a new society.[12] Our
preaching needs to bring this positive vision unapologetically.

Practicality

The Sermon is full of practical examples of kingdom living, with comments
about divorce, beggars, use of money, praying, and so on. There are two
opposite dangers for the preacher.

The first danger is in treating these examples legalistically, as though the
sermon were a compendium of rules, when it is actually something much
bigger. Not that rules or commandments are bad in themselves (indeed the
Sermon is a positive affirmation of the goodness of the Old Testament law,
and Matthew ends his Gospel by speaking climactically of Jesus' own commands, 28:20).[13] Nor is the Sermon irrelevant for the church when the latter
formulates its rules and disciplines; on the contrary (see e.g. Paul's use of
Jesus' teaching on divorce in 1 Cor. 7:10–11). But still a bigger vision is presented in the Sermon, which is much more positive and encouraging than a
list of rules.

The second danger is in preaching vaguely. The Sermon gives concrete
examples of kingdom living; we must not preach generalizations but need to
preach practically. So the Sermon gives the illustration of saying *raca* (worth-
less fellow) to my brother; today we might talk about bullying via social net-
working sites. The Sermon, having warned against moth and rust's affecting
earthly treasures, encourages laying up treasures in heaven. That has often
been interpreted generally as teaching that we should have heavenly priorities;

---

12. Later published as *The Message of the Sermon on the Mount* (Leicester: Inter-Varsity
Press, 1992). Other notable expositions include D. A. Carson, *The Sermon on the
Mount: An Evangelical Exposition of Matthew 5–7* (Grand Rapids: Baker, 1978; Carlisle:
Paternoster, 1978), and the older classic, D. M. Lloyd Jones, *Studies in the Sermon on
the Mount* (London: Inter-Varsity Press, 1959). See also R. A. Guelich, *The Sermon on
the Mount: A Foundation for Understanding*, WBC (Waco: Word, 1982).

13. Matthew may well have had in his sights Christians who were in danger of ditching
the OT law and indeed all law, on the grounds of freedom in Christ. In an age
when many Christians have a negative view of the OT and many churches give
extremely little attention to it, we do well to notice Jesus' immensely positive view
of the OT as a divine book, even in the details, which he 'fulfilled' and which his
followers 'fulfil' when they do Jesus' teaching.

but Luke 12:33–34 points in a distinctly practical direction, and the modern preacher will likely be preaching about ethical investment and indeed ethical disinvestment ('sell your possessions').

The serious challenge

The preacher needs to convey the Sermon's challenge to a different lifestyle, as something eternally important. The Sermon is neither depressing nor comfortable. It contains serious warnings especially at the end, where Jesus warns of empty discipleship, of saying 'Lord, Lord,' yet not doing the Lord's will. In preaching the Sermon we are not offering people a pleasant lifestyle choice, but the way that leads to life, as opposed to the way that leads to destruction. It is a rock on which to build.

The sermon has a lot of references to judgment and to hell: for example, 5:20, 22, 29, 30; 6:15; 7:1, 13, 19, 23, 27. 'It fell with a great crash' are the last solemn words of the Sermon, referring to those who fail to do what Jesus has commanded. Preaching in those terms today does not come easily to us. It does not come easily to those who cannot easily imagine God's saying 'I never knew you' to anyone. Nor to those whose understanding of conversion and regeneration sits uncomfortably with Jesus' saying 'Away from me' to any disciples. But Jesus' warnings are unmistakable, as elsewhere in his teaching; for example, in the parables about faithful and unfaithful servants, where the unfaithful are thrown into outer darkness (24:45 – 25:30). We may conclude that such servants were never real disciples, but Jesus' words are clearly directed to signed-up and apparently effective followers.

This teaching of Jesus is not a contradiction of grace. But it is a warning against a cheap view of grace and discipleship that suggests it does not really matter what I do.[14] Jesus is in the business of bringing in the kingdom of God and producing people whose lives are transformed by the rule of God in their lives – he is not in the business of generating religiosity.

The preacher's integrity

Jesus' saying about those who say 'Lord, Lord' is especially relevant to preachers and Christian leaders who may do mighty things in Jesus' name (7:15–23). These evidently impressive Christian leaders (on the outside at least) are sent away by Jesus as 'evildoers'. They have no integrity. Perhaps the most important thing to say about preaching the Sermon is that we need first to listen to

---

14. See famously Dietrich Bonhoeffer's *The Cost of Discipleship* (London: SCM, 1959).

it ourselves, so that we can then, with integrity, bring its serious, but seriously exciting and attractive, teaching to others.[15]

© David Wenham, 2013

---

15. Do the Matthean and Lucan forms of the Sermon teach us anything about how to preach? The evangelists were undoubtedly more interested in the content than the form (and in any case could not have given us much more than a synopsis of Jesus' original sermon with extracts). But, although we would be unwise to see the form as in anyway prescriptive, we may nevertheless be impressed by the striking opening (the Beatitudes), the structured and relevant teaching at the heart of the Sermon, the use of vivid, pictorial, provocative and memorable ways of making points, and the crystal-clear presentation of the challenge of Jesus' way at the end of the Sermon.

6. THE CHALLENGES AND OPPORTUNITIES FOR PREACHING FROM THE ACTS OF THE APOSTLES

Christoph Stenschke

Introduction

The book of Acts is the first place to look for examples of preaching the New Testament, as this book contains a selection of the first sermons preached by Christians.[1] It records Peter's sermons on the day of Pentecost (2:14–36), in the temple (3:12–26) and before a Gentile audience in Caesarea (10:34–43), and Paul's sermons in the synagogue of Pisidian Antioch (13:14–41), in Lystra and Athens (14:15–17; 17:22–31), and also his one and only sermon to a Christian audience in Miletus in Acts 20:18–35. These sermons have been analysed in detail in New Testament scholarship. In addition to the insight they offer into Luke's theology, they have been a source of inspiration for many Christian sermons. We may, for instance, gather from them how to preach the gospel in different circumstances.[2]

---

1. Other sources of inspiration have been the sermons and teaching of Jesus. Some of the NT letters (e.g. 1 Peter and Hebrews) have been understood as written early Christian sermons (homilies).

2. A representative example is D. Flemming, *Contextualization in the New Testament: Patterns for Theology and Mission* (Downers Grove: InterVarsity Press, 2005), pp. 56–88, who considers Paul's sermons in Acts 13, 14 and 17 as 'compelling

Many readers and preachers are attracted to Acts, as 'most sectors of evangelical Protestantism have a "restoration movement" mentality. We regularly look back to the church and Christian experience in the first century either as the norm to be restored, or the ideal to be approximated.'[3] John Stott describes the benefits of doing so:

> It has, in fact, been a salutary exercise for the Christian church of every century to compare itself with the church of the first, and to seek to recapture something of its confidence, enthusiasm, vision and power. At the same time, we must be realistic. There is a danger lest we romanticize the early church, speaking of it with bated breath as if it had no blemishes. For then we shall miss the rivalries, hypocrisies, immoralities and heresies which troubled the church then as now. Nevertheless, one thing is certain. Christ's church had been overwhelmed by the Holy Spirit, who thrust it out to witness.[4]

This great appreciation of Acts raises some of the hermeneutical issues involved in applying and preaching the book.

The challenges of preaching the book of Acts

The task of preaching from Acts seems straightforward.[5] After all, Acts contains many inspiring accounts of the spread of early Christianity and many

examples of evangelistic contextualisation' (p. 57). Flemming notes that 'Luke probably intends Paul's evangelistic speeches in Acts to provide a model for how the gospel approaches various groups of people, which his readers can appropriate in their own witness to the world. Likewise, the church today has much to learn from these first-century narratives' (p. 85).

3. Gordon D. Fee and Douglas K. Stuart, *How to Read the Bible for All Its Worth*, 2nd ed. (Bletchley: Scripture Union, 1998), p. 95.

4. John R. W. Stott, *The Message of Acts* (Leicester: Inter-Varsity Press, 1996), p. 10. Stott's exposition is helpful in that it is particularly sensitive to questions of contemporary application. Others with a similar orientation are W. R. Larkin, *Acts*, IVPNTC (Leicester: Inter-Varsity Press, 1995); and A. Fernando, *Acts*, NIVAC (Grand Rapids: Zondervan, 1998).

5. For discussions of the application of Acts see B. Witherington, *The Acts of the Apostles: A Socio-Rhetorical Commentary* (Grand Rapids: Eerdmans; Carlisle: Paternoster, 1998), pp. 97–102; Fee and Stuart, *How to Read*, pp. 105–110; Larkin,

passages that seem directly applicable: read them, explain them, add a few illustrations and apply them to the present needs of the congregation. Tell the audience to do likewise or to avoid sins such as that of Ananias and Sapphira (5:1–11), or the murmuring of Acts 6:1. While this procedure may work well with some passages, there are several problems involved.

1. In spite of how Acts is often used, Luke is a *narrator* and not a *systematic theologian*. He does not offer a handbook on church planting and church growth, nor a manual for pastoral ministry. Luke obviously mentions issues such as evangelism, baptism, church order and leadership (areas where we might wish to have a 'biblical' precedent for our own practice), but he does not provide clear guidelines for all occasions. He offers a selection of what happened under specific circumstances over a period of time, not necessarily of what *should have happened at the time, or should always happen*. There is little authorial evaluation of what is narrated. Take, for example, issues of leadership: we read of the apostles leading the church in Jerusalem; later James and a group of elders appear in leadership roles. Who these elders were and how they were qualified is not mentioned, nor how they were installed and by whom. The congregation chose seven men for special service who were to be 'of good repute, full of the Spirit and of wisdom' (6:3 ESV). The qualifications mentioned here probably apply to all office bearers of the church (and we rightly expect that to be the case!), but Luke does not say so. At the end of the first missionary journey Paul and Barnabas installed elders in the newly founded churches (14:23). Were they nominated by the congregations, as in Acts 6? How were they qualified for their task? Is this to be the pattern for finding the right people under similar circumstances?[6]

What are we to make of Luke's descriptions?

> The question . . . is *how* we are going to interpret these narrative passages? For some of them are not self-interpreting, and contain within themselves few if any clues as to what we are intended to learn from them. Are they necessarily normative? Is the behaviour or experience recorded in them meant to be copied? or perhaps avoided?[7]

Acts, pp. 13–17; and I. H. Marshall, *The Acts of the Apostles*, NTG (Sheffield: JSOT, 1992), pp. 101–105.

6. For other examples see Fee and Stuart, *How to Read*, pp. 95–101.

7. Stott, *Message of Acts*, p. 12 (his italics). Fee and Stuart, *How to Read*, p. 105 (their italics): 'Does the book of Acts have a Word that not only *describes* the primitive church but *speaks as a norm* to the church of all times?'; cf. pp. 106–110.

While not a detailed blueprint, Acts is more than mere history. Witherington observes that Luke 'is striving to be a reliable and careful narrator of the material he is conveying, not only because he is a good historian but also because *he believes that this material can and should be used for instruction in his own day*'.[8] Witherington continues:

> It is also hard to doubt that Luke believes that God continued to act in his own day in similar fashion to the way God in the person of the Holy Spirit is portrayed as acting in Acts. There is no hint, for instance, that Luke takes the so-called apostolic age as somehow totally unique and unrepeatable, and so to be radically distinguished from the time in which he wrote insofar as either belief or behaviour or even the miraculous activity of God is concerned.[9]

Acts does provide examples and patterns to be followed by later Christians. While not everything *can* or *should* be closely copied, there are many accounts and examples that may inspire Christians of all ages. Again Witherington:

> Though characterisation is not a *major* concern of Luke, it is fair to say that he intends his own Christian audience to follow in the footsteps of people like Peter . . . in terms of their words and deeds. In other words, the vast majority of the behaviour of the *Christian* characters in the story is probably meant to be seen as exemplary. This is not always the case of course, as the example of John Mark's abandoning of the missionary journey or of Ananias and Sapphira shows. Thus, even the Christian characters in the narrative have to be scrutinised on the basis of Christian standards or ideals listed in the text.[10]

As a guideline for distinguishing between what Luke sees as normative and what he sees as merely historically important, Witherington advises: '1) look

---

8. Witherington, *Acts of the Apostles*, p. 97 (my italics).

9. Ibid., p. 98.

10. Ibid., p. 99 (his italics). Witherington continues, 'By standards and ideals, I mean the sort of material we find in the summary passages in Acts 2:43–47 or 4:32–37. It is widely recognized that these are Lukan redactional summaries meant to boil down into a few phrases some of the essential positive characteristics of the Jerusalem church. These standards can be used to evaluate, for example, Ananias and Sapphira, or the uneven distribution of food to the widows in Acts 6, in a negative way. There are then internal clues as to what Luke sees as a norm for Christian behaviour' (ibid.).

for positive repeated patterns in the text, or 2) look for when there is only one pattern, or 3) look for when there is clear divine approval or disapproval in the text for some belief or behaviour or experience or religious practice.'[11] Before preachers take one or the first occurrence of one particular issue in Acts as normative and proclaim it accordingly, they must check whether Luke addresses the same issue elsewhere, and, if so, what he says about it in other places. One instance needs to be interpreted in view of the others and guidelines should be generated considering all occurrences. In some cases, such 'guidelines' will have to be general in order to accommodate all occurrences.

Fee and Stuart also offer helpful guidelines for dealing with 'historical precedent'.[12] They conclude:

> The decision as to whether certain practices or patterns are repeatable should be guided by the following considerations: First, the strongest possible case can be made when only one pattern is found (although one must be careful not to make too much of silence), and when that pattern is repeated within the New Testament itself. Second, when there is an ambiguity of pattern or when a pattern occurs but once, it is repeatable for later Christians only if it appears to have divine approbation or is in harmony with what is taught elsewhere in Scripture. Third, what is culturally conditioned is either not repeatable at all, or must be translated into the new or differing culture.[13]

In addition to helpful clues within the narrative, Stott emphasizes the difference between didactic and descriptive parts of Scripture.[14] The *descriptive*

---

11. Ibid., p. 100. Witherington goes on to discuss as examples Acts 2:43–47, 4:32–37, the chronological and/or theological relationship of the reception of the Spirit and water baptism, and the relationship between Acts 2 and 10. The need for repentance and faith serves as an example of only one positive pattern in Acts. Paul's persecution of the Christians is an example of clear divine disapproval (pp. 100–102). Fee and Stuart, *How to Read*, pp. 101–105, use Acts 6:1–7 and 8:1–25 as examples. Marshall, *Acts*, pp. 103–104, tackles issues head on and discusses Acts 5:1–11.

12. Fee and Stuart, *How to Read*, pp. 110–112.

13. Ibid., pp. 111–112.

14. Stott, *Message of Acts*, p. 11. Stott continues, 'It is here that the didactic must guide us in evaluating and interpreting the descriptive. We have to look for teaching on the issue, first in the immediate context (within the narrative itself), then in what the author writes elsewhere, and finally in the broader context of Scripture as a whole.' The primacy of the narrative of Acts should be noted.

account of Acts (*what actually happened*) must be related to the *prescriptive* passages (*what should happen and how it should happen*) in the New Testament letters
and be interpreted in view of these.[15] The didactic passages should guide the
interpretation of descriptive accounts. While this works well for a number of
issues raised in the descriptions of Acts, it is difficult to find didactic passages
related to other descriptions in Acts. In addition, Marshall cautions that

> we need to be aware of the danger of feeling at liberty to relativise the teaching
> of any part of Acts if we have a mind to do so, simply by looking for other NT
> teaching which can tone down its impact for us. Where the teaching of Acts stands in
> harmony with the central teaching of the NT, then there is all the more reason to take
> it seriously.

2. Closely linked to the previous point is a further challenge in applying Acts, namely the character of the events being narrated. Many events
recorded in Acts are unique and cannot be repeated: 'We have to recognise
the historical peculiarities of Scripture, especially of the "salvation-history"
which it records.'[16] We may preach about their consequences, but cannot
suggest or demand that they be repeated regularly, or in the same manner in
today's church and world. The resurrection of Jesus, his post-Easter teaching ministry and his ascension were unique events, as were his incarnation,
ministry, suffering and death. The eleven or twelve apostles were a unique
group of people with unique qualifications and callings (1:21–22). Although
some comparable events recur later in Luke's account, the coming of the Holy
Spirit at Pentecost was a unique event and fulfilment of a particular promise
(quoted at length in Acts 2:17–21). In some ways, the encounter of Paul and
his conversion or calling were unique events; other aspects thereof belong to
every conversion to the risen Christ.

While for most readers of Acts this will seem clear for the examples just
used, the matter becomes more difficult in other cases; for instance, should
other or even all Christians of all times attempt to heal people in the manner
in which Peter and John did (3:6–7; 5:12–16)? Should they share their goods
in the same manner and to the same extent as was practised early on in

---

15. Marshall, *Acts*, p. 102, notes that 'on this view the problem [of interpreting
   narrative] is not significantly different from dealing with teaching passages which
   themselves must be understood in the light of other teaching'.

16. Stott, *Message of Acts*, p. 11. After a number of examples Stott concludes, 'We have
   no liberty to copy everything they did,' p. 11.

Jerusalem? Should we always expect direct manifestations of the Holy Spirit when people come to faith, as was the case in Acts 2:1–4; 8:15–17; 10:44–46; and 19:6? What criteria should be used in deciding what can and must guide Christians *of all ages*, and what was unique to the people and period narrated by Luke?[17]

3. Furthermore, only on a few occasions does Luke describe the everyday life of the early church and its mission. We hear of the church in Jerusalem in summary fashion in Acts 2:42 and 4:32–34, of a prayer meeting after persecution (4:24–31), of the good works of a female disciple in Acts 9:36 and of an (admittedly unusual) evening service in Troas in Acts 20:7–12. Rather than describing the usual life and mission of the church, Acts narrates the *exceptional* events in a unique context, in particular places over a period of about three decades. The ordinary life of the church is mentioned only in passing when it is related to particular events.

Due to this selection of material in Acts, arguments from silence for *the* practice of the early church are questionable. Should what Luke records once or twice in particular circumstances automatically be presupposed for all later occasions? On a literary level this is true for some accounts: the relatively detailed account of Paul's missionary speech in Pisidian Antioch (13:16–41) is probably meant to be understood as representative of his preaching in a Jewish Diaspora context.[18] While his ministry in other synagogues is mentioned regularly, his sermons are not recorded in detail. However, does what Luke says also apply in other instances? For example, he twice mentions the fellowship of goods in the early Christian community in Jerusalem (2:44–45; 4:32 – 5:11). Does he presuppose this as self-evident and normative for all later Christian communities? While this cannot be proven, the emphasis on the radical use of material goods in Luke's version of the teaching of Jesus

---

17. See the instructive discussion in I. H. Marshall, *Beyond the Bible: Moving from Scripture to Theology* (Grand Rapids: Baker, 2004).

18. It should be noted that this and (perhaps more clearly) other sermons in Acts are context specific: in order to communicate the message, they address particular people at a particular time and under particular circumstances. This poses challenges for interpretation and present-day application, but also reminds us that preaching is not abstract communication of an abstract truth. In this way these sermons provide fine examples and set a standard for Christian preaching. Marshall, in *Beyond the Bible*, describes and rightly critiques the common approach of abstracting from texts by identifying 'timeless truths' in time-bound biblical texts in order to reapply such 'principles' in other contexts.

(e.g. Luke 12:13–34) indicates that the portrayal of Acts is not mere description, but an ideal to be followed.[19]

4. We also need to note that Acts is the second volume of a two-volume work (Acts 1:2).[20] Luke presumes that his readers know his Gospel. The Jesus who is active in Acts – directly, through the Holy Spirit and his disciples – is the risen and exalted Jesus who is the central figure of the first volume. The fulfilment of God's promises in Acts is a continuation of 'the account of the things that have come to fulfilment among us', as Luke writes in the preface to both volumes (Luke 1:1, my tr.). If we want to be faithful to Luke, the overall purpose(s) of Acts and its broad salvation-historical perspective should guide preaching and application. For the sake of emphasis and clarity one might distinguish between *preaching from individual passages of Acts* and *preaching the message of Acts*. Individual passages should be preached in view of all of Acts and with reference to the larger narrative of which they are part.

5. While Acts also notes failures of individual Christians, problems in the course of the spread of the gospel and the at times fierce and deadly resistance the disciples faced (e.g. Stephen's martyrdom), the book as a whole is in many ways a success story with a repeated emphasis in the summaries on growth (2:47; 4:4; 9:31; etc.). In some parts of the world, readers can easily identify with this story as it corresponds with (at least some of) their own experiences. Other Christians may read Acts with a sense of nostalgia, a deep yearning and/or a sense of frustration. If only their own lives, witness, experiences and churches were more like those recorded in Acts! In such contexts, preachers will have to take these sentiments seriously (perhaps address them directly) and present the successful course of the gospel and its Lord (not necessarily of individual Christians!) in Acts in such a way that Christians will be strengthened in their faith and be equipped to live and continue the mission of the church in their own circumstances. In order to do so they may heed the call of the risen Christ to be his witnesses, and claim his promise of receiving the power of the Holy Spirit (1:8).

---

19. See B. E. Beck, *Christian Character in the Gospel of Luke* (London: Epworth, 1989), pp. 28–54.

20. See the discussion in I. H. Marshall, 'Acts and the "Former Treatise"', in B. W. Winter and A. D. Clarke (eds.), *The Book of Acts in Its Ancient Literary Setting*, AFCS 1 (Grand Rapids: Eerdmans; Carlisle: Paternoster, 1993), pp. 163–182.

The opportunities for preaching Acts

Despite, and in particular *because* of, its unique character, Acts should be proclaimed. It is our only canonical, historically reliable and tremendously inspiring account of early Christianity. Acts also testifies to the continuity between Jesus and the early church.[21]

There are specific opportunities for preaching Acts and preaching from Acts.

1. Luke's salvation-historical perspective and the assurance that Gentile Christians indeed, and legitimately, *belong to the people of God* are still fundamental for Christian identity. Christians of all ages need to know where they come from: how they are related to God's people of Israel and the promises given to them, and how it came about that the Jew Jesus of Nazareth came to be the universal Saviour and Lord. Luke's story starts in Jerusalem's temple (Luke 1:5–25) and closes with Paul's proclamation of the kingdom of God and teaching about the Lord Jesus Christ in Rome (Acts 28:31), a clear indication of whose kingdom really counts and who the real Lord of the earth is.

2. Luke wrote to provide certainty about the origin and course of salvation (Luke 1:1–4). This is a timely reminder that Christian faith is related to God's revelation in history. Christians do not believe in myths, but their faith is based on history and reliable accounts thereof. The events of Acts did not occur 'once upon a time in some distant country', but are firmly placed in a particular time and at particular places. With his preface to both volumes Luke indicates that he wants his account to be understood as history. Recent studies have reaffirmed the historical reliability of Acts. Luke's historical concern serves an immense theological purpose. Luke has rightly been called *historian and theologian*.[22] Preaching from Acts should affirm this historical foundation of Christian faith.

3. Luke's focus is on the plan and will of God behind all events.[23] He acts directly or through Jesus, the Holy Spirit and people. Says Squires:

> Seen in this way, the book may well be understood as the Acts of God. In Acts, Luke reveals how he understands the purposes of God are being worked out through the various people who make up the messianic Jewish movement which was begun by

---

21. For the value of Acts see Stott, *Message of Acts*, pp. 9–10.

22. I. H. Marshall, *Luke: Historian and Theologian*, 3rd ed. (Exeter: Paternoster, 1988).

23. Summary in E. F. Harrison, *Interpreting Acts* (Grand Rapids: Baker, 1986), pp. 436–439.

Jesus of Nazareth. He shapes the narrative so that it constantly unveils the workings of the divine in ordinary human events.[24]

Johnson has noted:

> Luke's Apology is rather in the broadest sense a theodicy. His purpose is to defend God's activity in the world. Luke-Acts ostensibly addresses a wider audience in the clothing of Greek literature; but the main interest is to construct a continuation of the biblical story for Gentile believers in order to help them come to grips with the profound puzzle generated by their own recent experience.[25]

Our preaching must reflect this God-centredness of Acts, rather than consist of a mere concentration on the *human* protagonists and their different activities, interesting and inspiring as they may be. Acts is primarily about God's granting salvation to Israel and the nations in fulfilment of his promises.

4. In addition, the supreme role of the Holy Spirit is noteworthy.[26] Many passages in Acts describe how the Spirit came and manifested himself in varying circumstances. The presence and power of the Spirit drives the events of Acts. The Spirit in Acts is the Spirit of prophecy who directs and enables bold witness. In his first homily on Acts, John Chrysostom (AD 349–407) said of the book, 'For indeed it may profit us no less than even the Gospels; so replete is it with Christian wisdom and sound doctrine, especially in what is said concerning the Holy Ghost.'[27] He particularly notes

> the mighty change which is taking place in the disciples now that the Spirit has come upon them . . . Here again you will see the Apostles themselves, speeding their way as on wings over land and sea; and those same men, once so timorous and void of understanding, on the sudden become quite other than they were; men despising wealth, and raised above glory and passion and concupiscence, and in short all such affections: moreover, what unanimity there is among them now; nowhere any envying

---

24. John T. Squires, 'Acts', in J. D. G. Dunn and J. Rogerson (eds.), *Eerdmans Commentary on the Bible* (Grand Rapids: Eerdmans, 2003), pp. 1213–1276.

25. L. T. Johnson, *The Acts of the Apostles*, SP 5 (Collegeville: Liturgical Press, 1992), p. 7.

26. See Harrison, *Interpreting Acts*, pp. 442–444.

27. P. Schaff (ed.), *A Select Library of the Nicene and Post-Nicene Fathers of the Christian Church*, vol. 11: *Saint Chrysostom: Homilies on the Acts of the Apostles and the Epistle to the Romans*, repr. (Edinburgh: T. & T. Clark; Grand Rapids: Eerdmans, 1989), p. 1.

as there was before, nor any of the old hankering after pre-eminence, but all virtue brought in them to its last finish . . .[28]

Next to this mighty change, the Spirit also appears in other contexts: while the gift of tongues occurs after Acts 2 particularly as a sign to (Jewish) believers of inclusion into the people of God of people hitherto unexpected, other occurrences are not excluded. Luke speaks of direction and comfort of the Spirit, of many signs and wonders, the Spirit's assistance in challenging situations and of early Christian prophets and their prophecies.

5. The open ending of Acts suggests that the story is not completed.[29] Several issues raised by the narrative remain open. Paul has fulfilled his calling and reached Rome, although under other circumstances than he has imagined (cf. Rom. 15:22–32). However, the charge of Jesus to be his witnesses 'in Jerusalem and in all Judea and Samaria, and to the end of the earth' (1:8 ESV) still stands and remains to be fulfilled. All Christian witness stands in continuity with that described in Acts and carries the same promise of Jesus. What may be learnt from the witness recorded in Acts?

6. We have seen above that Acts offers many challenging examples of Christian behaviour that can be applied today. I have briefly described the hermeneutical care that is necessary in presenting the behaviour of Christians in Acts as examples for today (see below). The application will often be more general than the specific behaviour described by Luke.

7. Many passages in Acts contain the norm in Christian belief that is foundational in preaching: 'the heart of the faith has to do with the narrative of Jesus' life, death, and resurrection . . . and the sending of the Spirit. . . . the belief that God is a God of all peoples and individuals, and that God shows no partiality'.[30]

How will we preach Acts?

Does Acts itself provide guidelines on how one should preach (from) it?

1. Luke did not write a letter to his readers as other early Christian authors did. Rather, he wrote an extended *narrative* in order to get his point across. He

---

28. Ibid.

29. See T. M. Troftgruben, *A Conclusion Unhindered: A Study of the Ending of Acts Within Its Literary Environment*, WUNT 2.280 (Tübingen: Mohr Siebeck, 2010), pp. 151–178.

30. Witherington, *Acts of the Apostles*, p. 100.

chose to let a carefully crafted narrative speak for itself, with little authorial comment. In the last two decades scholars have applied the insights of literary criticism, in particular of *narrative criticism*, in order to appreciate and understand Luke-Acts. The approach has also been applied to other Gospels and the narrative books of the Old Testament. Narrative criticism helps to appreciate Acts as a *story*, to see how Luke worked out his theological purposes and characterized people and events.[31] The quest itself is promising and offers fresh perspectives. Many useful insights gained in this way still need to find their way into commentaries and popular discussion. Taking Acts as narrative does not deny its historical value or reliability.

Acts should not be read and preached as if it were a detailed, crafted argumentative text such as, for example, Romans. The narrative genre *of* Acts should be reflected in preaching *on* Acts. Narrative criticism and other recent literary approaches have shown how biblical narratives involve their readers in their stories and challenge them to change their own attitude and behaviour. That potential of Acts should be recognized and used.

In addition, some in the audience may take more to listening and reflecting on a well-told story than to analysing a complex argument, or seeing a moving story turned into a set of abstract points. Obviously, explanation and illustration have to be provided, so that listeners today can understand the point of Luke's account and receive guidance on how to apply it to their particular circumstances.

2. Luke offers selective accounts of the biographies of Jesus, Peter and Paul, and glimpses of the ministry of people such as John, Philip and Barnabas. There is no full coverage of individual people; they appear only in so far as they serve the overall purpose of Acts. In addition, Luke places his protagonists in a larger context (Israel, the disciples, the Jerusalem community or other congregations). Nevertheless, narrative criticism has led to an appre-

---

31. For recent surveys see R. Parry, 'Narrative Criticism', in K. J. Vanhoozer (ed.), *Dictionary for Theological Interpretation of the Bible* (London: SPCK, 2005), pp. 528–532; J. C. Robinson, 'Narrative', and C. Long Westfall, 'Narrative Criticism', in S. E. Porter (ed.), *Dictionary of Biblical Criticism and Interpretation* (London: Routledge, 2007), pp. 236–237 and 237–239 respectively; M. A. Powell, 'Narrative Criticism', in J. B. Green (ed.), *Hearing the New Testament*, 2nd ed. (Grand Rapids: Eerdmans, 2010), pp. 240–258. Examples of studies that apply narrative criticism to the book of Acts are F. S. Spencer, *The Portrait of Philip in Acts: A Study of Roles and Relations*, JSNTSup 67 (Sheffield: JSOT, 1992); and R. C. Tannehill, *The Narrative Unity of Luke-Acts: A Literary Interpretation*, vol. 2: *The Acts* (Minneapolis: Fortress, 1990).

ciation of the importance and the techniques of characterization in narratives. While there are, for example, no descriptions of outward appearance (such as of Paul), people are characterized through their words and actions, as is the case in Old Testament narratives.[32]

Luke's full characterization of individuals is worth examining. Individual scenes of a life need to be seen as part of the full portrait. Readers are not only to appreciate outstanding *activities*, but are to see and emulate the *character* of these early Christians. What kinds of people were used by God in such tremendous ways? While simple psychologizing of the characters is hazardous, Luke's portrayals invite preachers to focus on the protagonists and other figures and deduce the implications. People enjoy hearing about other people and how God used them. In doing so, one should (1) note and emphasize the communal aspect of all events; (2) remember that these figures were unique people in unique contexts – therefore, not all of what they did or said can be applied to all Christians (see above); (3) keep in mind the God-centredness of Acts (see above), and (4) consider the full characterization and its implications for the readers. Although the positive behaviour of Christians serves as an inspiring example to us, Acts must not be reduced to a set of motivating accounts of exemplary early Christians from which to choose whatever affirms us and ignore whatever may challenge us. Greater care is needed when we examine the implications of the negative behaviour of Christians (used as a warning[33]) or the behaviour of non-Christians (e.g. applying Gamaliel's counsel of Acts 5:35–39 to conflicts within the church).[34]

---

32. What R. Tate's description of Hebrew narrative also applies to Acts; Luke 'is less interested in presenting the appearance of a character than in guiding the reader to discover what kind of a person the character is' ('Characterization', in R. Tate, *Interpreting the Bible: A Handbook of Terms and Methods* [Peabody: Hendrickson, 2006], p. 59). See also J. A. Darr, *On Character Building: The Reader and the Rhetoric of Characterization in Luke-Acts* (Louisville: Westminster / John Knox, 1992).

33. See Marshall, *Acts*, pp. 103–104, on Acts 5:1–11.

34. This use of Acts, rather than drawing on positive Christian examples, is more culturally conditioned. For example, in cultures where exorcism and magic are common, the experience of the seven sons of Sceva in Acts 19:13–17 and the ensuing reaction of the Ephesian Christians will be more relevant than in other contexts. In situations where dictators or ideologies demand absolute allegiance and veneration, accounts such as the death of Herod Agrippa in Acts 12:20–23 will be particularly relevant. The reasons for the persecution of Christians and the fate of their enemies will help audiences who face similar challenges today. For the

3. The many sermons *in* Acts, and the reactions to which they led, serve to inspire and motivate all preaching *on* Acts and other parts of the New Testament. Acts vividly portrays God and Christ-centred preaching, in all boldness, on the basis of Scripture and faithful witness, the activity of God and the Holy Spirit in the preacher and in the audience, and the concrete results of the word of God proclaimed. Like few other books in the Bible, Acts encourages preachers and instructs them as to the content *and manner* of their sermons. It was Peter's sermons that led to mass conversions in Jerusalem. Philip's sermon led to the eunuch's conversion and baptism, and to his going on his way rejoicing (Acts 8:39).

However, Acts also reminds us that preaching (even by apostles!) will not always be successful. Preaching can cause division and may even trigger fierce resistance, so that preachers have to join the prayer of the Christians of Jerusalem 'and grant to your servants to continue to speak your word with all boldness' (Acts 4:29 ESV). Despite all the efforts of preachers, as was the case with Lydia in Philippi (Acts 16:14), it is God who opens the hearts of their listeners.

© Christoph Stenschke, 2013

---

significance of Acts in a global context see the discussions in B. Tat-siong Liew, 'Acts', in D. Patte, J. Severino Croatto, Nicole Wilkinson Duran, Teresa Okure and Archie Chi Chung Lee (eds.), *Global Bible Commentary* (Nashville: Abingdon, 2004), pp. 419–428; and P. M. Kisau, 'Acts of the Apostles', in T. Adeyemo (ed.), *Africa Bible Commentary* (Nairobi: Word Alive; Grand Rapids: Zondervan, 2006), pp. 1297–1348.

7. PREACHING PAUL'S LETTERS

Justin K. Hardin and Jason Maston

Because the letters of Paul comprise a major portion of the New Testament and their influence has been significant throughout church history, it is vital that preachers come to grips with how to preach from them. For some, it may be tempting to proof-text one's favourite verses while ignoring the rest of the letter entirely. For others, the tendency may be to spend weeks and weeks in a particular Pauline letter with the aim of unpacking every word and phrase in painstaking detail. In this chapter by setting out some guidelines for preaching Paul's letters we encourage preachers to avoid both these extremes.

In this regard we hope to answer three primary questions: (1) What literary genre are we dealing with, and how does this genre affect how we understand and preach from this portion of Scripture? (2) What are some good practices to encourage and pitfalls to avoid when preaching from Paul's letters? (3) How specifically might we prepare to preach from the Pauline corpus? When we come to this final question, we will focus on 1 Corinthians 1 – 4 to illustrate how our method might be fleshed out in practice.

Letters in the ancient world

Of course, we must first begin with a brief word on the literary genre we encounter. Paul wrote neither a narrative history (like the Gospels and Acts) nor an apocalypse (like Revelation); rather, he wrote letters to churches and individuals, providing theological and scriptural responses to the various practical issues arising in his churches.[1] Letters were, after all, a common form of communication in the Greco-Roman world, just as they are today (especially if we include electronic messaging), and they served a variety of purposes, including business transactions, personal communication and philosophical discourse. In the light of recent studies we can make at least three observations about Paul's letters that should also affect how we preach them.[2]

First, although Paul wrote for a variety of reasons, his letters were written as a substitute for his personal presence (2 Cor. 13:10). In many instances he wrote because he was unable to be physically present, and therefore his letters were meant to carry the same authority as if he were there (cf. 1 Cor. 5:3).

Secondly, Paul's letters are both timely and timeless. They are timely in that they address specific situations that arose within specific congregations. Paul's correspondence with the church at Thessalonica, for example, was meant to encourage the church as they endured persecution, whereas his two surviving letters to the church at Corinth addressed division and 'worldliness' in the church.[3] While there is certainly theological overlap between Paul's letters, the situation controlled what and how Paul wrote. The letters assume 'insider' knowledge and reflect one side of the conversation.

These writings are also timeless in that we believe Paul was inspired by God when he wrote them. Although the letters are addressed to specific groups and tackle specific problems, they both provide guidance for today's church and carry with them theological freight. As inspired Scripture, they speak into the life of the church today.[4]

---

1. As in the Hellenistic letters of his day, Paul also provided personal details regarding his current circumstances, sometimes even asking for prayer from the churches (Rom. 15:30–33) or providing them with his travel itinerary (Rom. 15:23–29; 1 Cor. 16:5–9).

2. On Paul as a letter writer see E. R. Richards, *Paul and First-Century Letter Writing: Secretaries, Composition and Collection* (Downers Grove: InterVarsity Press; Leicester: Apollos, 2004), and M. L. Stirewalt, *Paul, the Letter Writer* (Grand Rapids: Eerdmans, 2003).

3. For a very helpful discussion on the differing outlooks between the Thessalonian and Corinthian congregations see esp. J. M. G. Barclay, 'Thessalonica and Corinth: Social Contrasts in Pauline Christianity', *JSNT* 47 (1992), pp. 49–74.

4. For a recent treatment of God's Word as inspired Scripture see N. T. Wright, *The*

Thirdly, despite our common practice of reading Paul's letters in bite-sized portions, Paul's letters were intended to be read aloud in one sitting (although the evidence suggests Paul's letters were several times longer than the typical Hellenistic letter). When studying Paul's letters in one's private study, one should therefore bear in mind how they would originally have been heard.

A brief guide to preaching Paul's letters

In the light of these general remarks about letter writing in the ancient world, we can now offer a brief guide when preparing to preach from Paul's letters.

First, we should make every effort to *preach thought units* and not simply individual words or sentences. Many sermons unfortunately get lost in the nitty-gritty of Paul's arguments and leave the hearer with the false impression that Paul wrote in single-sentence paragraphs, despite our observation above that ancient letters were not intended to be read piecemeal. Although Paul's argument might turn on a single sentence, phrase or word, it is the context of Paul's argument that makes this single point so important. For this reason, we should be careful not to lose the forest for the trees when plodding through Paul's argument.

As a corollary to this first point, secondly, we should *follow Paul's argument* as best we can. The best way to understand any single part of Paul's argument is to understand the whole. In this regard, we should endeavour to link one section to the next. We can make much better sense of Romans 9, for example, when we read it in the context of Romans 9 – 11, which in turn is better understood if interpreted in the light of the rest of Romans. As we read, we should observe carefully Paul's transitions and how these may signal a logical connection between sections (e.g. Rom. 12:1) or a change in focus or topic (e.g. 1 Cor. 7:1).[5] Understanding the flow of Paul's thought – the place of individual paragraphs within developing arguments – will surely help us to preach from Paul's letters more effectively.

Thirdly, it is important to *appreciate the distance* between the first-century context of these letters and our contemporary setting. Stated positively, appreciating the distance means presenting our listeners with a fuller awareness of

---

Last Word: Scripture and the Authority of God – Getting Beyond the Bible Wars (Grand Rapids: Zondervan, 2006).

5. To be sure, we must be careful neither to force nor to create connections where they do not exist.

the relevant culture and events of the ancient world for understanding Paul's argument. When discussing idol meat in 1 Corinthians 8 – 10, for example, it would be immensely helpful for our listeners to know that in Roman Corinth (as was customary in the Greco-Roman world) meat was sacrificed at the temples before being sold in the marketplace.

Stated negatively, appreciating the distance between their world and ours means acknowledging that sometimes we cannot so readily cut and paste their context into our contemporary setting. The preacher should thus not feel the need to impose an application about meat sacrificed to idols that does not work in a contemporary Western context. To be sure, 1 Corinthians 8 – 10 speaks volumes on the exercise of one's 'rights' within the church community, which is certainly a relevant topic in today's culture. If preachers know their congregations as well as Paul seemed to know his, they will doubtless be in a position to make close connections between Paul's Corinthians and the contemporary setting.

Sometimes, of course, appreciating the distance may require that we acknowledge a lack of understanding. It is, after all, not a sign of weakness to admit to our congregations that Paul's letters are difficult (2 Pet. 3:16) and that we are sometimes uncertain what exactly he means or what precise historical occasion stands behind Paul's discussion. Although often we may be able to provide informed answers to our congregations, sometimes – perhaps more than we would like to admit – the appropriate answer is, 'I don't know.'[6]

And yet Paul's letters are surrounded by a cloud of able interpreters throughout the centuries. So, fourthly, we would do well to *learn from our predecessors in our interpretation of Paul's letters* by reading the great expositors of the church to help inform our own reading of the Pauline material (e.g. John Chrysostom, Augustine, Thomas Aquinas, John Calvin). Such heavyweights who have gone before us can provide guidance and insight, especially on some of the thorny passages within the Pauline corpus.[7] We are after all not

---

6. Here I am reminded of St Augustine's resignation on the vexed issue of the man of lawlessness in 2 Thess. 2:1–12: 'I honestly confess that I do not know what he meant' (*Ego prorsus quid dixerit me fateor ignorare*) (Augustine, *City of God*, 20.19, my tr.).

7. A variety of resources are now available that make previous interpretations more accessible, including the Blackwell Bible Commentary Series, which brings together the history of interpretation, and both the Ancient Christian Commentary on Scripture series (ed. T. C. Oden) and the Reformation Christian Commentary series (ed. T. George), which provide easy access to the comments of previous interpreters.

the first to read Paul's mail, the first to struggle with it or the first to allow it to speak to our issues.

Seeing Paul's letters through the lenses of others, of course, may result in blurred vision, as the history of interpretation can easily predetermine one's interpretation of the text. Often the meaning we ascribe to the text is determined by our theological persuasion, and this influence can hinder us from reading Paul afresh on his own terms. Of course, our task is not to preach Paul's letters via a great reformer or a contemporary preacher, even if we would be remiss simply to ignore the secondary literature. Rather, we should read those interpreters who have gone before us with critical lenses, being willing to affirm or challenge their readings of Paul.

In this regard we would do well to pause here briefly to suggest how busy preachers might navigate their way through the mass of secondary literature, especially given the multitude of commentaries on offer. While there are some helpful bibliographies available (some of which are helpfully annotated[8]), one should bear in mind a few basic principles with regard to commentary reading in sermon preparation.

- We would do well to read commentaries not only from our favourite theologians, but also from those outside our own tradition. Among other things, this exercise provides a broader awareness of other views and helps us to identify weaknesses in our own.
- Some of the better commentaries for sermon preparation are those that not only engage with the details of the text, but also explain the development and flow of the letter.
- We should perhaps not turn too hastily to 'application commentaries' or commentaries composed of other sermons. These commentaries can assist us in bridging the gap between the ancient world and our own, but a premature consultation with this sort of commentary can too easily result in an underdeveloped sermon.[9]

---

8. See e.g. D. A. Carson, *New Testament Commentary Survey*, 6th ed. (Grand Rapids: Baker Academic, 2007). The most up-to-date source is http://www. bestcommentaries.com, accessed 3 July 2012, which ranks commentaries based on a comparison of recommended lists. One should note, however, that this online resource often ranks theologically 'conservative' commentaries above others even when the 'conservative' ones are not the best at engaging with the text.

9. Several of the volumes in Zondervan's NIV Application Commentary series

In the end, one important reason to consult the commentaries is to help us understand Paul's argument better and thus to help us apply the Scriptures better in our contemporary setting.

Fifthly, our preaching of Paul's letters should revolve around the central point of Paul's theology: *Jesus the Messiah is Lord.* Paul can summarize his preaching to the Corinthians as 'Jesus Christ and him crucified' (1 Cor. 2:2). This does not mean that Paul spoke only of what happened on Good Friday (cf. 1 Cor. 15; Acts 17:16–33). Rather, in Paul's mind the whole of his preaching (and theology) is Christocentric. Our preaching of Paul should imitate Paul by calling people to imitate the crucified, buried and raised Messiah (1 Cor. 15:3–4).

Finally, when preaching Paul's letters, and indeed when preaching from any biblical text, we should *preach to both mind and heart.* After all, Paul's ethical charge in Romans hinges on a renewal of one's mind (Rom. 12:2). Our hearers must always be challenged in their thinking processes so they are drawn to understand and love God more deeply. The congregation may not know Greek and Hebrew; neither will they most likely have read the latest systematic theology. In our experience, however, they greatly desire to experience God through the reading of his Word. In addition, Paul's arguments are often filled with emotion and passion.[10] Our preaching of Paul's letters should travel comfortably between the mind and the heart so that our hearers are moved by the glorious gospel of hope and redemption that satisfies the deepest longings of humanity.

Going forward

Moving from the theory of interpretation to the writing of the sermon is understandably difficult, and so in this final section we would like to propose a model for preparing to preach from Paul's letters. To be sure, this is simply one way of approaching Paul's letters for the task of preaching, but we nevertheless commend it as a helpful way forward. In particular, we suggest four questions to help one transition from Paul's ancient letter to the contempor-

---

are exceptions to this general rule, as they provide some good examples of solid exegesis.

10. One might think here of the biting rhetoric of Galatians or the motherly compassion of 1 Thess. 2:6–9 (although Paul's maternal concern for the churches extends to the Galatians as well; see Gal. 4:19).

ary setting. This model attempts to take seriously the fact that Paul's writings are letters written to specific communities and therefore address specific issues, while also recognizing that our task in preaching is ultimately to bring the words and thoughts of Scripture to bear on the present. In the following paragraphs we will explain these questions and use 1 Corinthians 1 – 4 as an example of how we envision each being utilized.

What is the situation?

When interpreting Paul's letters, we should begin by attempting to understand the situation that prompted Paul to write his letter. Although we can never develop a full picture of the situation, Paul's letters usually provide enough details to piece together a coherent picture if we listen to his side of the conversation. Of course, we make two assumptions here: (1) that Paul had accurate information regarding the situation, and (2) that he has not exaggerated or skewed the situation in his discussion. Both of these assumptions, however, we believe are valid since Paul's extant letters seem at least to have been followed and cherished from very early on in the life of the church. It seems unlikely they would have done so if Paul had been either wrong or wrongheaded.

For many, this step may seem unnecessary or too speculative to provide any firm conclusions. Working towards a fuller understanding of the original situation, however, can help us to understand not only the content of his response but also the way in which Paul chose to respond. In any case, recognizing the limitations of our abilities to reconstruct the historical situation should not be an excuse for ignoring the historical rootedness of the text.

The value of some historical awareness can be seen through the example of 1 Corinthians 1 – 4.[11] Some church members from Chloe's household

---

11. For an overview of this letter see J. K. Hardin, '1 Corinthians', in M. Williams and K. Berding (eds.), *What the New Testament Authors Really Cared About: A Survey of Their Writings* (Grand Rapids: Kregel, 2008), pp. 150–157. Our exegesis of 1 Cor. 1 – 4 has been particularly informed by several excellent studies and commentaries on Paul's letters, including R. E. Ciampa and B. S. Rosner, *The First Letter to the Corinthians*, PNTC (Grand Rapids: Eerdmans, 2010); D. E. Garland, *1 Corinthians*, BECNT (Grand Rapids: Baker Academic, 2003); D. Litfin, *St. Paul's Theology of Proclamation: 1 Corinthians 1–4 and Greco-Roman Rhetoric*, SNTSMS 79 (Cambridge: Cambridge University Press, 1994); A. C. Thiselton, *The First Epistle to the Corinthians: A Commentary on the Greek Text* (Grand Rapids: Eerdmans, 2000); B. W. Winter, *After Paul Left Corinth: The Influence of Secular Ethics and Social Change* (Grand Rapids:

had informed Paul that the Corinthian church was rife with division since members were aligning themselves under their favourite personalities – Paul, Peter, Apollos, and even the Messiah (1 Cor. 1:10–12). In particular, some of the believers were favouring a Jesus-follower called Apollos over Paul (1 Cor. 3:4–9; 4:6–7).[12]

But who was Apollos? According to Acts 18:24–28, Apollos, a native of Alexandria (a city renowned for its education), was a 'learned man' who knew the Scriptures well. When Priscilla and Aquila travelled to Ephesus, they instructed Apollos more clearly in the way of God. Soon thereafter Apollos made his way to Corinth to strengthen the church further, and there became well known for his public debates, proving from the Scriptures that Jesus was the long-awaited Jewish Messiah.

After hearing Apollos, some in the church at Corinth preferred the rather polished Apollos to the 'rough and ready' Paul. Indeed, at its heart, this division was rooted in the Corinthians' preference for an orator, and Paul's physical appearance and public speaking abilities fell miserably short. In 2 Corinthians 10:10 Paul revealed this criticism explicitly: 'For some say, "His letters are weighty and forceful, but in person he is unimpressive and his speaking amounts to nothing."'

But why would the Corinthian believers have preferred oratory and not simply have judged Paul by the content of his message, which of course they had accepted as true? In Paul's day, society highly valued the skill of public debate, and those who were well trained in rhetoric often lived as 'Hollywood superstars'.[13] Upon their arrival in a city these celebrities would gather the citizens together and declaim publicly upon a particular topic. Upon a successful performance, the wealthy citizens would then register their children to learn the art of rhetoric under this orator, since public discourse was a crucial skill for aspiring young citizens.

What is more, one must appreciate the social stigma of crucifixion in Paul's day.[14] In short, it was a brutal form of punishment, often linked with

---

Eerdmans, 2001); *Philo and Paul Among the Sophists: Alexandrian and Corinthian Responses to a Julio-Claudian Movement*, 2nd ed. (Grand Rapids: Eerdmans, 2002).

12. Garland, *1 Corinthians*, pp. 44–51, is probably correct that the primary cause for disunity was a Corinthian preference for Apollos over Paul (cf. Ciampa and Rosner, *First Letter to the Corinthians*, pp. 78–82).

13. See e.g. Litfin, *St. Paul's Theology of Proclamation*, and Winter, *Philo and Paul Among the Sophists*.

14. See the programmatic study by M. Hengel, *Crucifixion in the Ancient World and the*

scourging, and could span several days. Crucifixion was a form of punishment reserved primarily for those of lower social status, most notably criminals and slaves. It was a humiliating punishment as the victim was often exposed naked at a prominent location, such as at crossroads, and was often left unburied.

Here we see that even the slightest historical awareness can improve our understanding of this text. Some knowledge about the emphasis placed on rhetoric in the ancient world helps us to appreciate the complex social situation of the Corinthian church. We are better able to understand how the church's preference for a public orator was wreaking havoc in the believing community, despite the fact that Paul and Apollos were not rivals, but were fellow ministers of the gospel of the Messiah. Recognition of the shamefulness of crucifixion brings greater clarity to Paul's statements about the folly of the cross.

What is Paul's pastoral response to this situation?

Once we determine the situation as best we can, we should attempt to trace Paul's pastoral response to this situation. Here our aim is to understand the flow of Paul's argument and to detect specifically how he addressed the situation. At this stage, we are seeking to understand Paul as a 'pastor'.

Again, using 1 Corinthians 1 – 4 as an example, we see that Paul responds to this situation in three major sections.

The problem defined: the Corinthians desire eloquence (1:10–17)
Paul first appealed to the congregation to rid themselves of divisions and instead live in unity as believers in Jesus. Paul reminded them that none of them was baptized into the name of their favourite leaders; they were all baptized into the name of Jesus their Messiah, who could not be divided. Indeed, Paul was sent not to baptize, but to preach the gospel without relying upon so-called wisdom and eloquence.

The root of the problem revealed: the cross versus human widom (1:18 – 3:23)
Paul then revealed the theological problem in the church. Although they had accepted the message of the cross, they were unwilling to let the 'foolishness' of the cross transform their outlook in society. He therefore reminded them that the cross is the power of God for those who believe its message (1:18–25). This reality explains why Paul was determined to preach the cross

---

Folly of the Message of the Cross (London: SCM, 1977); repr. in *The Cross of the Son of God* (London: SCM, 1986), pp. 93–185.

not with human wisdom and eloquence, 'so that your faith might not rest on human wisdom, but on God's power' (2:1–16, here 5).

The wisdom of God expressed in the folly of the cross is brought to bear on the Corinthians themselves, for God has not chosen the wise and rich but the lowly and poor (1:26–31). Here we see Paul the pastor at his best. Having made the theological claim about God's wisdom in the folly of the cross, he revealed to the Corinthians the impact this reality should have in the church at Corinth. In short, the Corinthian community was being called to embody God's reversal of human expectations.

By seeking the world's wisdom and oratory, however, the Corinthians were indeed being very immature in their faith. In chapter 3 Paul thus rebuked the church for their divisions, which revealed their ongoing adoption of 'worldly' values (3:1–4). What is more, Paul redefined Christian leadership over against worldly leadership (3:5–23). Paul and Apollos were servants and co-workers of God. The church was therefore behaving like 'mere humans' (3:3) when they were judging Paul and Apollos on the basis of their external appearance and performance. They had forgotten that the 'wisdom' of the world (i.e. their desire for oratory) is foolishness to God.

The problem addressed: Paul and Apollos are both servants of the Messiah (4:1–21)
As a result of their worldly attitudes, Paul finally instructed the church to stop 'judging' (i.e. rating the external performance) Apollos over against Paul. They were both servants of God, who would test the motives of their hearts (4:1–7). Paul then rebuked the church's arrogance by sarcastically contrasting the 'wise' Corinthian believers with the 'foolish' Paul and Apollos (4:8–13). He concluded this major section by appealing to the church to imitate him and by warning those who were 'arrogant' when evaluating Paul vis-à-vis Apollos (4:14–21).

What is the theological–scriptural ground for Paul's response?
When tracing Paul's argument, one should pay careful attention to the theological–scriptural grounds of Paul's response. The goal here is to understand the underlying presuppositions of Paul's argument. We are attempting therefore to penetrate the depths of Paul's thought so we can understand how he brought theology and Scripture to bear on the individual situations in his churches. In most instances a better grasp of the theological basis for an argument leads to a better understanding of the significance of that argument. At this point then we are focused on Paul as a 'theologian'.

To be sure, this crucial step can easily be overlooked as one seeks to turn from the text to the contemporary application. But doing so can easily lead to a dogmatic 'do this; don't do that' interpretation of Paul, which is devoid of the theological foundation that undergirds Paul's exhortations. The problem with missing out this theological step is that one cannot properly apply Paul's response to a contemporary situation without knowing how Paul was arguing theologically.[15] By carefully tracking Paul's theological argument and his use of Scripture, however, we can learn how to provide stronger theological reasoning to our own actions and those to which we call our congregations.

If we turn again to 1 Corinthians 1 – 4, we observe that Paul firmly grounded his instructions in the theological conviction that God does not operate within the same rules as the world and that his wisdom is much more powerful than that of humanity. As a result, the believers in Corinth were wrongheaded in their preference for oratory in the gospel's proclamation. After accepting the 'foolish' message of the cross, why would they look to society to inform the values they should have as believers? Paul appealed to the cross because they needed to be reminded that they had already accepted a message that was foolishness to the world (following a crucified man), and they should therefore disregard the 'rules' of society that valued rhetorical prowess. Indeed, the power of the cross entails the reversal of human expectations and the transformation of one's theological perspectives.

Paul supported this theological outlook by drawing on several scriptural texts from the prophets (Isa. 29:14; 40:13; 64:4) and from the wisdom literature (Job 5:13; Ps. 94:11). In response to God's superiority in his ways, humanity is not to boast in their wisdom (Jer. 9:24). These scriptural passages furthermore suggest that because God's wisdom and strength are far superior to the wisdom and strength of humanity, the Corinthians should not have placed their stock in the values of society (e.g. eloquence).[16] Such a theological–scriptural argument would have provided a necessary antidote to the Corinthians' 'worldly' behaviour. They had not been influenced by the Scriptures, but by the world, and Paul therefore summoned the Scriptures to

---

15. For the importance of theological interpretation of Scripture see e.g. K. J. Vanhoozer, *The Drama of Doctrine: A Canonical Linguistic Approach to Christian Theology* (Louisville: Westminster John Knox, 2005); and M. Bockmuehl, *Seeing the Word: Refocusing New Testament Study* (Grand Rapids: Baker Academic, 2006).

16. See the very helpful discussion on each verse in question in Ciampa and Rosner, *First Letter to the Corinthians*, who conclude, 'The citations, allusions, and echoes of Scripture are not illustrations or occasional exclamation points but rather the substance of Paul's argument' (p. 72).

support his response that they must no longer be puffed up one against the other on the basis of worldly values such as oratory.

How might this response apply to situations in our contemporary context?
Our final task is to determine the situation in our contemporary context that Paul's text might address. Here it should perhaps be stated that what often applies most directly to one's congregation is not the surface problem being addressed, but the theological underpinnings that drove Paul's response. Pastors must therefore think creatively about how the argument and theology evidenced in Paul's letters apply to their congregations. Here pastors must have the pulse of their congregations so that the preaching event can touch upon the lives of the community and not stop short of this essential step in preaching.

Conclusion

The writings of the apostle Paul have stood at the centre of Christian thought and have been read publicly in Jesus-believing congregations for almost two thousand years. Preaching Paul's letters is by no means a straightforward task, but we believe it is ultimately a very rewarding one. In this chapter we have sought to provide some salutary guidelines for preaching them today. We first argued that recognizing their literary genre is instructive in the preaching task. We then provided a brief guide, including some common pitfalls to avoid when preparing to preach from Paul's letters. In our final section we set out a particular method – from historical occasion to contemporary setting – that one might want to consider when preaching them. However one deals with these issues we have raised in the above discussion, we wish to encourage every minister to preach heartily from the Pauline corpus. The revelation of the glory of God in the Messiah Jesus, a message we find again and again in Paul's letters, is certainly a message worth proclaiming.

© Justin K. Hardin and Jason Maston, 2013

8. PREACHING FROM THE PASTORAL EPISTLES

I. Howard Marshall

In the Church of Scotland, Reformed in its theology and Presbyterian in its practice, the process of authorizing its ministers includes a preliminary stage when candidates are licensed as preachers of the gospel by the presbytery. At one such service in Aberdeen some half-dozen or so candidates were each presented with a Bible, and the moderator, Alan Main, gave each of them an appropriate scriptural verse. The verses were chosen from the three Pastoral Epistles (PE); Alan clearly had no difficulty in finding different apt verses for each candidate, and there were doubtless further suitable verses to be found there if needed. Thus the PE demonstrated their continuing relevance to the task of ministry today.

The addressees – including us!

The reason, of course, why this trio are collectively called 'Pastoral Epistles' lies in the fact that they were written by one older pastor to two junior pastors who were being put into positions of greater responsibility. Nowadays the term 'pastoral letter' tends to refer rather to a letter written by a person acting in a pastoral capacity to the members of a congregation under his or her care. Here, however, the letters are addressed to pastors themselves to aid and direct them regarding their pastoral duties, although they are also pastoral in the modern sense of the term in that Paul is actually acting as a pastor to pastors, taking care of them and giving them advice. 1 Timothy and Titus are more in the nature of what are termed 'mandates', written accounts of duties entrusted to the recipients; 2 Timothy is more a personal, friendly letter of encouragement.

This personal character does not confine the contents of the letters to being relevant simply to the named recipients, Timothy and Titus. Three indications of their wider relevance may be noted.

First, both recipients were to be involved in the appointment of other people to carry on pastoral work, whether in order to share out responsibilities that were becoming too great for single individuals, or to widen out the mission areas, or with an eye to the future when successors to the named addressees would be needed, just as they themselves were being prepared for being successors to Paul himself. Thus the letters in their original settings contained material that was to be shared by a wider group than just the two named recipients.

Secondly, the letters also contain clear indications that they were to be read to and shared with the congregations supervised by Timothy and Titus. In each case the closing benediction is concerned with 'you' plural and not 'you' singular, despite the misunderstandings of some early scribes. The congregations could overhear the letters, and they could expect their pastors to elaborate on their contents over time.

Thirdly, the analysis I have just given rests on the prima facie identification of the letters as communications from Paul to his named colleagues. Nevertheless, those of us who would accept the letters as such would doubtless assume without argument that it is fair to apply them to other persons than the named recipients and the two groups of secondary recipients, namely the pastors and congregations who form the church in subsequent generations. But in the eyes of many scholars the letters are in fact compilations by an author or authors later than Paul; syntheses of what Paul himself may have said or written to Timothy and Titus and other people in similar positions are presented for the benefit of pastors and congregations in the post-Pauline period, and Timothy and Titus are to be understood as representing these later pastors. On this scenario, the letters were from the beginning intended to be read by post-Pauline Christians. Either way, therefore, we are looking at letters we are justified in treating as being written for our instruction and therefore as being foundations for our preaching.

The situation then

The problem of their specific situation then raises its head. Timothy and Titus are to deal with opponents of Paul's teaching by measures that include appointing godly persons as overseers and deacons; refuting error by appropriate teaching; silencing the opponents by forbidding them to teach; encouraging the congregations simply to ignore what the false teachers say and not enter into debate with futile positions; expelling the opponents as a last resort; and yet treating them in such a way that they may come to see the error of their ways, repent and find entry back into the fellowship. The false teaching itself included spinning of strange ideas based on myths and genealogies, which are probably to be understood as fantasies based on the Pentateuch; the forbidding of marriage and childbearing; some food bans; and the claim that the resurrection had already taken place. Alongside these false ideas were teaching and practice that were just straightforwardly sinful: insubordination over against the authorities recognized in that culture (slaves, wives, younger vis-à-vis older); greed; extravagance; power-seeking; lack of prayer; quarrelsomeness and argumentativeness. Some of these things are context-related examples of moral failures that are perennial; others are specific to the ancient situation. Some are cultural, in that they are tied to structures and authorities in ancient society that belong to a different context from ours.

Other specific needs in the congregations include provision for widows (presumably including elderly spinsters), seen as a duty of the church: this may not be a problem in the contemporary Western world, but it is not difficult to reapply it as the basic duty of the church to care for whatever vulnerable groups of people there may be within its ambit today. Another duty is the appointment of leaders who are presumed to act like householders; again the general principle is clear enough.

Types of exposition

My expository output on the PE includes about forty-five sermons and talks, and this compares with some sixty items on Romans. Thus I have preached proportionately more often on texts from the PE, though this may be explained by my deliberate policy of preaching particularly on books that I was studying academically at any given time. Even so the numbers confirm that the PE are a fruitful area for the preacher. The expositions have taken place at four levels:

1. Exposition of a single verse (or equivalent unit). In practice very often this becomes an exposition of the longer passage that provides the context, or that the verse summarizes (cf. how exposition of a verse from a parable usually becomes an exposition of the parable).
2. Exposition of a paragraph or comparable self-contained unit.
3. Exposition of a whole letter so as to get the impact of the letter as a whole. This may need to be spread over more than one preaching session so that it is not superficial. It can be done with a congregation that is prepared to listen with the Bible open in front of them. But I have also found it helpful with audiences of theological students.
4. Exposition of a concept running throughout one or all three letters. This is in effect expounding several verses united in expressing different aspects of one word or a concept that may be expressed in a set of words (e.g. 'conscience' might include 'heart'; 'love' might include 'kindness').
5. But I want to add another level (or perhaps another kind) of treatment here that I have not attempted as often as I should. This is to have an interactive session in which the preacher and the congregation work together, with the preacher handling the text to explain what Paul was saying and setting the congregation an agenda to apply this message to their contemporary situation. This may be done in house or other small fellowship groups, but it can also be done in a congregational setting by forming several small discussion groups on the spot. In general, small groups are not equipped for handling exegetical difficulties since they tend to lack the resources to do so, but they are certainly in a position to think of their own needs and to think creatively about what God is saying to them today.

What would we lose if the Pastoral Epistles had never been written?

What do we find in the PE that we do not get elsewhere, whether as regards topics not found elsewhere or regarding treatments from a different angle on topics treated elsewhere? My list would include such items as:

Christian belief
- The inspiration and usefulness of Scripture
- The apostolic deposit and passing it on
- Odd beliefs and sectarianism

- Aspects of Christology (Jesus as man and mediator; possibly Jesus as God [Titus 2:13]; epiphany)
- The universal provision of salvation

Christian living
- Conversion
- Conscience
- Commitment
- Wealth and poverty: rich believers and the use of wealth
- Care for needy people in the congregation
- Social groupings and Christian life in such structures
- The sanctity of marriage and childbearing
- Care for the family
- Martyrdom and persecution

Congregational life
- Orderliness in congregational organization and meetings of believers
- The practice of prayer in a congregational setting
- The universal scope of prayer
- Congregational leadership: the detailed qualities and functions of church leaders (including role models)
- Commissioning by laying on of hands
- The central place of teaching in church life
- Stipends or other provision for congregational and missionary workers
- Church discipline

Alongside the content of the PE on these topics, the preacher should also consider the 'shape' of the teaching, that is, the ordering of the topics and their relationship to one another. Has this anything to teach us, and how should it affect our preaching? Does it, for example, require us to teach through a letter from beginning to end, or is it sometimes better to reorder the material?

Problems and opportunities for the preacher

Honesty on critical issues or silence?
Recently a preacher in my own church began a sermon on gender issues by referring to what he called the two 'myths' of creation in Genesis 1 and 2 – 3. The congregation is mixed in composition with some who can take such terms in their stride and are not bothered by them; they know that 'myth'

refers to the *function* of a narrative rather than necessarily to its lack of literal historicity. But the more conservative members are worried by it and may switch off their attention and not turn up again the next time the same person is preaching. One learns to be careful not to speak in ways that create obstacles for the congregation and prevents them from hearing the Word of God. Even within a Tyndale Fellowship group there could be those who might stop listening to me if I were to suggest that the PE were the work of a disciple inspired by Paul rather than by the man himself. Indeed, I was once visited by a small deputation who had heard that I was about to publish a commentary that did not unequivocally declare Paul to be their author. I told them that I had to be honest about the facts so far as I knew them.

Nevertheless, when preaching on these letters I generally refer to the author as Paul, so as not to put an obstacle in the way of hearing them as the Word of God. There is nothing dishonest about this, since Paul is the person who is named in the letters as the author. The procedure might be likened to referring to the narrator of the Sherlock Holmes stories as Watson, although we know that the author was Arthur Conan Doyle. It is not appropriate to raise such a debatable technical issue in an expository sermon when it is irrelevant (I am tempted to say 'totally irrelevant') to the matter in hand and would cause a distraction. We do need on occasion to teach people something about the doubts concerning many points of biblical origins and the unlikelihood of some traditional positions rather than trying to assure them that there are no such problems. But we must not preach in such a way that we distract people from the spiritual lessons we are aiming to teach. Is there not a possibly apocryphal story about Karl Barth being asked whether he believed that there was a talking serpent in the Garden of Eden and his response that far more important than whether the serpent existed was the question of what the serpent said?

Time-bound teaching?

Some commands and related lifestyles seem dubious to readers today, both because they seem to be out of harmony with contemporary ethics, which is usually what alerts people to question them, but also because they may also seem to be out of harmony with other biblical teaching. The conspicuous example of this is the teaching regarding the limitations placed on women. It is a problem both for those who take the traditionalist interpretation, since they have to defend a mode of conduct that seems to defy common sense, and also for those who take the egalitarian type of interpretation, since they appear to be denying what appears to be the plain teaching of Scripture. Evangelical scholars and preachers will approach the text rather differently from those liberals who seem to want to make the teaching appear to be contradictory to that of Jesus and as irrational and unacceptable as possible: they will ask how it is to be applied positively in a different situation and shown to be extensible to men as well as to women. This is too big an issue to discuss here (see the 'Further reading' section at the end of this chapter).

Balances

Frequently in preaching I have to indicate the balance that must be achieved in Christian living between competing ideals. This applies especially with regard to the teaching in the PE regarding the point just mentioned, namely the requirement for the women to be silent. Elsewhere in the New Testament it is clear that women did prophesy, preach and teach, or at the very least were not silent (Acts 18:26; 21:9; 1 Cor. 11:5) despite what appear to have been some local, cultural restrictions.

The teaching in 1 Timothy 2 must be balanced against that in 1 Corinthians 11 and 12 – 14 according to the different situations addressed. If the PE stress the need for trained teachers with authority to teach, this must be placed alongside the spontaneity of utterance inspired by the Spirit in 1 Corinthians 12 – 14. Charisma and office must both have their places. The PE tend towards what is called 'institutionalization', the process of developing orderliness in organization and procedures for the growing Christian network and coping with the defence of orthodox teaching and exposing the dangers of false teaching. But alongside them stand places where freedom to exercise charismata is much more open, and congregations today must find ways of incorporating the elements of both freedom and good order.

Similarly, if the PE exclusively stress the duties of slaves to their masters, this must be seen alongside the directions to masters in Ephesians, Colossians and Philemon. All scriptural teaching must be understood in the context of the canon as a whole, and we must not expound the PE in isolation, particularly in view of their unusual situation.

Context

The PE must not be expounded on the basis of an assumed theological background, common to all biblical authors, which may not be appropriate. For example, they appear to teach clearly enough the universal provision of salvation for everybody (1 Tim. 2:6; 4:10; Titus 2:11). Prima facie this goes against the concept of a 'limited atonement' (alias 'particular redemption') characteristic of Augustinian and Calvinist theology. Some expositors believe this concept is silently present throughout the New Testament and that this provision of salvation is solely for the company of God's elect people, and they argue that the PE must be understood in harmony with such a theology, even though the result may be to embrace unnatural interpretations of the verses in question. This is a dubious procedure, and it may be more satisfactory either to show that the other passages in the New Testament can be interpreted more naturally in line with the PE or to recognize the existence of a tension that must not be forcibly broken. (The opposite situation also arises, when the PE need to be interpreted in the light of other passages in the New Testament as regards the roles of women alongside men.)

Variation

The PE offer interesting examples of the use of categories and vocabulary that differ from those used elsewhere in the New Testament. There is the theological language of epiphany and the moral language of piety and self-control which are used to convey the message in ways that would be understood in the Hellenistic world (both Greco-Roman and Jewish). Compare how the Gospel of John expresses the message of Jesus with very little mention of the kingdom of God but lots of reference to eternal life, whereas the Synoptic Gospels do precisely the opposite. This procedure may offer a model for the preacher today to attempt to find contemporary language to convey the gospel, but to do so in such a way that nothing of substance is lost or weakened.

By way of example

Jumping the centuries: the problems in the congregations (Titus 1:10–16)

This example of an application that fits our own time is not an excerpt from an actual sermon but from an academic session in which I was trying to summarize the teaching of Titus to a gathering of students and pastors and at the same time to raise questions and topics for them to explore. I invited my audience to consider what to do with the underlying reasons for the instructions given to Titus in this mandate letter.

> That *the congregations had serious problems* is evident from the very strong language used here and elsewhere (cf. Gal. 1 or Phil. 3) to castigate them. Such strong language is typical of polemic in the ancient world, and is not necessarily an example for us to follow. Timothy is in fact told to be gentle with his opponents, in the hope that some of them may repent (2 Tim. 2:24–25).
>
> If we put together the information that comes out implicitly from all three PE, there were three characteristics of these opponents, although it may be wrong to assume that they were all present in Crete.

First, some of them were trying to impose some odd kinds of lunatic-fringe Jewish belief and practice on the Christian congregations. According to 3:9 they were spinning weird ideas out of the stories and genealogies in the early parts of Genesis and teaching some kinds of commandments to follow rather than the gospel.

Two, according to 1 Timothy, some of them were keen ascetics, who were trying to impose some rigorous rules of conduct on Christians (such as abstinence from certain kinds of food and from marriage, 1 Tim. 4:3).

Three, some of them were teaching esoteric doctrines with practical implications in the church (cf. 1 Tim. 6:20), such as that the resurrection had in some sense happened already (2 Tim. 2:18).

No single group in the church or the world today corresponds exactly with these people, so that we can draw analogies or conclusions directly from Scripture to the modern world. But we can detect six characteristics in the references to Titus's opponents that can occur independently of one another and that individually have corresponding manifestations in the world of today.

1. These problem people in the church were rebellious. There was *a spirit of opposition to authority*, the kind of thing seen in rebellious young and old people who rebel against society and favour anarchy.

2. There were people going around, upsetting households by their odd teaching. Some Christian sects today *go round* the streets usually in pairs and speak to people on their doorsteps and lead some of them away from the orthodox Christian faith into Christian deviations.

3. Their teaching is summed up as consisting of Jewish myths. The nearest thing in the modern world is the doctrines of the New Age, *bizarre and irrational speculations* that make no sense, but captivate people. But I have also come across theologians whose interest is not so much protology as eschatology, trying to harmonize and interpret Daniel and Revelation on the assumption that the prophecies in these books must be literally fulfilled.

4. They pay attention to the commands of human people who reject the truth. The modern equivalent to this might be the so-called *messianic sects* in which a human leader gets the unquestioned obedience and devotion of his followers to the extent that he can even order mass suicide and is obeyed.

5. Their minds are corrupted and whatever they touch they make dirty. The original reference here may be to the laws of purity in Judaism. Today some people find sexual innuendoes and dirty jokes in things that are pure and innocent and see the whole world from a perverted point of view. This is the growing realm of *pornography and filth*.

6. And, finally, there are the people who claim to know God but by their actions deny him. This has its modern equivalent in the *nominalism* of people who profess an attachment to the church, but whose behaviour is inconsistent with it and brings the

gospel into disrepute. There are sometimes people who make a great profession of being Christians and yet who belie it by the way they behave in business or in their family, the professing Christians who are dishonest or violent at work, the husbands and wives who batter one another, the Christian leaders who engage in pornography, or whatever.

This represents an attempt to show that the same types of sinful thought and behaviour manifest themselves today, so that preachers may be able to recognize them when they see them, and so that they may instruct their congregations not only to recognize them but also to take appropriate action regarding them.

Extracting doctrine (Titus 2:11 – 3:8)

My second example is from a brief Bible study that was meant to set the tone for a conference on the doctrine of salvation.

The passage before us is *the doctrinal heart of Titus* and, one might say, of all three letters. It consists of various sections. The first section, 2:11–14, forms the conclusion to the earlier part of the chapter which gave Titus instructions about the teaching that he was to pass on to various groups of people according to their particular situations. It provides the doctrinal backing that explains why they are to behave in these specific ways. Then comes a final recapitulation to the chapter in 2:15 that reinforces the command to Titus to teach these things. There is a fresh start in 3:1–2 that gives him instructions about how he is to train the congregation in general, and to urge them to the right kinds of relationships with people outside the church. This teaching in its turn receives a doctrinal backing in 3:3–8 that describes how God had saved the members of the church with the aim that they might do these right things in their daily lives. *Thus the doctrinal passages are included to give the basis for the ethics.*

In the context of this conference our concern is more with the doctrine in itself and with *what it has to say to us about the nature of salvation.* There are various notes to which we need to pay attention, as we discover incidentally, as it were, significant facts.

First, the passage underlines that *salvation comes from God and is due entirely to his grace, kindness and love.* If people are saved from their sins and receive eternal life, it is because of the kindness of God and only because of the kindness of God. Therefore, two things follow that are of importance.

The first consequence is that *there is one way of salvation for everybody.* God's grace has appeared to bring salvation to all people. I believe that the phrase 'to all people' is connected with the adjective 'bringing salvation' rather than with the verb 'has appeared', and I for myself believe that 'all' is to be taken straightforwardly to refer to every human being. But the implication of this is that, if God has provided a salvation for all, then no other way exists or is possible. This is the one and only way of salvation. All people can be saved only in this way. Or rather nobody can be saved, except in this way.

The second consequence is that *there is no other way to salvation than God's way*. This is emphasized by the writer's saying that we are not saved by good deeds that we have done but because of his mercy. He is, of course, saying nothing strange here. This is the united teaching of the New Testament, but it is expressed particularly pointedly and in absolute terms here. There is nothing we can do to save ourselves.

The second main point is that *salvation comes from God and is due to his grace expressed in the coming of Jesus*. God himself is called Saviour, and this title is shared with Jesus. Moreover, the actual title of God is used here for Jesus in 2:13 according to what I regard as the most likely exegesis of the verse (contra P. Towner). Such language leaves no room for any other Saviour. The description of the epiphany of God's grace in him indicates that a once-for-all action has taken place in order to redeem us from sin. No other Saviour stands anywhere on the horizon, although the ancient world knew of plenty of figures who were given this title.

The third main point is that *salvation comes from God but demands a human response*. It is for those who trust in God, and elsewhere in the letter the need for faith is made abundantly clear. ('Faith' is in fact the most used theological concept in the PE.) It leads to a changed life in which people abandon ungodliness and embrace the practice of goodness and godliness. Thus there are visible signs of a changed life. Certainly, some of these signs may be seen in people who are not saved; goodness is not confined to Christian believers. But the point is that if these signs are not evident, then the individual's experience of salvation is seriously called in question. One particular point that is singled out is that this change in behaviour is due to renewal by the Holy Spirit. A changed life is due to divine empowering.

From these three points can be drawn *some conclusions for our conference context*.

First, *salvation is a present experience that involves a changed life and a present knowledge of God*. It is arguable that too often the question of salvation in other religions or apart from the Christian revelation is couched in terms of 'final salvation', 'acquittal at the last judgment'. But salvation is present as well as future, and present salvation appears to involve factors that cannot be present apart from knowledge and experience of the divine grace shown in Christ. Therefore, whatever we may believe about the final end of people who have not heard the gospel, there is ample justification for evangelism in bringing them to experience the present blessings and joys of salvation.

Secondly, salvation is due to divine grace that expressed itself in the decisive act in Christ. *There is no way to salvation without the redemption from sin that he achieved*. Clearly those who believe in God through Jesus are saved because of this act of redemption. What is not clear anywhere in the New Testament is what happens to people who have not heard of Jesus. But we have to say that ordinarily people who hear the gospel and reject it are regarded as lost, and that all people are regarded as in need of salvation; the preaching of the gospel never contains the comment 'This message is needed only by some of you; others of you are all right even though you have never heard it before.'

Thirdly, it follows that *we have an obligation to take the gospel to people who adhere to other religions as much as to people who have no religion at all.* With all that must be said about respect and toleration for other religions – and there is some need to emphasize this! – and with all that must be said about recognizing the goodness and even the godliness of professors of other religions, it is nevertheless our inescapable duty to present the gospel to adherents of other religions. The New Testament example of preaching the gospel to Jews and proselytes, adherents of the religion that is surely the nearest to Christianity and that was, until Christ came, the one, true religion, is an invincible argument for the need to preach the gospel to all people everywhere. All have sinned, and all need to be saved.

But, fourthly, this raises the question *If all have sinned, what does God do about those who never hear the gospel?* Especially if, as this passage says, the salvation offered in Christ is open to everybody. To this question our passage gives no answer. But it stands in a letter that deals with the need to preach the gospel, and that obligation rests upon us. When people asked Jesus, 'Lord, are only a few people going to be saved?', he replied, 'Make every effort to enter through the narrow door' (Luke 13:23–24). Make sure you are saved! I fancy that if Paul were asked the equivalent question 'Can people be saved apart from the gospel?' he would reply, 'Strive to preach the gospel; woe is me if I do not preach the gospel.' 'The secret things belong to the LORD our God, but the things revealed belong to us and to our children for ever, that we may follow all the words of this law' (Deut. 29:29). Nevertheless, we believe that the secret nature of God is the same as his revealed nature, which is holiness and grace, and we trust in his mercy towards the world, while at the same time we fulfil his command to proclaim the gospel.

Both of the above excerpts are bare skeletons that can do little more than show how a logical structure may be developed out of a text, and they would need development in a normal preaching situation. The former shows the need for contemporary application. The latter shows the preacher examining the text for its implications in reconstructing the early Christian doctrine of salvation. It is assumed that this will be binding upon preachers today.

Further reading

DAVIES, M., *The Pastoral Epistles*, Epworth Commentaries (London: Epworth, 1996); faces up to the difficulties posed by these letters.

LIEFELD, W. L., *1 and 2 Timothy, Titus*, NIVAC (Grand Rapids: Zondervan, 1999); exegesis with discussions on bridging the gap to contemporary exposition.

MARSHALL, I. H., 'FEET Bible Readings: 1. Titus 2:11 – 3:8', *EJT* 4.1 (1995), pp. 11–17.

—— (in collaboration with P. H. TOWNER), *A Critical and Exegetical Commentary on the Pastoral Epistles*, ICC (Edinburgh: T. & T. Clark, 1999); detailed exegesis of Greek text but leaves exposition to the reader.

MONTAGUE, G. T., *First and Second Timothy, Titus*, Catholic Commentary on Sacred Scripture (Grand Rapids: Baker Academic, 2008); eminently practical and challenging.

MOUNCE, W. D., *Pastoral Epistles*, WBC (Nashville: Nelson, 2000); detailed exegesis of Greek text but leaves exposition to the reader.

ODEN, T. C., *First and Second Timothy and Titus*, Interpretation (Louisville: John Knox, 1989); thematic studies with history of interpretation.

STOTT, J. R. W., *Guard the Gospel: The Message of 2 Timothy*, BST (Leicester: Inter-Varsity Press, 1973); probably the most useful for preachers.

——, *The Message of 1 Timothy and Titus: The Life of the Local Church*, BST (Leicester: Inter-Varsity Press, 1996); as previous entry.

TOWNER, P. H., *1–2 Timothy and Titus*, IVPNTC (Downers Grove: InterVarsity Press; Leicester: Inter-Varsity Press, 1994); brief but helpful.

——, *The Letters to Timothy and Titus*, NICNT (Grand Rapids: Eerdmans, 2006); excellent detailed exegesis and application.

TWOMEY, J., *The Pastoral Epistles Through the Centuries*, Blackwell Bible Commentaries (Malden, Mass.; Oxford: Wiley-Blackwell, 2009); hilarious romp through the history of exposition.

WITHERINGTON III, B., *Letters and Homilies for Hellenized Christians*, vol. 1: *A Socio-Rhetorical Commentary on Titus, 1–2 Timothy and 1–3 John* (Downers Grove: IVP Academic; Nottingham: Apollos, 2006); lively exposition but tends to be patchy.

9. THE CHALLENGE AND OPPORTUNITY OF PREACHING HEBREWS

Charles A. Anderson

Perhaps no other part of the New Testament offers the challenge and yet the opportunity for contemporary preaching as the letter to the Hebrews. It is not an easy book for us today. It is long for an epistle. Its structure is complex. Its argument draws heavily on the Old Testament, but also from ancient philosophy. Yet for all the difficulties, Hebrews can contribute uniquely to our preaching. Like Romans, it offers a rather comprehensive picture of salvation, though in a different key. Combine that with its reliance on the Old Testament, and to preach Hebrews is to unfold the whole of God's plan to honour his Son and save a people. Even more to the point, Hebrews is so helpful for our preaching precisely because it is preaching. It alone presents a canonical, divinely inspired example of a sermon to a first-century church. This chapter will thus primarily investigate how to preach *as derived from* Hebrews.[1]

We will start by looking at the ways in which Hebrews is so challenging for preaching today. What about this letter makes it difficult for contemporary audiences? Then we will explore how Hebrews offers rich opportunity for preaching. First, that means investigating what we may learn from Hebrews

---

1. Anthony T. Selvaggio, 'Preaching Advice from the "Sermon" to the Hebrews', *Them* 32 (2007), pp. 33–45, also derives homiletic lessons from Hebrews. This chapter differs in its more technical focus on how Hebrews functions as a sermon.

as a sermon for the sake of our sermons. Secondly, and more briefly, we will consider its benefits for our doctrine and practice.

The challenges of preaching Hebrews

For all its size and significance, Hebrews seems relatively neglected within evangelical preaching. Such a judgment is admittedly subjective, though ministers whom I queried agreed they have rarely preached from it.[2] It is not for lack of resources: research on Hebrews has proliferated in recent years, including many excellent commentaries being published.[3] The lack of preaching is more likely due to the challenges it poses for contemporary audiences. First, it famously has uncertain historical origins. William Barclay described it as coming to us like Melchizedek, without father or mother.[4] The author and the recipients are not specified, although certain clues emerge.[5] Thus the historical markers normal for most other epistles are absent. To the extent then that we must build from the original historical context to determine a text's meaning, such an effort proves more difficult for Hebrews.

A second challenge for preaching Hebrews arises from its complex structure. Other epistles often break down along the lines of doctrine and practice, the indicative, then the imperative. Think, for example, about Ephesians

---

2. I am grateful to the East Midlands Evangelical Ministers' Fraternal, Jonathan Griffiths, George Guthrie, Peter O'Brien and the editors for their feedback and suggestions on improving this chapter.

3. Commentaries that should prove particularly helpful for interpreting and preaching Hebrews include the following: Harold W. Attridge, *The Epistle to the Hebrews: A Commentary on the Epistle to the Hebrews*, Hermeneia (Philadelphia: Fortress, 1989); Craig R. Koester, *Hebrews: A New Translation with Introduction and Commentary*, AB (New York: Doubleday, 2001); Peter T. O'Brien, *The Letter to the Hebrews*, PNTC (Grand Rapids: Eerdmans, 2010). For a guide to recent scholarship see George H. Guthrie, 'Hebrews in Its First-Century Contexts: Recent Research', in Scot McKnight and Grant R. Osborne (eds.), *The Face of New Testament Studies: A Survey of Recent Research* (Grand Rapids: Baker Academic, 2004), pp. 414–443.

4. Quoted in Richard N. Longenecker, *Biblical Exegesis in the Apostolic Period* (Grand Rapids: Eerdmans, 1975), p. 158.

5. E.g. 10:32–34; 13:23. For a plausible reconstruction of the recipients being a Roman congregation in the mid-60s see William L. Lane, *Hebrews*, 2 vols., WBC (Dallas: Word, 1991), li–lxvi.

1 – 3 on God's cosmic plan to save a people in Christ, and chapters 4–6 on how they should live up to their calling. Hebrews is not as clear. It alternates between doctrine and practice, or to put it better, exposition and exhortation, and themes are raised only to disappear and then reappear. Numerous structural outlines have been proposed, but its complexity probably contributes to its neglect.[6] When a preacher and congregation find it difficult to get a handle on how the text fits together, that makes them hesitant to engage and less likely to understand it.

The difficulty of Hebrews extends beyond its structure to include its content. This third challenge occurs in at least two ways. First, there is the question of the letter's conceptual background. It shows apparent affinities to Platonic philosophy, Philo of Alexandria, Qumran, apocalyptic Judaism, Greco-Roman honour–shame culture, and the list goes on. That many of these influences are present, or that there are overlapping traits, is not in dispute. The question is whether any of them constitutes the appropriate, major conceptual framework in which to understand the letter.[7] The complex mix of ancient philosophical and religious traditions probably eludes us without wider study (or at least good secondary literature). That constitutes a challenge for studying and preaching the book.

The second facet of this challenge from the content of Hebrews resides in its reliance on the Old Testament.[8] Simply put, in an increasingly biblically illiterate age it is difficult for us to make sense of Hebrews, given its deep scriptural roots. The argument for Christ's sufficiency builds through comparison with Moses, Abraham, Mount Zion, Kadesh-Barnea, the tabernacle, the Day of Atonement – all these and more feature in the letter. Readers approach the story as they would epic poetry – *in medias res*, in the middle of the action. God has already spoken in various ways and places (1:1). Without knowing that story the true significance of Christ and his work, as laid out in Hebrews, remains elusive. To the extent then that we do not know the Old Testament, understanding Hebrews will prove a challenge.

---

6. For a helpful overview see Barry C. Joslin, 'Can Hebrews Be Structured? An Assessment of Eight Approaches', *CBR* 6 (2007), pp. 99–129.

7. For a comprehensive treatment see L. D. Hurst, *The Epistle to the Hebrews: Its Background and Thought*, SNTSMS (Cambridge: Cambridge University Press, 1990).

8. This includes how the OT is interpreted. See the survey by George H. Guthrie, 'Hebrews' Use of the Old Testament: Recent Trends in Research', *CBR* 1 (2003), pp. 271–294.

The final challenge for preaching Hebrews stems from the distance between the original recipients and Christians today. The internal evidence indicates those first recipients had started well in the faith (2:3–4), even resisted persecution (10:32–34), but now were in danger from renewed external threats (12:4), and, even more significantly, from their own spiritual lethargy (5:11–12), to the point that potential apostasy loomed (3:12).[9] They may have been ethnically Jewish, tempted to revert to the synagogue and its practices. But that profile of the first recipients – embattled, persecuted, Jewish – is vastly different from that of most Western congregations. Relatively well off, Gentile Christians today in the West generally do not face substantial persecution, nor do they fret over whether Jesus deals with sin better than the Day of Atonement did. How to bridge that gap? Crucial to preaching the Word is finding those points of contact between the original recipients and our hearers. For Hebrews, the link lies in a spiritual malaise. Believers have not progressed as they should (5:12), some having neglected meeting together (10:25) and are in danger of drifting away (2:1). As Thomas Long memorably puts it, they are 'tired of serving the world, tired of worship, tired of Christian education, tired of being peculiar and whispered about in society, tired of the spiritual struggle, tired of trying to keep their prayer life going, tired even of Jesus'.[10]

Such a diagnosis rings true in both the first and twenty-first centuries. That Western believers today do not experience the same level of persecution is not necessarily an impediment – just as it is not for preaching Revelation or 1 Peter, which were also written to suffering churches. As for the specifically 'Jewish' dimension of the text, the main point of comparing Jesus to the patriarchs, or of explaining his sacrifice in terms of the Levitical system, is to show his supremacy. Moreover, Hebrews makes sense of how God prepared salvation history for his Son. This last challenge, while real, is well handled by emphasizing the problem of spiritual immaturity.

These four challenges of Hebrews – its historical origins, complex structure, difficult content, and remoteness of its recipients – require attention. Some of them are not quickly or easily answered. But they are well worth engaging, for the potential benefits from Hebrews, both for and in our preaching, are worth the effort.

---

9. Koester, *Hebrews*, pp. 64–72, frames it as three phases of the community's history.

10. Thomas Long, *Hebrews*, IBC (Louisville: Westminster John Knox, 1997), p. 3.

The opportunity of Hebrews as preaching

Hebrews as sermon: the genre question

First, Hebrews does not read like other New Testament books. Its distinctive-ness is apparent from the opening words. No author is given, no recipients, no greeting. Instead, there is a majestic declaration of how God has spoken in the Son, an introduction that captures attention, rather like a sermon should (1:1–4).[11] Yet the ending is much more epistolary with its greetings from various parties and personal details about future plans (13:22–24). Secondly, Hebrews emphasizes direct speech in a unique way.[12] The author speaks (5:11; 8:1). God speaks: the Father (1:1–2; 12:25), the Son (10:5–7) and the Holy Spirit (3:7). In fact, nearly everyone speaks – Scripture (4:12–13; 3:5), Christ's work at the cross (12:24) and church leaders (13:7).

Most significantly, the author describes his work as a 'word of exhortation' (*logou tēs paraklēseōs*, 13:22). Two other occurrences of the phrase help reveal the genre of Hebrews. The synagogue rulers in Pisidian Antioch, after the reading of the Law and Prophets, ask Paul and Barnabas for a *logos paraklēseōs* for the people (Acts 13:15). Similarly, Judas Maccabeus exhorts his troops from the Law and the Prophets with an 'exhortation by means of good words' (*tēn en tois agathois logois paraklēsin*, 2 Maccabees 15.11). This phrase seems to serve as 'an idiomatic designation for the homily, or edifying discourse, which followed the reading from the Law and the Prophets in the Hellenistic synagogues'.[13] Hebrews has the characteristics of, and describes itself as, a sermon. It is an early Christian homily to an existing congregation that exhorts them on the basis of Scripture.

Understanding Hebrews as a sermon, with certain epistolary modifications, opens up a valuable opportunity within the Bible for reflections on preaching. Nowhere else *within* Scripture do we have a book so focused on the exposition *of* Scripture.[14] We can learn by eavesdropping on how a gifted and inspired

---

11. William L. Lane, 'Hebrews: A Sermon in Search of a Setting', *SwJT* 28 (1985), p. 13.

12. Contrast Paul's emphasis on his letters as writing (Rom. 15:15; 1 Cor. 4:14; 2 Cor. 1:13). David G. Peterson, 'God and Scripture in Hebrews', in Paul Helm and Carl Trueman (eds.), *The Trustworthiness of God: Perspectives on the Nature of Scripture* (Leicester: Apollos, 2002), pp. 121–122.

13. Lane, 'Sermon in Search', p. 13.

14. R. T. France, 'The Writer of Hebrews as a Biblical Expositor', *TynB* 47 (1996), p. 246.

first-century theologian preached. There are six major expositions in Hebrews woven together to help create the one sermon:

1. Psalm 8:4–6 in Hebrews 2:5–18
2. Psalm 95:7–11 in Hebrews 3:1 – 4:13
3. Psalm 110:4 in Hebrews 7:1–28 (it lies behind 5:1–10 as well)
4. Jeremiah 31:31–34 in Hebrews 8:7 – 10:18
5. Habakkuk 2:4 in Hebrews 10:26 – 12:3
6. Proverbs 3:11–12 in Hebrews 12:4–13

All these sections work from a key Old Testament passage, often incorporating other verses as secondary exegesis along the way.

The next parts of this chapter will explore how the author preaches from Scripture and to what effect. Sometimes that will provide a biblical example or warrant for what many already do as best practice in preaching. At other times it may correct or provide something new.

Exposition in individual passages in Hebrews

John Stott provides a succinct definition of expository preaching, where the task 'is to bring out of the text what is there and expose it to view'.[15] That practice fits the way Hebrews handles the Old Testament text.[16] The author uses a relatively consistent pattern for his exposition: introduction, citation of an Old Testament text, exposition and exhortation or conclusion.[17] Hebrews 3:1 – 4:13 presents a clear example of this. The introduction (3:1–6) compares Moses and Jesus, by using Numbers 12:7. Both were faithful (*pistos*) with respect to God's house, that is, his people, who include both the ancient Israelites and the recipients of the letter (3:6). That prepares for the exposition of Psalm 95 in two ways: by establishing that the psalm speaks to the

---

15. John R. W. Stott, *Between Two Worlds: The Art of Preaching in the Twentieth Century* (Grand Rapids: Eerdmans, 1982), p. 126.

16. For more on specific exegetical techniques in Hebrews see Guthrie, 'Hebrews' Use', and Susan E. Docherty, *The Use of the Old Testament in Hebrews: A Case Study in Early Jewish Bible Interpretation*, WUNT 2.260 (Tübingen: Mohr Siebeck, 2009).

17. Harold W. Attridge, 'Paraenesis in a Homily (λόγος παρακλήσεως): The Possible Location of, and Socialization in, the Epistle to the Hebrews', *Semeia* 50 (1990), pp. 215–216. Lawrence Wills, 'The Form of the Sermon in Hellenistic Judaism and Early Christianity', *HTR* 77 (1984), pp. 277–299, charts this pattern across a range of Jewish and Christian texts.

letter's recipients, since they also belong to God's people, and by foreshadowing the issue at hand: whether they will prove faithful. After the citation of Psalm 95:7–11 in 3:7–11, the exposition follows in two parts. First, unbelief, if unchecked, will prevent them from entering rest, just as it did the Israelites in the wilderness (3:12–19). Then, secondly, in 4:1–10, that rest they are to enter is explained, via Genesis 2:2 (on the rabbinic principle of *gezera shewa*, 'Scripture interpreting Scripture'), as God's own rest, which means to rest from their work and experience his salvation. The exhortation comes in 4:11 for them therefore to do all they can to enter such rest and not to disobey. Mentioning rest and disobedience ties the two sections of the exposition together. Finally, the conclusion reflects on the power of God's Word and its function in judgment (4:12–13). The exposition as a whole, therefore, draws from Psalm 95 the crux of faith and the promise that those who have it find rest. Along the way the author incorporates other scriptural texts in a way that presupposes an overall coherence as God's word.[18]

Examples could also be drawn from the four other expositions. But the point is clear. The author of Hebrews builds his sermon in large part, though not exclusively, by means of interpreting and applying Old Testament passages to this congregation. But if we intend to glean lessons for our own preaching from Hebrews, we need to see more than just the author's pattern of exposition in individual passages, and consider the principles that guide such work.

Underlying hermeneutical principles of exposition in Hebrews

The hermeneutics of Hebrews is famously difficult.[19] Here we will focus on two underlying axioms relevant for preaching.

The first principle is that the author interprets Scripture within the framework of redemptive history. Redemptive history, or salvation history, expresses the idea that God has acted progressively in history to bring about salvation, which the Bible gradually unfolds and reveals.[20] Hebrews reads

---

18. Docherty, *Use of the Old Testament*, p. 190.

19. See Guthrie, 'Hebrews' Use', pp. 283–290. On the charge that Hebrews interprets Scripture in ways no longer valid see Stephen Motyer, 'The Psalm Quotations of Hebrews 1: A Hermeneutic-Free Zone?', *TynB* 50 (1999), pp. 3–22.

20. See Brian Rosner, 'Salvation, History Of', in Kevin J. Vanhoozer (ed.), *Dictionary of Theological Interpretation of the Bible* (Grand Rapids: Baker, 2005), pp. 714–717. In particular, Hebrews reads redemptive history typologically: OT figures, events and institutions are patterns now fulfilled in Christ. On this,

the Old Testament in the light of this progression, where the sequence in which texts are written and events take place bears on their interpretation. Hebrews 4:8 alludes to Joshua 23:1 with the latter's declaration that Israel had rest in the land under Joshua. But the author reasons that such rest must not have been ultimate, because after that Psalm 95 held out the promise of 'today' entering God's rest. Since Psalm 95 was written after Joshua 23:1, there must still be another rest for the believers to enter (4:9–10). Elsewhere, the author infers that perfection must not have been possible through the Levitical priesthood, for if it were, there would have been no need for a priest in the Melchizedekean order (7:11), which was established after the Levitical (7:28). That points to the earlier priesthood's ineffectiveness (7:18). The same dynamic holds true for the covenants (8:13) and sacrifices (10:8–9). In numerous places therefore Hebrews extracts meaning from the sequence in which things occur in Scripture and history.

Sequence alone though might make Hebrews historical but not necessarily redemptive. For redemption we must consider what kinds of texts the author chose. George Caird proposed that the main Old Testament texts in Hebrews all point to their own inadequacy. That is, they indicate in themselves that they are incomplete. Each passage 'declares the ineffectiveness and symbolic or provisional nature of the Old Testament religious institutions'.[21] A set of unfulfilled conditional statements shows how these Old Testament figures and institutions could not provide genuine, lasting salvation: 'if Joshua had given them rest' (Heb. 4:8; Ps. 95); 'If perfection could have been attained through the Levitical priesthood' (7:11; Ps. 110:4); 'if that first covenant had been faultless' (Heb. 8:7; Jer. 31); if everything were actually under humanity's rule (Heb. 2:8; Ps. 8).[22] Hebrews reads Old Testament history as an era of salvation promised but not yet delivered. What comes later, that which is newer, is better.

A strategy of argumentation that prioritized newer as better may seem obvious to us. But in the ancient world it was counter-intuitive. Their notion was older is better. The further back in history a practice went, the more credible it was. Susan Docherty notes how few parallels there are to this kind of newer

---

consult the still profitable Leonhard Goppelt, *Typos: The Typological Interpretation of the Old Testament in the New*, tr. Donald H. Madvig (Grand Rapids: Eerdmans, 1982), pp. 161–205.

21. George B. Caird, 'The Exegetical Method of the Epistle to the Hebrews', *CJT* 5 (1959), p. 47.

22. Ibid., pp. 48–49. He does not include Ps. 8 in his list.

is better approach in Jewish exegesis of the time.[23] So the author of Hebrews, though obviously educated in Greco-Roman and Jewish worlds, is overturning widespread conventions. What would motivate this redemptive-historical approach? In the answer lies our second hermeneutical principle for preaching.

Hebrews is Christ-centred in its redemptive-historical interpretation of Scripture. Jesus' death and resurrection necessitated a reversal of how to see things, so that this intrusion, foretold and foreshadowed, is better and surpasses what God did before. The Christ event becomes the interpretative fulcrum for these previously unfulfilled Old Testament texts and institutions. The author has two poles for exegeting Scripture: the Christ event and the original text, and no interpretation can be advanced that separates them or allows one to overpower the other. Although not yet fulfilled, Psalm 8 is on its way to fulfilment through the death and enthronement of Jesus, who will bring about his universal sovereignty. Jesus offers the Psalm 95 rest that God always intended. Jesus is *the* priest in the order of Melchizedek, according to Psalm 110:4, its true member by virtue of his resurrection. The new covenant prophesied in Jeremiah 31 finds its mediator and guarantor in Jesus, whose self-sacrifice uniquely inaugurates it. That the righteous will live by faith (Hab. 2:4) is supremely exemplified by Jesus, 'the pioneer and perfecter of faith' (Heb. 12:2).[24] It is not just that these texts are interpreted in relation to Jesus, but that the implicit assertion is that it is *only* in relation to him that they can be interpreted and fulfilled. The patriarchs did not receive what was promised precisely because they were waiting for the better thing God had prepared: Jesus, who endured the cross to sit down at God's right hand (11:39–40; 12:2). Thus Hebrews' major Old Testament texts are read as fulfilled in Jesus, the centre point of redemptive history.

This redemptive-historical, Christ-centred approach is nothing new for evangelical hermeneutics and homiletics. Works by the likes of Graeme Goldsworthy, Sidney Greidanus and Edmund Clowney have been widely influential. Nonetheless, it is important to see these principles so clearly modelled in Scripture, particularly in preaching. Hebrews validates this way of interpreting the Bible and proclaiming its message. Our sermons need to have this same boldness and perceptiveness to point people to Christ from the whole Bible, as the one who fulfils God's promises and plans in salvation.

---

23. Docherty, *Use of the Old Testament*, p. 192.

24. Of the six major OT expositions in Hebrews, the only one not interpreted in a Christocentric fashion is Prov. 3:11–12. Yet the letter's wider teaching about the Son who suffers coheres with the exposition in Heb. 12 of how the Lord disciplines his children.

Sermon structure of Hebrews: argument from exposition

We have so far seen the pervasiveness and pattern of Hebrews' exposition of the Old Testament and some of the relevant underlying principles. The next steps are the wider questions 'How does such exposition work in the sermon as a whole? What difference does it make for our interpretation – and for our preaching – that the book is built around these expositions?' To answer these we need to look at the structure of Hebrews. I have already noted the difficulties above, so we need to confine ourselves to what is most relevant for learning from Hebrews as a sermon. The two keys are (1) how exposition constructs the argument of the sermon and (2) how exhortation determines that argument.

Hebrews is constructed from two types of discourse: argument and exhortation.[25] They are distinguishable by various criteria. The argument tends towards realized eschatology, while the exhortation is futuristic.[26] Spatial references come predominantly in the argument, not in the exhortation.[27] The author repeatedly addresses the recipients directly in the exhortation but only once in the argument.[28] These two types of discourse are clearly intertwined, and Hebrews is structured at the most general level such that argument and exhortation go together.[29] Yet this generic distinction is instructive for how to think about Hebrews as a sermon.

The Old Testament expositions in Hebrews do not create its structural

---

25. George H. Guthrie, *The Structure of Hebrews: A Text-Linguistic Analysis*, NovTSup 73 (Leiden: Brill, 1994), p. 115, with slightly different terminology.

26. Graham Hughes, *Hebrews and Hermeneutics: The Epistle to the Hebrews as a New Testament Example of Biblical Interpretation*, SNTSMS (Cambridge: Cambridge University Press, 1979), pp. 67–69; Guthrie, *Structure of Hebrews*, p. 121. E.g. argument: 2:10; 5:7–10; 10:14. Exhortation: 3:6; 6:10–12; 10:27; 13:4. Those passages that overlap between argument and exhortation correspondingly mix these eschatological views: 4:14, 16; 10:19–23.

27. Guthrie, *Structure of Hebrews*, p. 121. This is less clear, because 11:9–17 and ch. 12 are exceptions. E.g. heavenly references: 1:13; 2:5; 7:26; 8:1–2; 9:11–12; 10:12. E.g. earthly references: 2:9, 14; 5:1, 7; 8:4–5; 9:1; 10:5.

28. In exhortation, e.g. 3:12–13; 4:1; 5:11–12; 6:9–12; 10:32–36; and repeatedly in chs. 12–13. In argument, only 7:4.

29. Introduction, 1:1–4; Jesus as Son, 1:5 – 4:13; Jesus as offerer and offering, 4:14 – 10:25; live faithfully, 10:19 – 13:19; benediction and conclusion, 13:20–25. The diagram in Guthrie, *Structure of Hebrews*, pp. 14, is extremely helpful for showing the flow of thought in the structure.

framework. They run across both types of discourse: Psalms 8, 110 and Jeremiah 31 fit into the argument, while Psalm 95, Habakkuk 2 and Proverbs 3 fit into the exhortation. But the expositions of Psalms 8, 110 and Jeremiah 31 are the *means* by which the argument is made.[30] Interpreting these texts in a redemptive-historical, Christ-centred fashion is *how* Hebrews argues Christ is the surpassing Son who offers genuine redemption. The exposition is the argument. There is a spatial-logical movement in the argument that corresponds with the Old Testament interpretation.[31] In 1:5–13 the Son's superiority to the angels and involvement in creation, as advanced in the catena (a connected series of biblical quotes and citations) of Old Testament texts, point to his heavenly pre-existence. Yet he is temporarily lowered below the angels via the incarnation, and, even more specifically, his suffering death (2:5–18; Ps. 8). If the Son is going to deliver human beings from sin and death, and lead them to glory (2:10), he must identify with them (vv. 14–17). In 5:1–10 the Son is among humanity, for a high priest must be taken from the people (5:1), which in turn enables him to be appointed according to the order of Melchizedek, validated by his resurrection (7:1–28; Ps. 110:4). His appointment as high priest must logically precede his sacrificial work; hence the placement of the exposition here. The upward movement towards heaven resumes at 8:1–2 with Christ seated at the Father's right hand. Then, by means of Jeremiah 31, the argument is how Jesus' self-sacrifice inaugurates the new covenant (8:1 – 10:19). His sacrifice is earthly, and yet it is heavenly in order for it to be priestly (8:4; 9:11, 23–24). We can summarize the argument as the 'parabola of salvation': 'the glorious Son in heaven, the suffering Son on earth, and the triumphant Son ascended'.[32] And that movement, both spatially and logically, happens through the exposition of those key Old Testament texts.

To see how the exposition is the argument is to see something of its value for our own preaching. Expository preaching is so important precisely because it means the argument is made through what the Bible says. Preachers have authority for their claims in so far as they are demonstrably derived from Scripture. To borrow categories from Hebrews, we might say that since God speaks in Scripture, we want to communicate a message to people that is God's speaking to them, so they will heed his voice. Hebrews shows us how to build the argument in a sermon by exposition.

---

30. France, 'Writer of Hebrews', pp. 254–255.

31. See the excellent argument for this in Guthrie, *Structure of Hebrews*, pp. 120–127.

32. Daniel Harrington, S. J., *What Are They Saying About the Letter to the Hebrews?* (New York: Paulist, 2005), p. 13, paraphrasing Long, *Hebrews*, pp. 21–23.

Sermon structure of Hebrews: argument for the sake of application

What then is the relation between the argument and the exhortation? A first clue is in the pattern found by Guthrie when the exhortation semantically depends on the preceding argument.[33] Since the Son is superior to the angels (1:5–14), the revelation through him is superior to the one through them, and the recipients must pay attention to it (2:1–4).[34] Yet even more than individual instances, the overall thrust of the argument and the exhortation fits together.[35] Recall that the problem for the recipients is the danger of their not pressing on to the end (2:1). An emphasis in the argument on the eternal nature of salvation is therefore fitting. By virtue of his resurrection, Jesus can be a priest for ever (7:16, 24) with the pay-off that he can save completely those who come to him because he always intercedes for them (7:25).[36] He mediates the new covenant, so that those called can receive the eternal inheritance (9:15), and his sacrifice makes them perfect for ever (10:14). For those tempted to give up their faith, that promise of eternal salvation could rouse and motivate them to press on to the end.

The exhortation, in a sense, follows Jesus on his journey through the cross to the right hand of the Father, the second half of the parabola of salvation. He is the 'pioneer' (*archēgon*), perfected through suffering (cf. 5:9), blazing the trail for believers to follow to glory (2:10). The congregation therefore should consider Jesus (3:1) and fix their eyes on him (12:2). Just as he endured the cross, they should go to him outside the city gate (13:13). If they follow him through such suffering, the promise is that they too will reach that heavenly homeland.

The argument is calibrated to encourage the embattled, wearied believers to persevere. Under the new covenant, as the Son made high priest for ever, whose offering God has accepted, Jesus has obtained genuine redemption. Thus believers should press forward and carry on. The argument is 'a powerful motivation'[37] and 'the presupposition and grounding for exhortation'.[38] In that light, the aim of Hebrews is ultimately pastoral. The hearers need to find strength to carry on. Accordingly, they are shown, through Old Testament exposition, how Jesus is greater. The need of the hearers shapes and determines the argument.

---

33. Guthrie, *Structure of Hebrews*, pp. 140–141.
34. Hughes, *Hebrews and Hermeneutics*, pp. 7–8.
35. Guthrie, *Structure of Hebrews*, pp. 141–145.
36. Peterson, 'God and Scripture in Hebrews', p. 129.
37. Guthrie, *Structure of Hebrews*, p. 145.
38. Lane, *Hebrews*, p. c.

Exhortation drives the argument. This is a dynamic more acknowledged than applied in our preaching. We often invert the relationship. We spend the bulk of time and energy in finding insights into the passage, and they are what drive the sermon. We put far less effort into determining how those insights apply, why they should matter for people today. Application is hurriedly tacked on at the end, as time runs out. I am not advocating we read the meaning we want into the passage, or that we go looking for a passage just to support the application we already have in mind. Instead, this lesson from Hebrews means at least two things: first, we have not truly studied a biblical text until we know how it applied to its original hearers. Secondly, sermon writing should start at the end, with the need of the hearers, and how they should apply the passage. Bryan Chapell offers a helpful model for this.[39] The key for moving from Bible study to sermon preparation is finding what he calls a Fallen Condition Focus. The FCF is the bridge between the original hearers and an audience today. Chapell defines it as the need they both have, by virtue of the Fall, 'that requires the grace of the passage'.[40] It represents the 'so what', a reason, often the sin problem, why the Scripture was given. Finding and preaching to the FCF ensures we are faithfully handling the biblical text in its original context and truly applying it in our own context. The FCF should act as the rudder for our preaching: it guides the entire direction of the sermon. The opening illustration will expose the FCF in the hearts of our hearers so they realize their need and listen. The main truth of the passage will be formulated so it is applied to the FCF. The FCF provides the focal point of our actual application. Hebrews marshalled its biblical exposition to craft an argument meant to change the people who received it. Using something like the FCF may help ensure our own interpretation and preaching of Scripture does the same.

Other lessons for our sermons from the sermon to the Hebrews
And what more could we say about learning preaching from Hebrews?[41] I do not have space here to tell of the careful composition, its rhetorical force and artistry, even the avoidance of digressions (9:5), and going on too long (11:32), so that we learn so that how we say things in our sermons matters; or about the mix of warning and comfort (e.g. 6:4–9), so we do not become mono-

---

39. Bryan Chapell, *Christ-Centered Preaching: Redeeming the Expository Sermon*, 2nd ed. (Grand Rapids: Baker Academic, 2005), esp. pp. 48–57.

40. Ibid., p. 50.

41. Selvaggio, 'Preaching Advice', pp. 38–44, develops these points further.

chromatic in approach but instead make sure both to afflict and console; or about the identification of a preacher with the congregation (e.g. 3:6; 10:25), so we demonstrably stand alongside them under God's word; or about speaking to the congregation as a congregation, not just an aggregate of individuals (3:12–13; 10:24–25), so they grasp that to live the Christian life is necessarily to live with each other. May our sermons be worthy of them, so our preaching is strengthened and Christ is honoured.

The opportunity in preaching Hebrews

We turn now, briefly, to preaching Hebrews itself rather than learning from Hebrews how to preach. Hopefully, even through my discussion of homiletic lessons, some of the benefits that can derive from preaching Hebrews have begun to emerge. How might a congregation benefit and grow from a series through this book?

A first benefit of preaching Hebrews lies in Christology. Our view of Jesus should expand and our hearts should be more satisfied with him as we work through this book. Some of the Bible's greatest statements of his deity and intimacy with the Father are found in these pages (e.g. 1:2–4; 8:1; 13:8). At the same time, Hebrews brings the Son's humanity into sharp focus. He is clearly one of us, especially in his knowing what it means to suffer (2:18; 5:7). His two natures come together, as indeed they are together, in the strongest encouragement that Hebrews offers its recipients for pressing onwards: 'the character of the Lord who cares for them'.[42] He identifies with them and released them from the fear of death (2:10–16); he is the champion and perfecter of faith (12:2), empathetic with their weaknesses (4:14–15), because he himself suffered (2:18), and when he cried out to God because of his suffering (5:7), he found resurrection rather than pain's immediate removal. The rousing call of 12:1–3 to fix our eyes on Jesus and follow him is predicated on the applicability of his life and mission to ours. But it must be both a fully divine and fully human life in order to make a difference for us.[43] For me, and probably for many others, the invisible God may seem distant at times in the midst of pain.

---

42. Lane, 'Sermon in Search', p. 18.

43. On this proto-Chalcedonian approach in Hebrews see Richard Bauckham, 'The Divinity of Jesus Christ in the Epistle to the Hebrews', in Richard Bauckham, Daniel R. Driver, Trevor A. Hart and Nathan MacDonald (eds.), *The Epistle to the Hebrews and Christian Theology* (Grand Rapids: Eerdmans, 2009), pp. 15–36.

But Hebrews encourages us to come again and again to the Son who is God, glorified at the Father's right hand, who at the same time has known hardship, temptation and pain, and intercedes and sympathizes.

Secondly, Hebrews helps us get to grips with how the Bible fits together. It is not just that it builds its argument by means of exposition of the Old Testament. That alone is important, as we are exposed to significant parts of Scripture, some of which we may not know well. Preaching through Hebrews should familiarize us with Israel's rebellion in the wilderness, the enigmatic figure of Melchizedek, the tabernacle and the system of sacrifices under the Mosaic cult, not to mention the Old Testament overview of chapter 11. Even more, the kinds of texts chosen and how they are interpreted are instructive. The redemptive-historical, Christ-centred approach offers a concrete way for our congregations to understand how to read the whole Bible as one story. The very first verses set out this 'anticipation–consummation' motif for how God acted in the Old Testament and how he acts now in the Son.[44] To see how Hebrews reads the Bible is to learn how we likewise might read it. Preaching through Hebrews offers us a course in Christian hermeneutics.

Related to the prior point, a third benefit from engaging with Hebrews is its emphasis on the new covenant. The new covenant features at key junctures in the New Testament (e.g. Luke 22:20), yet at other times seems hidden from view, and is often absent in New Testament and systematic theologies. Precisely as we engage with how the Bible fits together, and how Hebrews reads the Old Testament, we come to the centrality of the new covenant. For Hebrews, only with the new covenant, with its emphasis on interiority and genuine forgiveness of sins, does Christ's sacrifice at the cross accomplish redemption. The joy of living in the new covenant may well up all the more in the congregation when they hear preaching that goes through Hebrews.

Finally, as a fourth benefit, Hebrews makes ongoing obedience an imperative in the Christian life. It sets out high moral standards for those who follow Jesus (10:26–27). One can see how some in the early church relied on it to argue against any welcome back for those who had publicly recanted their faith under persecution.[45] But we do not need to go that far to see the high value set by the book on 'persevering faith'; indeed, the phrase is almost inseparable: neither faith nor perseverance exists without the other (6:12). In the same vein, there is the emphasis in hortatory sections on the future nature of salvation. Christ will appear a second time to bring salvation (9:28), and '[w]e

---

44. Longenecker, *Biblical Exegesis*, pp. 174–175.

45. Koester, *Hebrews*, p. 23.

have come to share in Christ, if indeed we hold our original conviction firmly to the very end' (3:14). In times and places prone to easy believism, where people can pray a prayer and then rest confident that God accepts them, no matter what their next sixty years may look like, we need to remind ourselves that the only truly saved person is one who carries on in the faith and does not lose sight of how the Bible holds together the past, present and future dimensions. Preaching through Hebrews, and hearing its high standards, helps this process.

Conclusion

Hebrews will undoubtedly pose a challenge for those who study and work through it. But the lessons it offers for our preaching are significant. It demonstrates how to preach. If, as J. I. Packer said, the Bible is God preaching,[46] then Hebrews is God preaching an actual sermon. A sermon built from biblical exposition, discerning Christ in the text through a redemptive-historical approach, and orientating and guiding the argument on the basis of the need of the hearers. Our own efforts should find Hebrews an encouragement and spur us on in the high purpose and value of preaching. And in so preaching Hebrews in this renewed, sharpened way, we may encourage our hearers to lay hold of Christ and trust in his work to see them through to the end. As we do so, our preaching may take heart that its basis, God's Word, is 'alive and active. Sharper than any double-edged sword, it penetrates even to dividing soul and spirit, joints and marrow; it judges the thoughts and attitudes of the heart' (4:12).

© Charles A. Anderson, 2013

---

46. Cited in Stott, *Between Two Worlds*, p. 103.

10. PREACHING THE GENERAL EPISTLES

Mariam J. Kamell

As a group, these seven epistles may well be the least preached section of the New Testament. But six of them are presented as coming from, if not actually from, three of the named pillars of the Jerusalem church (Gal. 2:9), and two are traditionally from brothers of Jesus. That means these epistles derive from the forefront of the developing Christian movement, from people shaped by very close relationships with Jesus himself, and each shows the influence of Jesus' teaching in various ways. Meanwhile, the principle that these epistles were grouped together because of Paul's comment in Galatians on the pillars – James, Peter and John – inspires respect for these texts that is often unconsciously lacking. In some ways it is ironic that the Protestant tradition, which places such an emphasis on Scripture, has largely neglected these epistles from those closest to Jesus because they read so differently from those of Paul, and for the sake of the full witness of Scripture it is worth hearing these voices again.

There are several difficulties when one approaches the General Epistles, including simply grouping these disparate texts. Preachers, bogged down by background questions, often cannot even get to the text, and simply throw up their hands in despair. For the sake of brevity, I will not spend undue time with questions readily debated in commentaries, but will focus on authorship and structure in so far as those things help give a point of entry into the texts, a potential guide to bring these epistles out of obscurity.

It is also worth considering the imaginative exercise of a differently shaped canon. The earliest complete canon listing, in the thirty-ninth Festal Letter of Athanasius (AD 367), lists 'the seven so-called catholic epistles of the apostles' immediately after the Gospels and Acts, an order still used by the Russian Orthodox Church. Placed before the letters of Paul the missionary, this makes profound sense: the gathering of epistles from the leaders described so often in Acts, the men who fronted and guided the shape of the entire early church. It can be a helpful exercise to make a congregation aware of our propensity to read all of the New Testament through the lens of Paul by having them imagine how they would hear Paul if they read his letters *after* James and 1 John. This is a simple imaginative exercise that may help people engage these epistles as they were read in earlier generations of the church, and recognize the authority and respect these authors held in the early church.

There are seven 'General' Epistles, written to believers in an unspecified area, potentially all of known Christendom.[1] This means they read differently from Paul's letters to specific congregations. To help with preaching these epistles, I will speak briefly about each one, providing some threads – authorship, context, structure, key themes – that should help the preacher feel more confident when presenting these texts.

James

The epistle of James often garners a very mixed response. It is an immensely practical book, which is clear from a first reading. So some love it because it gives immediate applications without requiring a great deal of interpretation. On the other hand, some hate it and deem it 'bossy'. Particularly since Luther's time, anyone who wishes to teach James cannot simply preach the text but must also be engaged in an apologetic for it. There are several notes, however, that can significantly help with the process.

First, it can be worth clarifying the author of the epistle. Scholarship is widely varied on authorship and date, ranging from the brother of Jesus in the 40s to a Pauline community in the 150s.[2] I would argue there is a cohesive

---

1. See John Painter, 'The Johannine Epistles as Catholic Epistles', in Karl-Wilhelm Niebuhr and Robert W. Wall (eds.), *The Catholic Epistles and the Tradition* (Waco: Baylor University Press, 2009), pp. 245–251, for a discussion of the grouping of the 'catholic' epistles.

2. Respectively, see e.g. Ben Witherington III, 'James', in *Letters and Homilies for Jewish Christians: A Socio-Rhetorical Commentary on Hebrews, James and Jude* (Downers Grove:

case for authorship by James, the brother of Jesus and leader of the Jerusalem church, and a date at least by the mid-50s (if not before the Apostolic Council of AD 49), a position well attested in critical scholarship. So the preacher need not feel defensive if he or she wishes to present this James as the author.[3] The *literary* intention in the epistle certainly evokes the character of this James 'the righteous' and, indeed, there is near unanimity about the intended referent of 1:1.[4] That said, we have a towering figure from the early church to invoke, a man noted for his consistent and fervent prayer,[5] his nature as a peacemaker,[6] described by Hippolytus as the 'bishop of Jerusalem', a man who received his own resurrection appearance (1 Cor. 15:7), and given the titles in the early church of 'the Just', the 'bulwark of the people' and the 'Righteous'.[7] This man lived his life aware that 'we who teach will be judged more strictly' (Jas 3:1). His words and his life matched, and the church recognized him as its leader and teacher. This is the character that stands behind the text: a peacemaking authority who prayed constantly and sought justice.

IVP Academic, 2007), p. 401; or Douglas Moo, *The Letter of James* (Grand Rapids: Eerdmans, 2000), p. 25; Margaret M. Mitchell, 'The Letter of James as a Document of Paulinism?', in Robert L. Webb and John S. Kloppenborg (eds.), *Reading James with New Eyes: Methodological Reassessments of the Letter of James* (London: T. & T. Clark, 2007), pp. 75–98.

3. See Richard Bauckham, *James: Wisdom of James, Disciple of Jesus the Sage* (London: Routledge, 1999), pp. 16–25. Peter H. Davids, *The Epistle of James* (Grand Rapids: Eerdmans, 1982), p. 22, sees at least the source material as originating from this James. See Alicia Batton, *What Are They Saying About the Epistle of James?* (New York: Paulist, 2009), pp. 28–43.

4. See Karl-Wilhelm Niebuhr, 'A New Perspective on James? Neuere Forschungen zum Jakobusbrief', *TLZ* 129 (2004), p. 1030.

5. See Hegesippus, who describes James as 'he used to enter alone into the temple and be found kneeling and praying for forgiveness for the people, so that his knees grew hard like a camel's because of his constant worship of God, kneeling and asking forgiveness for the people' (Eusebius of Caesarea, *The Ecclesiastical History*, tr. Kirsopp Lake and J. E. L. Oulton, LCL [Cambridge, Mass.: Harvard University Press, 1975], 2.23.6 [p. 171]).

6. See Scot McKnight, *The Letter of James* (Grand Rapids: Eerdmans, 2011), pp. 17–18.

7. Again, Eusebius, *Ecclesiastical History* 2.23.4–7. See Richard Bauckham, 'James and the Jerusalem Church', in idem (ed.), *The Book of Acts in Its First Century Setting*, vol. 4: *The Book of Acts in Its Palestinian Setting* (Carlisle: Paternoster; Grand Rapids: Eerdmans, 1995), p. 449.

Textually, James fits within the developing blend of wisdom and prophetic traditions. Its genre is best described as paraenetic wisdom, with style and emphases similar to that of Proverbs (control of tongue, charity to the poor and a need for wisdom),[8] but it is also related to the prophetic tradition (several have noted a relationship to Deut. 10:12–21; but Isaiah, Jeremiah and Zechariah also have echoes in James, particularly on the subject of justice for the poor), and James even has a thread of apocalyptic (the emphasis on coming judgment as a motivation for proper behaviour now).[9] Moreover, Johnson has argued that James is a sermon on Leviticus 19:9–18,[10] and Morgan notes that 'there is not one section of the Sermon on the Mount that James does not reflect' and that the entirety of James mirrors the words of Jesus.[11] James even cites God's covenantal self-description from Exodus 33:19. By highlighting these canonical relationships the preacher is able to move James from its typical reception as anti-Pauline (and therefore potentially not Christian) and place it into the consistent witness of Scripture and the teaching of Jesus himself.

Structurally, the cyclical nature of the text, where ideas are reiterated and developed, allows for thematic or textual preaching. One option is to read James for its understated theology. As a wisdom text, the theology of James rests in the background, like the unseen framing of a house. But from 1:5, 17–18 and 21 we can develop a picture of God as the unchanging giver of good gifts, the greatest of which is his choice to give new birth to his people, in contrast to the natural birth-cycle of sin and death, a new birth by his word, which has the power to save the souls of those who receive it.[12] God is one who hears and responds to requests for help by generously giving the wisdom we need (1:5; 3:16–17), desires humility and repentance from his people (1:21; 4:6–10; 5:19–20), answers prayers offered in trust in his unchangingly good

8. Martin Dibelius, *James*, tr. Michael A. Williams (Philadelphia: Fortress, 1975), p. 21.

9. Patrick A. Tiller, 'The Rich and Poor in James: An Apocalyptic Ethic', in Benjamin G. Wright III and Lawrence M. Wills (eds.), *Conflicted Boundaries in Wisdom and Apocalypticism* (Atlanta: SBL, 2005), pp. 169–179.

10. Luke Timothy Johnson, 'Use of Leviticus 19 in the Letter of James', in *Brother of Jesus, Friend of God* (Grand Rapids: Eerdmans, 2004), pp. 123–135.

11. Christopher W. Morgan, *The Theology of James* (Phillipsburg: P. & R., 2010), p. 37; see pp. 31–37 for his outline. See Bauckham, *James*, for his unpacking of the relationship between James's teaching and that of Jesus.

12. Patrick J. Hartin, *James* (Collegeville: Liturgical Press, 2003), pp. 104–105.

nature, yet opposes those who arrogantly seek to usurp his power (1:5–8; 4:1–4, 11–12; 5:12–18).

The ethics in James flows from a changed reality: his audience is a people who have been given, by God's free choice, the word implanted in a new birth that has the power to save them, *if* they choose the path of obedience and humility before God. He is concerned because the audience members are acting as 'hearers only' who have not therefore received this word and, by disobedience, envy and pride are placing themselves in danger of the judgment of the God who has the power to save and destroy (4:12). In a word, this epistle seeks to encourage the hearers *to be what they are*, a newborn people shaped to the image and character of God himself.[13] The repeated language of 'knowing' and of 'self-deception' encourages the hearers to live in the reality of being a new covenant people, born of grace but called to obedience.

1 Peter

1 Peter throws a number of obstacles in the way of its interpreters, from questions of authorship and context to difficulties with submission passages, and with Christ preaching to the spirits in prison. This is a text, however, that can provide a great deal of encouragement to congregations, particularly in the West, struggling with how to live in an increasingly post-Christian and even occasionally hostile environment. Focusing on the overarching theme of the text – affirming one's identity in Christ and therefore remaining a faithful and good witness despite persecution[14] – can help one avoid getting lost in the difficulties.

This text also begins with a statement of authorship: 'Peter, an apostle of Jesus Christ' (1:1). There are a number of questions regarding authorship and context,[15] but this need not be a defining problem, as early church tradition and many modern scholars argue for Peter's authorship.[16] Here is a letter

---

13. For this argument in greater detail see Mariam J. Kamell, 'The Implications of Grace for the Ethics of James', *Bib* 92 (2011), pp. 274–287.

14. Cf. J. Ramsey Michaels, *1 Peter*, WBC (Waco: Word, 1988), pp. xxxv–xxxvi; Ralph P. Martin, '1 Peter', in *The Theology of the Letters of James, Peter, and Jude* (Cambridge: Cambridge University Press, 1994), pp. 87–90.

15. John H. Elliott, *A Home for the Homeless* (Philadelphia: Fortress, 1981), p. 270.

16. E.g. Karen H. Jobes, *1 Peter* (Grand Rapids: Baker Academic, 2005); Michaels,

purportedly from the impulsive yet profound disciple of Jesus, one of the closest followers who heard all of Jesus' teaching and became the first spokesperson for this new movement as the Spirit arrived at Pentecost. In 1 Peter a significant leader of the early church writes so that the scattered communities might understand how Christology supports believers to persevere in the face of persecution.

Contextually, some scholars argue that the hardships described were not empire-wide focused persecution of Christians under Domitian or Trajan, but were unfocused, local hostility by those who did not appreciate the changed lifestyles of these Christians.[17] As such, the opening call to holiness (1:13 – 2:10) combined with the consistent challenge to live rightly and not give cause for accusations to stick (cf. 2:11–12, 19–20; 3:4–6, 13–14; 4:3–4, 12–16, 19) together give a guiding thread through the entire epistle. The themes of holiness and conduct together depict a distinct people living according to the example of Christ (3:21–25), who has himself already witnessed to judgment (3:18 – 4:6)[18] and will return to judge everyone and restore his people (4:16–19; 5:10). Because of what Christ has already done, believers can have confidence that he will restore his people despite current hardships.

Canonically, it is worth mentioning the dependence 1 Peter has on Isaiah, as the apostle consistently quotes or alludes to the prophetic text. This is the earliest example of Isaiah 53 being applied to Jesus[19] – this from the man who originally tried to rebuke Jesus in Mark's Gospel for speaking of his death! 1 Peter also develops themes from Jesus' teaching, particularly the beatitude in Matthew 5:10–12 (par. Luke 6:22–23).[20] Likewise, there are echoes of a common teaching source with Paul (e.g. 1 Pet. 4:10 and Rom. 12:4–8, the household codes) and with James (e.g. common themes of endurance based on prior grace and future hope, citations of Prov. 3:34 and 10:12). 1 Peter brings these threads together to teach that as Christ suffered to redeem his people, believers may also suffer, but by holy conduct must follow in the pattern of Christ and work for the good of their society.

---

1 Peter, p. xxxiv, who notes that 'the external attestation for 1 Peter is as strong, or stronger, than that for any NT book'.

17. Reinhard Feldmeier, *The First Letter of Peter: A Commentary on the Greek Text*, tr. Peter. H. Davids (Waco: Baylor University Press, 2008), pp. 2–13.

18. Peter H. Davids, *The First Epistle of Peter* (Grand Rapids: Eerdmans, 1990), pp. 138–141.

19. Jobes, *1 Peter*, p. 192.

20. See Davids, *First Epistle of Peter*, pp. 26–27; Michaels, *1 Peter*, p. xli.

Much like James, 1 Peter begins with an exposition on endurance in the context of future hope: endurance is based on recognizing the new reality into which one has been born (1:3–9). With Grudem, it is worth considering 4:19 as a good summary verse of the epistle's intention: the suffering with which the epistle concerns itself is that which is according to God's will and for doing good.[21] The author has no interest in suffering earned through poor behaviour! But when suffering for right living, one should reaffirm faith in God's goodness and control and *continue* to do the right thing, despite the opposition. And this right living has two purposes: the holy character of the church as strangers and aliens who care for each other in a crumbling society,[22] but also the power of right living and ordered relationships for evangelistic witness.[23] Important to all of this, of course, is the necessity of understanding the massive claim in 2:9–10 of being a chosen people, recent recipients of God's mercy. This restatement of identity is crucial, both then and now: understanding who believers are *in Christ* as a *new* people should give them the encouragement they need to persevere in righteousness despite hardships.

2 Peter

Following canonical order here presents some difficulties, as it is generally agreed that 2 Peter most likely depends on Jude; thus Jude and 2 Peter, not 1 and 2 Peter, are often combined in discussions.[24] However, although the relationship between Jude and 2 Peter should be acknowledged, there is also much unique about the latter that should be brought to the church.

The authorship of 2 Peter is in deep question, because the grammar and

---

21. Wayne Grudem, *The First Epistle of Peter* (Leicester: Inter-Varsity Press, 1988), p. 184.

22. See Elliott, *Home for the Homeless*, particularly chs. 1 and 2.

23. As in William J. Webb, *Slaves, Women and Homosexuals* (Downers Grove: InterVarsity Press, 2001), p. 107, where he notes that in 1 Peter 'a wife's submission is explicitly linked to purpose statements about evangelism and Christian mission'.

24. Nineteen of Jude's verses are found in some fashion in 2 Peter but the material has not been consistently imported, making it possible that they are drawing on common preaching imagery of the time; see Michael Green, *The Second Epistle General of Peter and the General Epistle of Jude* (Leicester: Inter-Varsity Press, 1987), pp. 61–63.

style of the epistle is significantly different from that of 1 Peter.[25] The writer is again presented as the apostle Peter, referencing the transfiguration itself (1:17–18) and thereby affirming himself as a witness to that moment of divine glory. If 1 Peter was written with the help of an amanuensis (possibly Silvanus, 1 Pet. 5:12), perhaps 2 Peter was written by Peter on his own, or with another scribe. Scholars also often point to 2 Peter 1:15 as indicating a possible use of the testamentary genre, wherein 'an erstwhile colleague of Peter's, who writes Peter's testament after his death, [writes] in his own way but [is] confident that he is being faithful to Peter's essential message'.[26] 2 Peter is presented as the apostle Peter's final testimony as he faces the reality of his death.

In this epistle Peter seeks to re-establish his hearers in the truth in the face of false teachers who deny the second coming of Christ.[27] His concern centres on their eschatology because it affects how one lives.[28] 2 Peter 3:2–4 acts as a guide to the three approaches the author uses to combat the false teaching: 3:2 echoes the call to remember the teaching of the prophets (1:12–21); 3:3 warns of the nature of the false teachers and their mockery (2:1–22); and 3:4 gives the content of the scoffing, which is then answered by a reminder that God's timing is not like ours (3:5–14). And indeed, 3:8–10 provides a beautifully preachable answer to the problem of evil, that despite how we perceive God's slowness, his patience stems from 'not wanting anyone to perish, but everyone to come to repentance' (3:9); for when he comes, the time for repentance will be past. This realization encourages the hearers to trust God's faithfulness to his promises. It also serves as a reminder that God is the sole judge and the hearer's job is to call others to repent![29]

2 Peter 1:4 could read as endorsing a Gnostic escapist paradigm, but verses 5–8 warn that participation in the divine nature means *acting according to his character now*.[30] 2 Peter 1 encourages its hearers to grow in good qualities, so that they may not be 'ineffective and unproductive in [their] knowledge' of

---

25. See the arguments in Peter H. Davids, *The Letters of 2 Peter and Jude* (Grand Rapids: Eerdmans, 2006), pp. 123–130.

26. Richard Bauckham, *Jude, 2 Peter* (Nashville: Thomas Nelson, 1983), p. 147.

27. Ralph P. Martin, '2 Peter', in *The Theology of the Letters of James, Peter, and Jude* (Cambridge: Cambridge University Press, 1994), p. 134.

28. Bauckham, *Jude, 2 Peter*, p. 334.

29. See Davids, *Letters*, p. 274–287, on this section. He comments, Christians 'do not rejoice in the death of any evil person, but rather hope against hope for their repentance' (p. 282).

30. Michael Green, *Second Epistle General*, pp. 73–75, 80–81.

Christ (1:8). Unproductive persons are not heavenly minded, but are instead described with the covenantal failure language of blindness and as 'forgetting that they have been cleansed from their past sins' (1:9). The audience is called instead to 'confirm [their] calling and election', for it is in the doing of these things that they reach the kingdom (1:10–11). The epistle returns to this notion in the conclusion, warning the audience to 'be on [their] guard' that they not be led astray and 'fall from [their] secure position' (3:17), a warning we do well to heed in our postmodern age of relativism. There is a point where truth is critical, and one can, like the Israelites of old, repudiate one's calling.[31]

Because of this danger, Peter in his final letter seeks to correct their eschatology so that they live properly now. Ultimately, audiences then and now are called to 'grow in the grace and knowledge of our Lord and Saviour Jesus Christ' (3:18). The epistle ends as it began, with the encouragement to grow while giving glory to Christ, the proper focus for all we do.

1 John

This letter begins a grouping of three epistles whose relationship is uncertain. This first epistle is anonymous, while the second and third originate from 'the Elder' and are addressed to different audiences. It is probable that the same author penned all three epistles,[32] the same author as the Gospel of John.[33] The question remains whether 'John the Elder' is a distinct person from John the apostle (qua Papias),[34] for the majority of early church witnesses support apostolic origin for all three epistles.[35] This would mean that the author of at least 1 John was one of Jesus' closest companions.

---

31. Gene Green, *Jude and 2 Peter* (Grand Rapids: Baker, 2008), pp. 284–285.

32. See Andrew Lincoln, *The Gospel According to St John* (London: Hendrickson, 2005), p. 55.

33. Craig S. Keener, *The Gospel of John: A Commentary* (Peabody: Hendrickson, 2003), pp. 124–125. Painter, 'Johannine Epistles', p. 265, suggests that the evidence of 'literary dependence . . . implies the use of the Gospel by the author of 1 John'.

34. See Raymond E. Brown, *The Epistles of John* (Garden City: Doubleday, 1982), pp. 14–30, who concludes that the Gospel and 1 John were by the same author, the latter significantly later, but 2 and 3 John by a separate author (p. 30).

35. E.g. Irenaeus, Tertullian, Clement of Alexandria and Origen all thought 1 John was from John the apostle despite its anonymous status, and no distinction was made between the 'apostle' and 'Elder' for authorship of 2 and 3 John until Eusebius'

Structurally, 1 John may be thought of as a sermon rather than a letter, with interweaving of themes that makes schematization difficult.[36] Kruse notes, 'As a piece of epideictic rhetoric, 1 John, not surprisingly, lacks a clear structure. Instead it revisits the same themes over and over, each time amplifying them further.'[37] While possibly an oversimplification, Painter's structure, based around three presentations of two tests of faith, an ethical and a Christological, may provide the best preaching outline (1:6 – 2:27; 2:28 – 4:6; 4:7 – 5:12).[38] Along with this, one can see the epistle unfolding and expanding three key themes wherein each test entails and develops the other two (cf. 3:23–24): keep the commandments (1:5 – 2:6; 2:28 – 3:10; 5:16–21); love one another (2:7–17; 3:11–24; 4:7–21); and believe in Jesus as the God-Man (2:18–27; 4:1–6; 5:1–15).

Whether one prefers a double helix or a triple spiral, the text reiterates the same themes – which fits with its origin as a sermon, because the repetitive development would help the hearers retain the main concerns. Instead of fighting this, the preacher is well advised to work with the text, preaching thematically or textually, in the latter case showing how the themes develop, expand and are inseparable. This latter approach requires careful planning to ensure the sermons themselves do not become redundant.

Contextually, the main concern of the epistle appears to be false teachers who deny Jesus' messiahship, sonship and incarnation (2:22; 4:3; 5:1, 5), and whose lives therefore do not reflect Christ (3:23–24; 4:7–8).[39] John seeks to correct this misguided Christology, but does so by directing the congregation into fellowship with God and one another: love for one's neighbour is the crucial test that proves one's love for God.[40] God is 'light' (1:5) and so those who walk in relationship with him will have confidence and be able to

quote of Papias. Andreas J. Köstenberger, *A Theology of John's Gospel and Letters* (Grand Rapids: Zondervan, 2009), pp. 86–89, concludes the author of the Gospel and the letters is 'John the son of Zebedee'. See also Colin G. Kruse, *The Letters of John* (Grand Rapids: Eerdmans, 2000), p. 11.

36. H. Windisch, *Der Katholischen Briefe* (Tübingen: Mohr, 1951), p. 136, viewed this epistle as a religious tractate meant for the whole of Christendom.

37. Kruse, *Letters of John*, p. 31.

38. John Painter, *I, II, and III John* (Collegeville: Liturgical Press, 2002), p. 118.

39. Stephen S. Smalley, *1, 2, 3 John* (Nashville: Thomas Nelson, 2007), pp. xxii–xxvi; Brown, *Epistles of John*, pp. 49–55.

40. John R. W. Stott, *The Letters of John* (Leicester: Inter-Varsity Press, 1988), pp. 53, 162–164.

discern falsehood (4:4–6; 5:1–5). But even more crucial, God is 'love' (3:11–24), ultimately demonstrated by Christ's incarnation and death. Given this model, fellowship with and love for God must be manifested in love for one another (4:7–12), and verbal confession of truth cannot be separated from the outward fruit of practical love for each other (3:11–24).

False teachers had begun to trouble this community, by threatening the author's authority, leading people towards a proto-Gnosticism that could not handle Christ's incarnation and did not promote love in the community.[41] To challenge this, the epistle drives the hearer towards a corrected theology of Christ's true, physical incarnation (1:1), while fighting against a workless theology that does not recognize the requirement to love. Ultimately, we are warned in 1 John that the one who does not love his neighbour does not love God (4:19).

2 John

Following the lengthy defence of the necessity of loving one's neighbour in 1 John, 2 John continues in similar vein.[42] The primary issue at stake here is the false teachers who have now 'gone out into the world' (v. 7), promoting a proto-Gnostic teaching that again denigrates Christ's humanity. This 'lady chosen by God' and 'her children', possibly a specific house church (see v. 13's parallel greeting) from whom the false teachers have seceded in order to begin their own work, are urged to be cautious in their dealings with the false teachers and not to offer them hospitality or welcome them (vv. 10–11). The epistle helps to refine further the notion of 'loving one's neighbour': love does *not* mean accepting everyone's opinions, as our culture likes to promote. Loving our neighbour and holding to the truth are not mutually exclusive, but loving God entails at times excluding from fellowship those who lead others astray.

The letter follows traditional epistolary form, beginning with a greeting

---

41. Brown, *Epistles of John*, p. 175, calls the opening lines 'an urgent manifesto called forth by struggle', wherein the author makes a 'polemically exclusive claim'.

42. Internal evidence points to this being from the same author as 1 John. See Kruse (*Letters of John*, p. 37), who observes close textual similarities (cf. 2 John 7; 1 John 2:18, 22), common emphasis on the love command (vv. 4–6; cf. 1 John 3:11, 23; 4:7, 21; 5:1–4a) and walking in truth (v. 4; cf. 1 John 1:3–4). Smalley (*1, 2, 3 John*, p. 323) argues that, while the subject matter may be closer to 3 John, the theological ideas 'in 2 John resemble those of 1 John very closely'.

that rejoices over the recipients' continued obedience. The blessing in verse 3 pairs the promise of Christ's presence with his 'truth and love'. The Elder then rejoices that they are 'walking in the truth' (v. 4), encourages them to 'love one another' (v. 5) and then defines that love as walking 'in obedience to his commands', commands summarized by the exhortation that they 'walk in love' (v. 6). Thus for this author, truth, love and obedience are all inseparably interconnected.[43] The second half of the epistle stands in contrast to these positive commands, as it excludes from fellowship those who would deceive the faithful (vv. 7–11). The warnings are so concerted because the Elder fears that the faithful could '"lose what [they] have worked for", losing God by running ahead of him and teaching incorrectly (vv. 8–9). Being deceived by false thinking has serious consequences!'[44] Ultimately, sharing communion with those who think and teach in a manner contradictory to truth (which is in Christ, v. 3) is sharing in wickedness (v. 11).

2 John is a prime example of the need to major on the majors: there are theological threads that cannot be compromised, here focused on Christ's physical existence (v. 7). While many churches would not recognize Gnosticism as a label for their thinking, the current preoccupation with 'getting to heaven' and the lack of concern for how we live *here* on earth, as though what we do with our bodies and our money is not of concern, reveals that strains of this dualism persist to this day. Likewise, obedience to Christ is to walk in love with one another, so practising ecumenism is a crucial movement in which Christians should engage. Ecumenism has limits, however, as 2 John makes very clear. 'Love' cannot mean 'unconditional acceptance' of those who contradict biblical teaching. Love and truth must always be held together.

3 John

Finally, in 3 John hospitality is again at issue, but now the letter's recipients are failing to welcome those who *are* faithful. This epistle provides an interesting balance to 2 John, for the Elder condemns Diotrephes for taking it upon himself to discern who should receive a welcome in the church, and the Elder calls the congregation to discern for themselves and not follow someone who is judgmental. In contrast, the Elder encourages Gaius for his spirit of welcome for 'the brothers', who appear to be faithful itinerant ministers.

---

43. See Stott, *Letters of John*, p. 210.
44. Ibid., p. 217.

There appears to be a power struggle between the Elder and Diotrephes (v. 10), and so the author encourages Gaius both to look at the actions of people in the congregation to discern who is from God, and to listen to the witness of the church at large.[45]

The epistle divides into three sections, each introduced by 'dear friend', paralleling the introduction and witnessing to the close friendship between the Elder and Gaius (vv. 1, 2, 5, 11).[46] In the first section the author rejoices to hear of Gaius' faithfulness. Verses 3 and 12 parallel each other in the importance of witnesses testifying well of another. In verses 3–4 the author emphasizes 'faithfulness to the truth' and 'walking in the truth' (twice), reminding the hearers of the importance of remaining in the truth despite opposition. The second section (vv. 5–8) encourages Gaius to continue offering hospitality to missionaries who have left everything 'for the sake of the Name' (v. 7). Verses 9–10 function as a hinge, for Diotrephes is condemned for his failure to offer correct hospitality and for his improper control of others in the church. This failure leads to the caution in verses 11–12 regarding imitation. In verse 10 Diotrephes provides the model of what *not* to imitate ('evil', v. 11). By contrast, the parallel works of hospitality and of leaving everything to preach the truth can be seen as the 'good' in this context (vv. 7–8).

The language of imitation has profound precedents,[47] from Deuteronomy 18:9 and the caution to Israel not to 'imitate the detestable ways of the nations' as they enter the land – which they fell into doing repeatedly. The consistent call to 'be holy, because [God is] holy' (Lev. 11:45; 19:2; 20:7, 26; cf. Matt. 5:48; Luke 6:36; 1 Pet. 1:15–16) echoes across all of Scripture, making the *imitatio dei* (imitation of God) the base for covenantal behaviour. When the Christian movement begins, Paul urges the Corinthians to imitate his humility and chosen humiliation for the sake of the gospel (1 Cor. 4:16), while the author of Hebrews – following commands similar to John's to 'keep on loving one another' and to 'show hospitality to strangers' (13:1, 2) – urges the hearers to '[r]emember your leaders. . . . Consider the outcome of their way of life and imitate their faith' (13:7).[48] Finding the proper models for imitation is a crucial

---

45. See Brown, *Epistles of John*, pp. 730–732, for the relationship between Gaius and Diotrephes. He adds that 'the real problem [is] not simply the inhospitality of Diotrephes but his rejection of the Presbyter', p. 730.

46. Stott, *Letters of John*, p. 222.

47. Brown (*Epistles of John*, p. 720) suggests 11a was a 'general non-Johannine maxim'.

48. This is one of only three other uses in the NT of the verb *mimeomai*, the other two being in 2 Thess. 3:7, 9. The noun is more common. See Smalley, *1, 2, 3 John*, p. 345.

step in faithfulness: pride, gossip, slander and inhospitality model evil. In contrast, those of whom only good is spoken reveal what one *should* imitate: hospitality, love and sacrifice for the Name. 3 John calls the hearers to be a discerning but lovingly hospitable people.

Jude

This last epistle may be the least-preached text of the New Testament. It is a challenge for anyone to preach, not only because the text is difficult with its quotation of Enoch and description of Michael's battling the devil, but also because it drives the audience to test teachers through a critique of their lifestyle. These false teachers have slipped in amongst the congregations, but they have exchanged grace for licence and in doing so deny Christ (v. 4). And so Jude, the servant of Christ (using the same title 'servant' as does James), brother of James and of Christ himself,[49] seeks to challenge – and humiliate – these impostors and encourage the congregation to test their leaders and ensure they hold fast to the truth.[50]

One of the main problems with preaching this epistle is its use of pseud-epigrapha. The legend of Michael and Satan's fighting over Moses' body (v. 9) probably comes from the *Assumption of Moses*, while in verses 14–15 Jude cites *1 Enoch* 1.9. Rather than trying to justify Jude's use of these texts, however, it is more important to see the *purpose* for which he uses them. In the former, Jude notes that not even an archangel would dare speak with the haughty abuse these leaders use. In the latter, Jude uses the prophet Enoch to warn that everyone will be judged for their ungodly acts and words, which he cautions that these false teachers are exhibiting. In each section the illustration serves to highlight *just how bad* the words and deeds of these false teachers are, followers of Cain, Balaam and Korah. Jude serves as a prime example of how illustrations can serve the preacher's point and the value of a relevant example![51] Moreover, the images in verses 12–13 show the disparity between truth and appearance: shepherds who feed only themselves, clouds that fail to rain, felled trees without fruit in autumn, foaming waves and wandering

---

49. See Richard Bauckham, *Jude and the Brothers of Jesus* (Edinburgh: T. & T. Clark International, 1990), pp. 45–133, for a comprehensive picture of the role of the relatives of Jesus in the early church.

50. Bauckham, *Jude, 2 Peter*, p. 41.

51. Michael Green, *Second Epistle General*, p. 179.

stars.[52] These people provide no stability to their congregation, but instead are simply form without substance. And so the bulk of the epistle, via *ad hominem* rhetoric, encourages the congregation to test their leaders, watch the fruit of their lives, test the quality of their speech and remove these false leaders from their midst. There is, and there must be, a limit to tolerance within the congregation for a life described as 'ungodly' (vv. 15, 18), even while seeking the restoration of that person.[53]

But there is another thread well worth exploring: the notion of 'keeping'.[54] In verse 1 the congregation are 'kept' (*tereō*) by Jesus Christ, whereas in verse 21 they are encouraged to 'keep' (*tereō*) themselves in God's love – in contrast to the angels in verse 6 who did not keep (*tereō*) themselves as they ought to and the outer darkness in verse 13 'reserved' (*tereō*) for those wandering leaders – but ultimately they are kept (*phylassō*), guarded by Christ, the only one 'able to keep you from stumbling and to present you before his glorious presence without fault and with great joy' (v. 24). The ones who failed to keep themselves as they ought to fell under judgment and will go to the place kept for them. But those who are *kept* by Christ, and *keep* themselves in Christ, *will be kept* by Christ until the very end, when they are presented as righteous.[55] And this triumphant benediction again returns the focus back to Christ, for Jude dedicates his hearers *to Christ*, the only one with the power to guard and keep them, even as they seek to keep themselves pure in a fully trinitarian faith (vv. 20–21). This should provide profound encouragement to those who want to follow Jesus fully!

---

52. Bauckham, *Jude, 2 Peter*, p. 7, notes that in vv. 12–13 when Jude cites the OT, he depends on the Hebrew text, although elsewhere he shows himself familiar with traditional Greek renderings.

53. Davids, *Letters*, p. 32; Bauckham, *Jude, 2 Peter*, pp. 117–118.

54. Cf. Scott J. Hafemann, 'Salvation in Jude 5 and the Argument of 2 Peter 1:3–1', in Karl-Wilhelm Niebuhr and Robert W. Wall (eds.), *The Catholic Epistles and the Tradition* (Waco: Baylor University Press, 2009), p. 339, for a covenantal reading of salvation in both Jude and 1 Peter.

55. Bauckham, *Jude, 2 Peter*, p. 124, describes the goal that they 'be found fit to be a sacrificial offering to God'.

Conclusion

Preaching these texts requires a great deal of humility on the part of the preacher, particularly since several of them directly challenge their respective audiences to evaluate their teachers and ensure the flock are following Christlike leaders. They all hold preachers or teachers to the accountability of a higher standard, requiring that they live the life described. But these are also texts that can be infinitely practical, which help to lead us into a life characterized by holiness, endurance and mercy, guided by the character of God and the example of Christ. Every one of these epistles focuses on the life and character of the recipients as the true witnesses to Christ's work and their status as a redeemed people. Lifestyle cannot be separated from theology, and all of these epistles also ground the ability to live correctly on the prior work of God in Christ. In this day both the world and the church direly need to hear the call to faithfulness and holy love from these epistles.

© Mariam J. Kamell, 2013

11. PREACHING FROM THE BOOK OF REVELATION

Ian Paul

Introduction: the problems and promise of preaching Revelation

The book of Revelation, more than any other in the New Testament, functions for many as a *mysterium tremendum et fascinans* (mystery that causes both trembling and fascination) – it draws people, mothlike, to the intense flame of its passion, yet repels others by its apparently grotesque imagery. But for both groups, rather than offering revelation, it more usually remains veiled, hidden behind a series of closed doors whose keys only a few possess. Some use these confidently, but most feel disempowered, since they feel they have no way of knowing how to evaluate different ways of reading the text, and are either locked in to one approach, or, lacking alternatives, give up on Revelation's having any value. I was confronted very directly by this range of experiences in 2011, as I preached through Revelation on seven consecutive Sundays. One person commented that, having read this as a teenager, it had remained a closed book for the previous thirty years until then. As I have preached and taught on this book in a wide variety of contexts, I have come across similar responses – either that there is only one correct way of reading it (usually what is known as a 'futurist' interpretation)[1]

---

1. This is one of four 'classical' ways of reading, the other three being 'preterist' (it

or that this book is more trouble than it is worth and is best left well alone!

This evading of the text is both expressed in and reinforced by the provision in the Revised Common Lectionary, used by a number of denominations as their pattern for reading the Scriptures in public worship. The RCL covers very little of Revelation; the Sunday provision is mostly in Year C, and covers the 'positive' passages of the opening vision of Christ in chapter 1, worship in heaven from chapter 5, the redeemed in chapter 7, and then some of the positive sections of the New Jerusalem in chapters 21 and 22. In addition the account of Michael in chapter 12 is read at Michaelmas (the feast of St Michael and All Angels) on 29 September each year. The thinness of this provision is clear when we note that Revelation, whilst around 13% shorter than Mark's Gospel, is the longest book in the New Testament after the Gospels and Acts.[2] (It is interesting to reflect on what might have happened to the text of Revelation in the church had *all* the books of the whole New Testament been arranged in order of length, as Paul's letters to churches are, with Revelation at the heart of the canon.) But perhaps of even more concern is the nature of the passages that have been selected. As Koester notes, Revelation alternates between scenes that are provocative and disturbing and those that are reassuring and encouraging. The lectionary omits the former and includes only the latter, which has the effect of flattening the text out and rendering these visions almost bland. 'The result is a rather pleasant selection of texts that minimizes the likelihood that anyone will be embarrassed or confused by Revelation's more bizarre or disturbing images.'[3]

Our failure to engage with Revelation has serious consequences both for

---

relates only to its first-century world), 'church historical' (it predicts the history of the church through the ages) and 'symbolic' (it expresses timeless truths and does not have any historical referents). For detail and evaluation of these see my *How to Read the Book of Revelation* (Cambridge: Grove, 2003), p. 30, or the introduction to any more 'traditional' commentary such as Craig Keener's: *Revelation*, NIVAC (Grand Rapids: Zondervan, 2000), p. 27. I am increasingly of the view that such categories are of little value in understanding Revelation itself.

2. The number of words of Greek text (Nestle-Aland, 26th ed.) in each book is as follows: Mark 11,304; Revelation 9,825; Romans 7,111; 1 Corinthians 6,829; Hebrews 4,953. Figures from Felix Just <http://catholic-resources.org/Bible/NT_Canon.htm>, accessed 27 June 2012.

3. Craig R. Koester, *Revelation and the End of All Things* (Grand Rapids: Eerdmans, 2007), p. 32.

individuals and the church as a whole. Whilst there has been a growing academic interest in the way other parts of the New Testament challenge patterns of imperial power and devotion, Revelation is a text that confronts cultural and ideological issues in society with a unique directness and clarity. As Western society emerges into an increasingly post-Christendom and post-modern context, and we still struggle to understand the cultural changes that have led to a haemorrhaging of church membership, this is a text that must engage and form us.

But there is another promise held out by this most intriguing of books. Because Revelation presents us with so many challenges in reading and inter-pretation, it forces us to reassess what exactly we are doing in interpreting Scripture more generally. If we need to consider Revelation's genre, don't we need to consider the genre of other texts? If we need to consider Revelation's historical context, don't we also need to do this for other parts of Scripture? We can get away with avoiding this in less 'problematic' parts of the New Testament, but Revelation will not let us off so lightly. In a similar way, because it is so challenging to preach on, engaging with Revelation presses us to ask what we are doing with *any* New Testament text when we preach.

Closing the gap between readers and Revelation

We observed in the introduction to this volume that one way of understand-ing the task of preaching is to close the gap between the contemporary listen-ers and the text itself, whether that gap was one of information, motivation, understanding or interest. At times these different aspects of the 'gap' are intertwined, and this is especially the case with Revelation – so that simple ignorance robs the reader of understanding, and as the text becomes more 'opaque', interest is lost. In my experience, the issues here can seem quite technical, but in fact many of them can be easily addressed, particularly if they are located within a framework of what we might call a common-sense approach to reading.

I will take each of these in turn, and give specific examples from the text of Revelation to illustrate them.

The importance of genre

A few years ago I had a memorable conversation with the head of the primary school that my children were attending. They had been commenting on how one of the classes in school had lost marks because they did not sufficiently distinguish between 'recount' genre and 'narrative' genre in their work! When

I asked the head, he explained that it was all about 'metacognition'; they were taking part in an educational experiment in partnership with a local university, where they raised awareness of what the children were doing when they were reading and writing different genres of literature. The main point was this: recognizing different genres of writing was something the children could do quite naturally. The school's aim was to make them aware of what they were already doing – and very effective it was too.

Most people in our churches need to engage in 'metacognition'. They are all experts in genre recognition; they do it every day when they open the post, and immediately see whether the letter before them is a demand from the bank manager, or a letter from a friend, before they have read a single word. And yet most are unaware of this – or unaware of its importance when they open their Bibles. Yet, in the view of Gordon Fee, this is one of the two key skills in Bible reading.[4]

An easy way into this question is to use the following, fictional, example of text:

The stars will fall from heaven,
 the sun will cease its shining;
the moon will be turned to blood,
 and fire and hail will fall from heaven.

The rest of the country will have sunny intervals
 with scattered showers.

Readers of this always find it amusing – but the amusement arises from nothing other than a perceived change of genre. This encourages the readers to understand that they are already experts at genre recognition – they just never realized it.

This relatively straightforward issue is enormously significant for the reading and preaching of Revelation, for three reasons, as follows.

1. Generally speaking, we learn to recognize different genres of writing by experience, rather than being taught. No one ever told me what a bank manager-type letter looked like; I learned by seeing examples. The first readers

---

4. See the preface in Gordon D. Fee and Douglas K. Stuart, *How to Read the Bible for All Its Worth*, 3rd ed. (Grand Rapids: Zondervan, 2003). The other key skill they note is the need to have an overview, to locate each passage in its place in the canon.

of Revelation would have been familiar with this kind of writing; no one expresses surprise when Jesus turns to this kind of speech in Mark 13, for instance. Yet for modern readers this genre is very strange, and we are puzzled by it in the first instance simply through lack of familiarity.

2. Revelation changes its microgenre from one place to another, and this is particularly marked in chapter 1, where we have apocalyptic (vv. 1 and 7), blessing (v. 3), doxology (v. 5), prophecy (v. 8) as well as clear markers of the epistolary genre (vv. 4 and 9). It is important to highlight such changes in preaching on this chapter.

3. Amongst the variety of genres within the text, Revelation claims three major genres for its identity.[5] As a *letter*, it is 'occasional' in the same way that, for example, Paul's letters are, so we need to preach it intelligently from its historical context. As an *apocalypse*, a revelation, it is giving us a fresh understanding of the world we would not otherwise know – a perspective that will both comfort those under pressure, but also challenge those who are comfortable. Our preaching should do the same. And as *prophecy* it stands in the tradition of the Old Testament in pronouncing God's perspective on church and society. But like the Old Testament tradition, it is concerned with the future not as some kind of heavenly horoscope, but in so far as the future will reveal the reality of the present.

The significance of historical context

Since Revelation is, in part, styled as a letter, this immediately implies that we should take seriously its historical context. This is immediately confirmed by the form of chapters 2 and 3, which contain messages (not letters, as they are often called – they take the form of royal pronouncements) to the *ekklēsiai* in seven specific locations.[6] As any standard commentary will point out, these locations were on main routes for trade and communication, and the mes-

---

5. It is worth noting that there continues to be considerable debate about the genre of Revelation, in particular the extent to which it really shares its identity with other 'apocalypses' (none of which actually uses the word of itself). For the argument that Revelation is in fact a form of 'testimony' see Sean Ryan's chapter in the forthcoming Catrin Williams and Chris Rowland (eds.), *John's Gospel and Intimations of Apocalyptic* (London: Continuum).

6. I prefer to avoid the word 'churches' for these communities, because this can suggest an anachronistic sense of developed institutional identity. The primary meaning of *ekklēsia* in the first century was the gathering of citizens of a *polis* (city) for the purpose of discussion and decision-making.

sages are addressed to them in the order you would visit while travelling in a clockwise direction around the roads linking them together.[7]

It was the work of Colin Hemer in the 1960s that promoted the idea of reading the messages to the seven cities in their historical context, though in fact he was building on the much earlier work of William Ramsay. As a result, the majority of popular devotional books on Revelation are on this section of the book – and yet the significance of the historical realities is still not widely known.

The best example of the difference context makes here is in the message to Laodicea. In Revelation 3:15–16 we read the warning 'I know your deeds, that you are neither cold nor hot. I wish you were either one or the other! So, because you are lukewarm – neither hot nor cold – I am about to spit you out of my mouth.' The contrast between 'hot' and 'cold' is most commonly understood as a contrast between those who are 'on fire', who are passionate and enthusiastic about their faith, and those who are 'cold' and indifferent, so being 'hot' is a good thing, but being 'cold' is not. But this cannot be a coherent reading of the text, since the risen Christ would prefer the hearers to be 'cold' rather than 'lukewarm', and this would imply that no faith is better than struggling faith. In fact, the context here is the water supply to Laodicea; you can still see the pipes and sections of aqueduct that brought the hot spring water down the hill to the city, by which time it was lukewarm and full of calcium deposits – enough to make you want to throw up if you drank it.[8] Laodicea contrasted with Hierapolis (modern Pammukale) across the valley with its hot, therapeutic water, and Colossae further up the valley with its cold, refreshing springs. It was not the Laodicean's *faith* that was under scrutiny; it was their *works* (or 'deeds') – the effect their lives were having on those around them. Being either 'hot' or 'cold' was good, since each was good for something (healing or refreshing). But being 'lukewarm' meant being good for nothing.

Though Hemer at times overstated his case, any reasonable commentary will highlight the issues of historical context that throw light on these

---

7. The sites are well worth visiting; though Thyatira and Philadelphia have small sites in town centres, the others have extensive ruins to explore. Ephesus is the best known and most extensive, but Sardis and Laodicea have both undergone significant excavation and restoration in recent years, and Pergamon is also impressive. Smyrna is now the thriving port of Izmir.

8. The article highlighting this is M. J. S. Rudwick and E. M. B. Green, 'The Laodicean Lukewarmness', *ExpTim* 69 (Mar. 1958), pp. 176–178; this has been followed up by Stanley Porter, 'Why the Laodiceans Received Lukewarm Water', *TynB* 38 (1987), pp. 143–149, available online at www.tyndale.ac.uk.

chapters. However, as with all use of historical information in preaching, it is vital not to pull the expert 'rabbit out of the hat', but to use the information to facilitate engagement with the text.

The influence of allusion to the Old Testament

All commentators agree that Revelation is saturated with allusion to the Old Testament, despite never formally quoting it. What is debated is whether the Old Testament supplies Revelation with its 'language arsenal' (Elisabeth Schüssler Fiorenza) or whether it is careful and deliberate use (Richard Bauckham).[9] If it is deliberate, the question then is whether Revelation carries Old Testament meanings unchanged into the new context (Greg Beale), or whether the writer freely reinterprets Old Testament texts for his own purposes (Steve Moyise).[10] What is clear is that John sees the world very much in terms set out by the Old Testament, and in fact his use of Old Testament texts is not dissimilar to the way they are used in other parts of the New Testament – which in turn is not dissimilar to the way biblical texts are often used in contemporary preaching.

There is some debate on how we might actually detect echoes of and allusions to the Old Testament, but by my reckoning (I spent a week counting them) the 404 verses of Revelation contain 676 allusions to the Old Testament. So the first hearers of this text, those who knew their Old Testament, would have heard constant echoes of it – in much the same way we might experience echoes of the Bible if we attended a prayer meeting where the habit was to pray using phrases from the Authorized Version. Again, this also explains why many ordinary readers find Revelation puzzling, since these allusions are lost to a generation much less familiar with the text of the Old Testament.[11] Effective preaching on Revelation will need to make

---

9. E. Schüssler Fiorenza, *The Book of Revelation: Justice and Judgement* (Philadelphia: Fortress, 1985), p. 135. Bauckham's position is argued and assumed all the way through his volume *The Climax of Prophecy* (Edinburgh: T. & T. Clark, 1993).

10. G. K. Beale, 'Questions of Authorial Intent, Epistemology, and Presuppositions and Their Bearing on the Study of the Old Testament in the New: A Rejoinder to Steve Moyise', *IBS* 21 (1999), pp. 152–180; Steve Moyise, 'Intertextuality and the Study of the Old Testament in the New Testament', in Steve Moyise (ed.), *The Old Testament in the New Testament: Essays in Honour of J. L. North*, JSNTSup 189 (Sheffield: Sheffield Academic Press, 2000), pp. 151–180.

11. It is striking how, even in churches that self-identify as evangelical, the OT is very much less read and less frequently preached on than the NT.

such background and allusions visible if it is to enable engagement with the text.

One of the surprising things to note about Revelation's use of the Old Testament is the list of books it draws from most often and the frequency with which it alludes to them. In my count, the pattern is as follows:

Isaiah	128
Psalms	99
Ezekiel	92
Daniel	82
Exodus	53

This suggests that key themes in Revelation are judgment and hope of return from exile (Isaiah and Ezekiel), true worship of the true God (Psalms), living faithfully under the power of hostile empire (Daniel) and journeying through wilderness in anticipation of a future Promised Land (Exodus, a theme also expressed strongly in Revelation's use of numerology). These are not always seen as central in Revelation, but faithful preaching of this text will locate individual episodes within these wider themes.

This will need to happen alongside noticing the particular uses of the Old Testament in the passage in question. In chapter 4 around half the images and ideas in the vision of heavenly worship come from the Old Testament, including elements of the Sinai theophany and Isaiah's and Ezekiel's visions of God as the Holy One of Israel. Chapter 7 draws from a constellation of Old Testament themes, including the censuses of Israel in Numbers 1 and 2 Samuel 24, the distinction of Israel as a special people in Exodus 19:5 and the description of the nations in Genesis 10:31. Chapter 12 integrates Old Testament characters (the people of God as a woman in childbirth, Isaiah 26 and 66 and Micah 4 and 5; the dragon/serpent from Genesis 3 and Ezekiel 29:3, Job 1:6 and Zechariah 3:1; and the male child from Psalm 2:9 and Daniel 10:13) with a story from pagan mythology. And chapter 21 draws together a wide range of themes not only from earlier in Revelation itself, but from throughout the Old Testament.

The role of cultural references
One of the less accessible features of Revelation is its polemical adaptation of cultic and magical formulae from first-century pagan rituals.[12] But its

---

12. This has been most helpfully explored by David Aune, 'The Apocalypse of John and Graeco-Roman Magic', *NTS* 33 (1987), pp. 481–501; though this useful material did not really carry through into his Word commentaries.

importance is seen in noting the fact that the phrases 'I am coming soon' (22:20), 'I hold the keys of death and Hades' (1:18) and 'I am the Alpha and the Omega' (1:8) are all unique to Revelation in the canon, have been influential in New Testament Christology, yet all originate in Greco-Roman magical cults, the first two particularly from the cult of Hekate, and the latter from wider cultic-magical interests.[13]

Alongside this is the pervasive influence of Roman imperial court ceremonial in the language of worship in Revelation, particularly in chapters 4 and 5. The setting of the scene in what appears to be a throne room (rather than an open space), with twenty-four elders (not priests), dressed in white (rather than the Old Testament colours of worship), casting their golden crowns and singing repeated choruses (rather than a psalm) are all highly redolent of the practices of imperial devotion – again, something the modern reader easily misses but that would have been immediately evident to first-century readers.[14]

The key point in this is not simply that Revelation speaks the language of its age and culture, but that it does so *polemically*, in the sense that it wrests power away from those who claim it over our lives, and says without negotiation that all power (however it is exercised) belongs to God alone. This is an interesting challenge for contemporary preaching, both in its form and its message. In one sense it is saying no more or less than Paul says in Romans 13 – that the 'powers that be' derive their authority from God. But where Romans 13 says this in a positive way, Revelation says it in a 'negative' one, which challenges us to consider issues relating to power in the modern world.

The identification of literary features and structure

If the previous issues have challenged readers, preachers and listeners at the level of information they have about the text of Revelation, then these last two issues offer a much more fundamental challenge to the way we think about the text.

The numbering of the *ekklēsiai* and messages, the seals, trumpets and plagues or bowls suggests that Revelation may be carefully structured and

---

13. In an intriguing irony of our technological, postmodern context, it is now quite easy to join the ancient cult of Hekate by doing an Internet search for websites and information about the initiation rituals.

14. Again, David Aune draws attention to this in 'The Influence of Roman Imperial Court Ceremonial on the Apocalypse of John', *BR* 18 (1983), pp. 5–26. This has been most fully explored in Wes Howard-Brooke and Anthony Gywther, *Unveiling Empire* (New York: Orbis, 1999).

organized. Such shaping goes well beyond explicit numbering, and in fact characterizes the whole of the text. On a large scale there are clearly different sections, each with a different 'feel'. As noted above, Koester talks of alternating scenes that are 'disturbing' or 'reassuring'. A number of commentators talk of sections such as chapter 7 and chapters 10 and 11 as 'interludes' in the numbered sequences, as if the sequences ask questions about the way the world is, and the interludes offer God's answer. David Aune goes so far as to identify clear discontinuity between the *dramatis personae* of the different scenes, and so returns to theories such as those of R. H. Charles in suggesting that these sections were in fact originally different visions, which have been edited together.[15] Whichever way you look at it, it is clear that Revelation has shape and structure to it.

Effective preaching on Revelation not only recognizes such structural features, but also takes advantage of them. For example, even a cursory reading of chapter 7 shows that it falls into three parts. After the introduction (with its echoes of the sealing of Ezek. 8) and the numbering of the servants of God by tribe, we read 'After this I looked . . .' (7:9), a clear marker of a new subsection. Then, following a scene of praise that echoes aspects of chapters 4 and 5, we find 'Then one of the elders asked me . . .' (7:13), again introducing a change of focus with its anticipation of 'the end' in chapter 21. So it might be natural for a sermon on this chapter to fall into three parts itself.

Again, considering chapter 12, it is very evident to readers of English Bibles that the chapter has a definite structure to it. Most English translations include paragraph breaks at the end of verses 6, 9 and 12, giving four distinct sections, and most also lay out verses 10 to 12 in a poetic metre. Whilst sections two (war in heaven) and three (the song of triumph) have a fresh focus, section four picks up the story of section one, with the dragon pursuing the woman. So whatever you think this episode is about,[16] it seems clear that there is one

---

15. I have demonstrated elsewhere (unpublished paper, 'Orthogonal Methodologies and the Structure of Revelation', presented to Revelation seminar group, British New Testament Conference, Sept. 2003) that this cannot be the case, since words with special frequencies (see below) occur throughout Aune's separate sections; so if they were edited together, this was done so carefully that you cannot see the joins. This kind of 'source critical' approach is anyway unnecessary – though it can be helpful in highlighting the structure.

16. The majority of English-language commentary sees this as referring to the 'Christ event', Jesus' birth, life, ministry, death and resurrection, though dispensationalist approaches see this as referring to some future 'end times' figure. For a critique

main 'storyline' in sections one and four, and the middle two sections appear to be 'epexegetical' (explanatory) of this main theme. Walking our listeners through these kinds of observations not only helps them to become more skilled readers of Scripture, but also builds confidence in skills they already had but were unaware of.

The case of numerology

Although Revelation's use of numerology is just one aspect of its socio-rhetorical context, it is sufficiently specialist and intriguing to merit some comment in its own right. It is also a subject that tests our hermeneutical discipline: Will we content ourselves with reading this text only in ways that John could have intended and his first readers could have understood (though of course it may have fresh implications in our day), rather than using it as a springboard for our own flights of fancy?

The secret here is to make disciplined use of our imagination. Revelation's world was one with relatively little textual material compared with ours, so people attended carefully to specific words in texts, and how often they occurred. It was a world where numbers were strange and powerful; with an incomplete number system, which did not include a 'zero', it was a place where Achilles was, apparently, unable to run past a tortoise (Zeno's paradox).[17] And, most crucially, it was a world without a separate number system, so that letters stood for numbers – which meant that every word has its own value, the sum of the values of its letters.

Revelation makes full use of all these ideas, and it requires us to read the text in a way quite different from our usual approaches to finding meaning. First, key words appear with special frequencies in the text, most commonly 4, 7, 10, 14 and 28 times.[18] So 'Jesus' appears 14 times, the number of perfect witness (14 is 2 × 7; 2 is the number of witness from Deut. 19:5 [see also John 5:31–32] and 7 is the number of completeness), which supports Revelation's claim that Jesus is the faithful witness in 1:15 and 3:14.

Secondly, we are used to 'square' numbers, those that could be arranged in a square array. But the ancients were also familiar with 'triangular' numbers

---

of dispensationalist reading see my *The Ethics of the Book of Revelation* (Cambridge: Grove, 2005).

17. The understanding of zero as a number is generally attributed to Indian mathematics in the ninth century AD.

18. For a fuller account of word frequencies see my *How to Read* (n. 1 above). For detailed analysis see Bauckham, *Climax of Prophecy*, ch. 11.

(15 red snooker balls can be arranged in a triangle) and 'rectangular' numbers (those formed by multiplying adjacent numbers such as 4 × 5, rather than multiplying a number by itself). Revelation uses square numbers (144,000) to represent the things of God, triangular numbers (666) to represent those opposed to God, and rectangular numbers (1,260; 42) to represent the people of God living under the rule of those opposed to God. We live in a world that belongs to God, but is shaped by opposition to God – a world of both the good and the bad, of both 'suffering and kingdom', in which faithfulness to the witness of Jesus calls for 'patient endurance' (Rev. 1:9).[19]

Thirdly, Revelation uses 'gematria' (the Hebrew term) or 'isopsephism' (the Greek term) to expose the true spirit of imperial power. A common scheme of allocating numbers to letters gives the value of 'beast' to be the same as the value of 'Nero Caesar', both totalling 666. The true work of Rome is not to bring peace and prosperity but to be the agent of Satan, opposing God and crushing his people.[20]

The most interesting pastoral aspect of this numerology is that it can communicate vividly to those who find more usual, verbal aspects of Scripture and preaching less effective. These are often people with a scientific interest who may struggle with other categories of theology.

Strategies for preaching

With so many technical issues involved, how might we go about preaching on texts from Revelation without either getting bogged down ourselves or bamboozling our listeners? There are three possible strategies.

Strategy 1: separate out the issues from the preaching
A very effective way of preaching without becoming entangled with the technicalities is to deal with them separately. This can work well in a larger

---

19. Failure to recognize this is behind the various (problematic) readings of the millennium in ch. 20. As the cube of 10, it belongs with other square and cube numbers signifying God's reign, so it is best understood as one of the visions of the eschaton, in this case drawing on rabbinical understandings of a final, thousand-year age of the Messiah. See Ben Witherington, *Revelation* (Cambridge: Cambridge University Press, 2003), pp. 245–246; and Michael Gilbertson, *The Meaning of the Millennium* (Cambridge: Grove, 1997).

20. For details on this see my *How to Read*, ch. 6, and Bauckham, *Climax of Prophecy*, ch. 11.

context, where there is a tradition of teaching on issues of the Bible and
its interpretation. This was the approach I took when preaching through
Revelation 2011, in the city centre, 'gathered' congregation I attend that has
a significant number of university students. The 'teaching' and 'preaching'
elements happened at the same point within the Sunday evening service, but
were different in form, with the teaching element involving small-group work
and interaction, and I indicated clearly when we reached the end of the first
stage and were moving into the second, which used a more 'traditional' monologue preaching format. The sermon series covered the issues and chapters as
shown in the table below.

Week	Issue	Text
1	Genre	Chapter 1
2	Historical context	Chapters 2 and 3
3	Use of the OT	Chapters 4 and 5
4	Cultural context	Chapter 7
5	Literary structure	Chapter 12
6	Numerology	Chapter 13
7	The millennium	Chapter 21

The separate task could also be tackled in other ways: perhaps by offering
sessions at another point in the day, or through written notes, or perhaps in
small groups within the church. My approach had the advantage that everyone
who heard the teaching also heard the preaching; the disadvantage was that it
involved a longer than usual time of listening.

Strategy 2: integrate issues and preaching but with clear explanation

A second approach is to keep the two tasks together in the sermon, but make
explicit reference to the process by which you have reached the conclusions
you have about the text. This is good practice for all preaching, because it
avoids the preacher's functioning as a 'priestly' intermediary between text and
congregation, holding privileged information others cannot know.

I have frequently preached on Revelation 7 in a number of different contexts, and always aim to do several things within the sermon:

- Comment on the place and function of this episode within the book as
  a whole.
- Draw out the threefold structure of the chapter, as described
  above.

- Identify the use of the Old Testament texts of census that form the background to the list of tribes.
- Comment on the list of tribes, which is distinct from all others in the New Testament.
- Clarify the meaning of *thlipsis*, translated 'tribulation' in the AV, noting its use in 1:9 and in Paul and the gospels as the lot of any who would follow Christ.
- Explore the phrase 'nation, tribe, people and language' (1:9) and how it works in Revelation.
- Note the anticipations of 'the end' in verses 15–17.

The threefold structure of the chapter has led me to centre these comments around three points:

- God's people as a disciplined army, ready for conflict (which relates to the purpose of the OT censuses)
- God's people as those who are suffering in 'tribulation' until Jesus returns
- God's people as the saints praising, partly for what God has done, but mostly for what God will do

Since these are three portraits of aspects of our identity, I have often used opening and closing illustrations about how we see ourselves and how others see us, perhaps relating this to actual portraits that have been in the news. But the essential in preaching this chapter has been to make clear the connections with the features of the text, showing how meaning for us emerges from the meaning for John and his first readers.

Strategy 3: fully integrate issues in preaching but in an overt way

I recently preached a fifteen-minute 'homily' in a Cambridge chapel, and in such a context with such a time constraint it was impossible to give separate time to the technical issues I had wrestled with. To make it more challenging, the subject was the numerology of Revelation!

Here it is still important to make your processes of engagement with the text explicit, but this must be done in a much more compressed, narrative way. And in order to avoid overwhelming listeners with technical details, it is also essential to allow application to flow quickly from this. Our goal is not to impart information, but to encourage transformation. So, following a short explanation of square, triangular and rectangular numbers, I included this section in my sermon:

The things of God come as squares, in particular the 144 (12 × 12) thousand of his people in chapter 7 and the New Jerusalem in chapter 21. The enemies of God come in triangles, in particular the number of the beast in chapter 13. (You could fit 666 balls on a snooker table large enough!). But the life we live in God now is marked by rectangles – the three-and-a-half years of Daniel becomes 42 perfect months, which are 1,260 days, both rectangular numbers.

What does this mean? Rectangles look a bit like squares, but they are also composed of two triangles; they share characteristics of both. In other words, we live between times – we are citizens of two worlds. The kingdom of God has come in the person of Jesus, the new age is with us now, and yet we live in a fallen world – the old age continues around us. Or, as John puts it in chapter 11 – the inner court is kept safe, whilst the outer court is trampled. The people of God are kept safe in a secret place (ch. 12), and yet the beast appears to trample them (ch. 13). Or, as John says at the very beginning, we share together both in the kingdom but also in the suffering – and so need patient endurance whilst we await our salvation. God is the God of peace and order, but it is a peace and order we do not yet see fully – so we continue to pray that God's kingdom will come, and his will be done on earth as it is in heaven.

The aim of this comment was to 'show my working' (as it were), to root Revelation in its Old Testament background, to make clear the connections with others parts of the book, to connect this with other themes of New Testament eschatology, and even to link it to the reason why we pray as we do. In this way we have travelled from the most obscure, technical point of New Testament exegesis all the way to the prayer that Jesus taught us.

Conclusion

Preaching on Revelation is probably one of the most demanding tasks facing the preacher – but also one of the most rewarding. I hope the examples here have given you confidence that it can be done, and done well. There is nothing quite like the experience of seeing the veil pulled back, this book dusted off, and pages that have been closed for many years opened once more. And as it happens, you will discover that this is truly a transforming text – of your world, of your congregation, and even of you yourself as you preach.

© Ian Paul, 2013

12. HOW ARCHAEOLOGY AND HISTORY CAN HELP WITH NEW TESTAMENT PREACHING

Peter Oakes

Archaeology and history offer resources that can be of value to a preacher both in engaging a congregation and in helping the congregation better appreciate what is at stake in a New Testament text. As a New Testament lecturer who is only an occasional preacher, I cannot offer expert advice on preaching. However, having spent considerable time on researching the New Testament in relation to various types of historical and archaeological evidence, and having come across some of the opportunities and pitfalls involved, I hope to be able to offer some helpful pointers for those who would consider bringing such evidence into the pulpit.

If I were to summarize the most important point towards which this chapter heads, it would be to argue that preachers should be rather wary of theories that use historical or archaeological data to offer specific scenarios for the reading of a New Testament book. Such theories continue to be very difficult to prove with a high degree of probability. Instead, a more valuable path for a preacher to follow is to use archaeological and historical evidence to gain (and communicate) a fuller and fuller picture of the issues of first-century life, whether that is in the fields of Galilee, listening to Jesus or in the house churches of the Greco-Roman towns and cities, the groups of people whom the writers of the New Testament texts had in mind as their audience.

Salvation on a coin

Buy a Roman coin, a first-century one. They are surprisingly inexpensive. I am sitting looking at a silver denarius of Vespasian. The reverse features a seated goddess and has the inscription *salus Aug*. Although I know roughly what *salus* means I have just looked it up in the *Oxford Classical Dictionary*. Jerzy Linderski's one-paragraph article describes *salus* as 'a deified "virtue", the safety and welfare of the state (akin to, and perhaps influenced by the Greek Soteria)'. He comments that '*Salus Augusta* or *Augusti*, the "Health" and "Saving Power" of the emperor, frequently appears on inscriptions and coins'.[1]

The physical object and the ideas it contains are both useful for preaching. Pass the coin round. The first century is not some fantasy era dreamed up by church ministers. The Gospels are not set in a fairy-tale world. Many people today may think the Gospels should begin with, 'Once upon a time . . .'. You need to convince them, intellectually and emotionally, that the New Testament documents are earthed in a real world. Coins and other archaeological remains can help with this, whether the congregation experiences them first hand or through pictures, maps, DVDs, websites or your own description.

This is not just an issue for the sceptical among your hearers, who may dismiss the New Testament world as unreal. Among the most devout there may be other types of fantasization of the text. The characters may be envisaged as inhabiting an implausible 'holy' reality, which does not engage with the nitty-gritty of everyday life. When Luke's Jesus says that he comes to 'proclaim release to the prisoners' (Luke 4:18), many in the congregation may give no thought at all to first-century prisoners, instead jumping instantly to a theological analogy of imprisonment by sin, as though the text was written in a social vacuum.

My ten-minute research project on the coin also turned up ideas that could form significant and engaging material for preaching. We must allow for a degree of uncertainty: from Linderski's article it would be unclear whether my coin celebrated the emperor's health or his saving power; we are also left uncertain about the degree of relationship between *salus* and the Greek *sōtēria*, which, as those with New Testament Greek will recall, means 'salvation'. Of course, these questions might (or might not!) be resolved by a month's research. However, that is not a

---

1. Jerzy Linderski, 'Salus', in *OCD*, p. 1350.

luxury available to most preachers. What can we do with what we have got?

What is clear is that the coin is an eloquent expression of a culture in which welfare and safety were deified, in which welfare and safety could be seen as depending on Greco-Roman religious practice (offerings at the temple of *Salus*), and in which the welfare and safety of the empire (and the world) could be seen as stemming from the emperor. The New Testament account of salvation was first proclaimed in a context with strongly established alternative accounts of salvation. It is good to stay aware of that when preaching on texts about healing or about salvation in a broader sense. Healing and salvation came through Christ and served the agenda of the kingdom of God, rather than coming either through the Roman emperor and serving the agenda of the empire, or through Greco-Roman gods and goddesses, whose favour was won by careful performing of ritual offerings. Part of the way in which we can understand the extent and shape of Christian ideas of salvation is by thinking of what the culturally available alternatives were or, indeed, now are.

Going via Corinth

As a student I sat many times under the preaching of Dick Lucas. One thing that impressed me was that he explained the biblical texts by a method I could understand. Sitting with my Bible open I could see how he derived from the text the points he was making. He was doing something we could do too, with other biblical texts, if we gave the same kind of close attention to them. The use of archaeological or historical information in preaching might be thought to undermine this process. It might be seen to undermine the possibility of the lay Christian's, without specialist expertise, reading the Bible properly.

Some years later I was in a training session for preachers, again led by Dick Lucas. He was speaking about the Corinthian correspondence. He drew a big diagram on a flip chart. It had a block representing the text and one representing us. He said words to the effect that as a preacher you should not simply go straight from the text to us. He then drew another block on the chart to represent Corinth. He drew arrows from the text to Corinth, and then from Corinth to us, and said something like, 'You have to go from 1 Corinthians to us *via Corinth*.'

I cannot now remember which particular issues were being discussed at the time, but one that I know would have been important to Dick Lucas relates to the passages on eating food offered to idols, in 1 Corinthians 8 – 10. He would have been concerned to impress on us that these texts carry vital messages for present-day Christians, even though we do not face the issue of idol meat. He argued that a key step towards understanding the significance of the texts for us is to understand the significance of the texts for the members of the Corinthian house churches. The way in which the texts related to issues facing them would help us understand how the texts could relate to issues facing us.

This does not require a PhD in study of Corinth. In fact, there is no specific level at which one suddenly reaches enough historical knowledge for preaching on a particular text. Instead, there is a continuous range of levels. Every preacher knows enough about ancient Corinth to have a reasonable basic understanding of some of the issues: Corinth was an ancient city in Greece; it was full of temples to various gods; ceremonies relating to these gods involved sacrifices. With a bit of reflection, the preacher preparing a sermon would also begin to realize how a refusal to eat meat from these sacrifices could cause various difficult issues in the life of a Christian, especially a first-generation Christian whose family had always participated in sacrifices to particular gods. For that kind of knowledge – and indeed much more detail than that – the preacher simply needs to watch a normal diet of popular television history programmes, read newspapers, and so on. At this level the preacher would, in fact, simply be drawing on the kind of archaeological and historical knowledge that some among the congregation might well already have, and applying it to help in understanding the text. In fact, those involved regularly in preaching from the New Testament also ought to take a little time to make sure they have a reasonably organized historical knowledge of the period, at least to the level of knowing which of the Roman emperors reigned when, and what happened in the 60s AD, particularly the great fire and Nero's persecution of Christians in Rome in 64, then the Jewish revolt against Rome in 66, culminating in the destruction of the Jerusalem temple in 70.

As a step beyond that level, preachers can bolster their sermon preparation by drawing on easily available resources. Easiest of all is the kaleidoscope of material – good, bad and downright crazy – available on the Internet. Web searches for the appropriate topics yield a wide range of useful material. Wikipedia can be very helpful if used cautiously. It is safer on relatively neutral subjects, such as the archaeology of Corinth, than it is on controverted ones such as the Gospels. The highly respected Perseus website (www.perseus. tufts.edu) hosts a range of valuable information. There are helpful links on www.ntgateway.com and www.biblicalstudies.org.uk. Tyndale House (www.

tyndale.cam.uk) offers a range of useful tools, which promises to broaden considerably in the near future through the development of the Scripture Tools for Every Person resources. Many respected seminaries and universities also make useful course material publicly available online.

For print resources, the more substantial modern commentaries are an obvious starting point. On 1 Corinthians, those by Gordon Fee and by Anthony Thiselton are good examples both of providing a good amount of historical information and of thinking through its implications for understanding the text.[2] Among other textual resources that preachers could have on their shelves are New Testament introductions, which all have some sections on context (a good example is by David deSilva[3]). There are more specific contextual introductions such as that of Simon Jones,[4] Moyer Hubbard,[5] or, from a social-scientific perspective, Dietmar Neufeld and Richard DeMaris's collection.[6] There are also biblical encyclopedic dictionaries such as the Inter-Varsity Press *Dictionary of New Testament Background*,[7] and classical reference works such as the invaluable *Oxford Classical Dictionary*, cited above. Further books and articles are noted below.

All these resources could be used by a preacher at the level of, say, a one-hour research project as part of sermon preparation. If there is a historical issue particularly relevant to a point in the sermon, the congregation might reasonably expect the preacher to go at least this far. On the idol-meat issue in 1 Corinthians, for this time commitment, the preacher would probably have encountered points such as the likely differences between the issues facing richer and poorer Christians over the issue. There would also be awareness of

---

2. Gordon D. Fee, *The First Epistle to the Corinthians*, NICNT (Grand Rapids: Eerdmans, 1987); Anthony C. Thiselton, *The First Epistle to the Corinthians*, NIGTC (Carlisle: Paternoster, 2000).

3. David A. deSilva, *An Introduction to the New Testament: Contexts, Methods and Ministry Formation* (Downers Grove: InterVarsity Press; Leicester: Apollos, 2004).

4. Simon Jones, *The World of the Early Church: A Social History* (Oxford: Lion, 2011).

5. Moyer V. Hubbard, *Christianity in the Greco-Roman World* (Peabody: Hendrickson, 2010).

6. Dietmar Neufeld and Richard E. DeMaris (eds.), *Understanding the Social World of the New Testament* (London: Routledge, 2009).

7. Craig A. Evans and Stanley E. Porter, *Dictionary of New Testament Background* (Downers Grove: InterVarsity Press; Leicester: Inter-Varsity Press, 2000).

the various specific cults in Corinth, including the emperor cult, which would raise interesting further possibilities for reflection.

Beyond this level lies the kind of more specialist study that should happen during ministerial training. At that level students should be writing essays on 1 Corinthians that draw on specialist monographs by scholars such as Andrew Clarke, John Chow, Bruce Winter, Gerd Theissen and David Horrell. Students should also be receiving at least a basic education in the overall first-century archaeological and historical context. In general, my impression is that too little is taught in this area, although I realize that there are many competing pressures on college time.

Two issues relate to this more advanced level of archaeological and historical study. The first is that ministers who reach a certain level of competence in this area during training can maintain that only by keeping on refreshing their knowledge. An element of that is to keep buying good commentaries throughout ministry, even though your shelves might have been full by the end of training. It is also worth periodically updating other reference works. For instance, Abingdon Press recently produced the *New Interpreter's Dictionary of the Bible* and InterVarsity Press are putting together an entirely new edition of *Dictionary of Jesus and the Gospels*.

The first issue implies a second: How, in preaching, can you make use of scholarship at the kind of level where the scholarly landscape tends to shift from time to time? This is, of course, an issue that relates to scholarly issues wider than just archaeological and historical ones. It underlies this whole volume. In terms of archaeology and history in particular, one piece of advice I would offer is to give attention to non-biblical scholarship on the issues. This will act as something of a caution against buying too easily into the sometimes rather wild gyrations of the archaeological or historical ideas that some biblical scholars espouse in defending particular theories about interpretation of various texts. If a biblical scholar's reading of a text is reliant on archaeological or historical standpoints that are not part of mainstream archaeological and classical scholarship (as represented in, for instance, *Oxford Classical Dictionary*), I would be cautious about using that view in preaching unless it was very clearly backed by strong primary evidence.

More broadly, as a preacher, you do need to exercise a degree of caution in drawing on scholarly views. Sometimes, this may mean using material in a somewhat illustrative rather than directly argumentative manner. This can still carry effective weight. We will stay with Corinth to consider a case in point.

Meeting and eating in house churches

Jerome Murphy-O'Connor very helpfully opened up the study of 1 Corinthians in relation to Corinthian archaeology in his book *St Paul's Corinth*.[8] In 1 Corinthians 11:17–34 Paul castigates the Corinthians for social divisions made apparent in the way in which the Corinthians eat when they all meet together. Murphy-O'Connor explains this with reference to the Anaploga Villa at Corinth, pointing out that, in such a setting, in order to accommodate a reasonable number of Christians, a few (probably the wealthy villa owner and his friends) would eat in the typically rather small dining room (*triclinium*) while the others ate outside in the courtyard (*peristylum*). It is clear that this scenario would relate in interesting ways to the concerns Paul raises about some people eating in a manner that effectively meant humiliating 'those who have nothing' (1 Cor. 11:22).

In 2004 David Horrell launched a powerful challenge to Murphy-O'Connor's use of archaeology. Horrell argued that the dining arrangements Murphy-O'Connor was drawing on at the Anaploga Villa actually dated from later than the New Testament period. Moreover, the setting was not of the social type most likely to be appropriate to the kinds of people in the Corinthian church. Horrell offered, as an alternative, an upper room in a street of buildings east of the theatre in Corinth.[9]

What is the preacher to do, faced with this kind of pair of competing views? The first answer is not to take the scholars' views too seriously. I am sure that Murphy-O'Connor and Horrell would agree with this. They are just offering reasonable scenarios for contextualizing the text. On the other hand, the preacher should take the scholars with great seriousness. Murphy-O'Connor is right that most first-century dining contexts encoded social hierarchy. Horrell is right that most first-century Christian groups would not have had access to the dining facilities of grand villas. Both scholars bring home the fact that early Christian dining practices should be considered in comparison with the norms of first-century life. Paul challenged the normal hierarchy of these practices in this passage that centres on the text recalling the Last Supper that is used at every Eucharist. For Paul, in 1 Corinthians, the Eucharist sacramentalizes the breaking down of division between rich and poor. This

---

8. Jerome Murphy-O'Connor, *St Paul's Corinth: Text and Archaeology*, 3rd ed. (Collegeville: Liturgical Press, 2002).

9. David G. Horrell, 'Domestic Space and Christian Meetings at Corinth: Imagining New Contexts and the Buildings East of the Theatre', *NTS* 50 (2004), pp. 349–369.

is an archaeologically informed message with extensive ramifications for our present-day congregations.

Focus on general context

I am writing a commentary on Galatians and trying to think through what are the most significant contextual issues for interpreting the letter.[10] There are a number of recent, very specific theories about the context of Galatians, focusing on key cults in the region. For instance, Susan Elliott draws on the cult of the Magna Mater, which involved castration of priests.[11] Thomas Witulski evokes the specific development of the imperial cult in Pisidian Antioch, a Roman colony in the south of the region.[12] I am dubious about such very specific contextual theories. It seems to me more important to keep in sight the general contextual point that the New Testament texts were written for members of first-century house churches (or, often, apartment churches). Reflection on the general context of life in such houses and apartments – who would be there, how they would relate to one another, what factors they would face in their lives – seems to me to be a more relevant and reliable concern for preachers than worrying too much about specific minority theories about context (although we do, of course, need to consider both the specific *rhetorical* context of Galatians, with its key issue of circumcision, and the context of Galatians in the history of the development of the early Jesus movement, as Gentiles became increasingly significant). Reflection on New Testament texts in their general house-church context will, in my experience, provoke consideration of significant issues for the church's witness in its current context.

The double archaeological and historical context of the Gospels

The Gospels raise a particular type of issue in thinking about the relevance of archaeology and history. The Gospels are mainly narratives of Jesus' minis-

10. Peter Oakes, *Galatians*, Paideia Commentaries (Grand Rapids: Baker Academic, forthcoming).

11. Susan Elliott, *Cutting Too Close for Comfort: Paul's Letter to the Galatians in Its Anatolian Cultic Context*, JSNTSup 248 (London: T. & T. Clark International, 2003).

12. Thomas Witulski, *Die Addressaten des Galaterbriefes: Untersuchungen zur Gemeinde von Antiochien ad Pisidian*, FRLANT 193 (Göttingen: Vandenhoeck & Ruprecht, 2000).

tering and teaching in Galilee and Jerusalem. The archaeology and history of these places is significant for understanding Jesus' life and message. Work by scholars such as Sean Freyne, for example, can help us understand the realities of Galilean life into which Jesus spoke.[13] This is clearly important for interpreting the Gospels.

On the other hand, most or all of the Gospels are probably products of the Greco-Roman urban environment, written in large cities such as Antioch, Ephesus and Rome. The archaeology of first-century urban life helps us to understand the concerns of the kinds of people who wrote the Gospels and for whom they were written. This too is important for interpreting the texts.

The way in which Luke 5:19 interprets the action by the friends of the paralysed man, who in Mark 2:4 dig through the roof, as being removal of tiles, probably gives some indication of Luke's urban assumptions. Roof structure is probably not an issue of great interest to preachers. However, the urban assumptions evidenced by Luke's reference to tiles are of considerable significance for understanding and preaching his Gospel. For instance, if a preacher (or scholar) is handling Luke's substantial material on tax collectors,[14] the temptation is to view this in purely Galilean and Judean terms, focusing solely on the role of tax collectors in that region. A common consequence of this is that interpreters give priority to the role of tax collectors as collaborators with an occupying power. This political characteristic is often seen as central to the issues relating to tax collectors in the Gospels. However, for Luke and his readers in the Greco-Roman urban world this would not be the main characteristic of tax collectors. Taxes, and consequently tax collectors, were indeed commonly resented in the provinces of the empire.[15] However, the most frequent complaint about tax collectors was of corrupt extortion, enabling them to get rich at the expense of the population.[16] This broader characterization of tax collectors actually fits Luke's text much better than a Judea-centred focus

---

13. Sean Freyne, *Galilee from Alexander the Great to Hadrian 323 BCE to 135 CE*, 2nd ed. (Edinburgh: T. & T. Clark, 1998). See also Stephen Travis, *The Galilee that Jesus Knew* (Cambridge: Grove, 2011).

14. The work of my PhD student Pyung-Soo Seo has recently brought this home to me.

15. Nicholas Purcell, 'The Arts of Government', in J. Boardman, J. Griffin and O. Murray (eds.), *Oxford History of the Classical World* (Oxford: Oxford University Press, 1986), pp. 560–591, here p. 582.

16. Ernst Badian, 'publicani', in *OCD*, pp. 1275–1276.

on collaboration. Luke's material on tax collectors is book-ended by John the Baptist's call for them to renounce extortion (Luke 3:13) and Zacchaeus' example of doing that and repaying money (Luke 19:8).

More broadly, Luke's extensive material on wealth and poverty should be considered not just in the Galilean context of Jesus' ministry but more broadly in the urban context in which Luke wrote. The practical implications of Jesus' manifesto launch at Nazareth (Luke 4:18–19) resonate for Luke throughout the life of the cities of the Mediterranean world. For the preacher, as well as understanding, say, Sean Freyne on Galilee, it is well worth getting your head around something like Peter Garnsey and Richard Saller's classic, *The Roman Empire: Economy, Society and Culture*.[17]

When archaeological and literary worlds collide

The kind of history that most commentaries make use of tends to be heavily literary. The development of commentary writing related closely to the development of classical scholarship. The great commentators of the nineteenth and twentieth centuries knew and used their Aristotle, Cicero and Seneca. The classical legacy enshrined in the great New Testament commentaries of the past, and passed on from those books to today, is vital but does have a major limitation. It sees the first-century world through the eyes of the elite Greek or Roman men who wrote the literary texts. Some of the distortions that is likely to introduce are obvious. For instance, the wide variety of levels of income and status among the non-elite are likely to be severely flattened out in a view of society as seen from the very high perches of senators and consuls such as Seneca and Cicero. Archaeological evidence of housing and its contents can help counterbalance this (and I have written on this area myself in relation to Pompeian housing and the interpretation of Paul's letter to the Romans[18]). Other distortions are subtler, and here archaeological evidence actually can reveal issues we might not otherwise detect.

One neat example is the issue of the relationship between associations and the urban authorities. Philip Harland defines associations as

---

17. Peter Garnsey and Richard Saller, *The Roman Empire: Economy, Society and Culture* (London: Duckworth, 1987).

18. Peter Oakes, *Reading Romans in Pompeii: Paul's Letter at Ground Level* (London: SPCK; Minneapolis: Fortress, 2009).

small, unofficial ('private') groups, usually consisting of about ten to fifty members (but sometimes with larger memberships into the hundreds), that met together on a regular basis to socialize with one another and to honour both earthly and divine benefactors, which entailed a variety of internal and external activities.[19]

Traditionally, scholars have seen these groups as typically having tense relationships with the authorities. This is based on Roman historians such as Tacitus, and office-holders, such as Pliny the Younger, who report bans on the meeting of *collegia*, the most common Latin term for associations. This idea of long-running tension between associations and authorities feeds into discussion of the grounds on which Christians may have faced persecution in the New Testament period.[20]

Harland, who was part of a major Toronto research project on associations,[21] shows that the extensive archaeological evidence for associations (in terms of buildings and inscriptions) overwhelmingly indicates positive relationships with the authorities. Many public inscriptions honour prominent civic figures supported by named associations.[22] Other publically visible inscriptions name associations and list their members (who can include civic officials).[23]

If we assume that New Testament texts, such as 1 Peter, which attest to Christians facing trouble, are written in a context where non-Christians would tend to see Christian groups as being like associations, should we go with the literary evidence and see the mere fact of their looking like associations as being likely to provoke trouble from the authorities? Or should we go with Harland and the archaeology and see associations as a normal, generally well-integrated part of the first-century social order – in fact, offering a model by which Christian groups could maybe find a degree of acceptance in society? Which wins – literature or archaeology?

The answer is that we need to construct our view of first-century life by

---

19. Philip A. Harland, *Dynamics of Identity in the World of the Early Christians* (London: T. & T. Clark, 2009), p. 26.

20. See e.g. E. T. Merrill, *Essays in Early Church History* (London: Macmillan, 1924), pp. 52–66.

21. See e.g. John S. Kloppenborg and Stephen G. Wilson (eds.), *Voluntary Associations in the Graeco-Roman World* (London: Routledge, 1996).

22. Philip A. Harland, *Associations, Synagogues, and Congregations: Claiming a Place in Ancient Mediterranean Society* (Minneapolis: Fortress, 2003).

23. E.g. the *cultores* of Sylvanus at Philippi. Peter Pilhofer, *Philippi II: Katalog der Inschriften von Philippi*, WUNT 119 (Tübingen: Mohr, 2000), nos. 163–166.

taking into account both types of evidence, with an awareness of the kinds of factors that affect the picture each type of evidence tends to produce. Take the literary evidence first. We are talking about instances in which associations appear in the writings of historians and politicians. Think of a rough modern equivalent. When do sports clubs appear in the news (other than during sports reports)? Apart from the occasional big-money managerial change, sports clubs tend to appear in the news if there is trouble. A decade or so back, there were repeated news stories in the UK about violence among soccer fans. Governments passed various pieces of legislation aimed at curbing the problem. The picture of sports clubs that would be produced if one put together excerpts of news coverage and political discussion would be very negative. In a similar way, associations are likely to turn up in the works of Roman historians and politicians only when there was trouble. Conversely, if we visit sports clubs and look at modern inscriptions outside sports grounds, almost always they will provide a glowing impression of the club and of its relationship with the community. 'The mayor, Joe Bloggs, laid this stone to inaugurate . . .' In a similar way, ancient-association inscriptions are bound to project a positive image of relationships with society.

In reality, both types of evidence, literary and archaeological, do make sub-stantive contributions to our understanding of the situation of associations. The inscriptions really were there, in many public places. Associations were generally not underground bodies, hiding in fear of discovery. On the other hand, the authorities clearly were wary of groups of people who met together regularly. Moreover, if trouble arose from one such group, the authorities were likely to take sweeping action that caught many innocent groups up with it, disrupting their normal activities. The early Christians behaved in various ways likely to arouse official disapproval. The authorities would then have had many precedents for taking actions that sought to shut a group down.

Text and people, then and now

The recent studies on associations make a broader point because they under-mine assertions that many scholars have made about some ways in which early Christianity was supposedly unique in its context. Like the early Christians, others could meet, eating together and honouring a deity. Associations could provide a sense of belonging and the opportunity to take official roles for those unable to do so in public life. Associations sometimes included quite a range of social statuses and sometimes had moral codes. There are many other ways too in which specific points of early Christian teaching and practice can be paralleled somewhere in the Greco-Roman world, with its wide variety of Jewish and Gentile practices and ideas. Preachers with insufficient awareness of the first-century context are sometimes too quick to claim uniqueness for various specific Christian ideas.

However, awareness of the first-century context makes it clear that something radically new was indeed going on in the advent of the Jesus movement. Radical changes were being brought about in the lives of thousands of people across the empire. For instance, although some associations might include slaves, there is no sign that becoming part of such an association would bring about anything like the radical change in experience that seems to have been brought about through becoming a member of one of the early charismatic house churches. Similarly, although we can find ancient parallels for some of Jesus' sayings, there is nothing like the overall package of teaching and hope expressed in the range of New Testament material on his teaching, life, death and resurrection.

The better our understanding of first-century lives, the better our understanding of just how the New Testament teaching could change those lives. The nature of those changes is important to reflect on as preachers because it helps us to think about the nature of the changes that can be brought about in lives today through the gospel.

To be specific, this means I would suggest that if a preacher is committing time to look at first-century archaeology and history, the key focus should be on people – ordinary people – their lives, experiences, expectations. By all means read about emperors, cities and philosophical movements. But do so with the constant question 'What did this mean in the lives of the ordinary people who made up Jesus' audience and the membership of the house churches?'[24] Shape your use of time to focus on this and keep this question in your mind as you study. A grasp of the lives of the ordinary people of the first century, in all their variety, will help bring the issues in the New Testament text into interaction with real life in a way that, I trust, will engage and inspire the present-day people you preach to.

© Peter Oakes, 2013

---

24. For a range of political approaches to these issues see Richard A. Horsley (ed.), *A People's History of Christianity*, vol. 1: *Christian Origins* (Minneapolis: Fortress, 2005).

13. PREACHING THE ETHICS OF THE NEW TESTAMENT

John Nolland

Introduction

A notable feature of the New Testament letters is their interest in concrete ethical matters. Attention to such is characteristically found in a final major section, as for example in Romans 12 – 16. Sometimes, however, as in the Corinthian correspondence, there is extended ethical discussion in the main body of the letters. As well, lists and clusters of virtues and vices can be found scattered liberally through the letters. A striking feature of the Sermon on the Mount is its ethical investment. Other parts of the New Testament also invest in encouraging virtue and discouraging vice.

Scholarly neglect

There is, however, surprisingly little New Testament scholarship on concrete ethical matters. We may take as an example the list of virtues in Galatians 5:22–23 that we know as the fruit of the Spirit. Attention to them has a place in popular literature, but one looks almost in vain for scholarly articles focusing on them.[1] One does no better in a search for broader-based study of virtue and/or vice lists in the New Testament.[2] For the catalogue of virtues in 2 Peter 1 we now have the published dissertation by Charles (1997), which has some useful material on a wider front; and Zaas (1988) has looked in a short article at list materials in 1 Corinthians 5 and 6, arguing that the materials have a contextual role.[3]

It is not just that the virtue lists as such have not become the focus of study. Broader study of New Testament ethics, Pauline ethics, ethics of Jesus, and so on seem rarely to make it down, except in passing, to the level of concreteness represented by the virtues to be found in lists and clusters throughout the New Testament.[4]

For some, 'since love is the "only fundamental ground for behaviour", all lists of individual virtues are superfluous'![5] The *sola fide* of the German Lutheran theological tradition has often resulted in embarrassment about

---

1. In the last twenty-five years of research output I have been able to identify only G. K. Beale, 'The Old Testament Background of Paul's Reference to "the Fruit of the Spirit" in Galatians 5:22', *BBR* 15 (2005), pp. 1–38; and B. L. Melbourne, 'Order and Disorder: The Structure of the Vices and Virtues in Galatians 5:19–23 Reconsidered', *St Nersess Theological Review* 7 (2002), pp. 85–99.

2. One has to reach back to B. S. Easton, 'New Testament Ethical Lists', *JBL* 51 (1932), pp. 1–12; A. Vögtle, *Die Tugend- und Lasterkataloge im Neuen Testament*, NTAbh 16.4–5 (Münster: Aschendorff, 1936); S. Wibbing, *Die Tugend- und Lasterkataloge im Neuen Testament und ihre Traditionsgeschichte unter besonderer Berücksichtigung der Qumrantexte*, BZNW 25 (Berlin: Töpelmann, 1959); E. Kamlah, *Die Form der katalogischen Paränese im Neuen Testament* (Tübingen: Mohr, 1964); N. J. McEleney, 'The Vice Lists of the Pastoral Epistles', *CBQ* 36 (1974), pp. 203–219; and cf. W. Schrage, *Die konkreten Einzelgebote in der paulinischen Paränese* (Gütersloh: Mohn, 1961).

3. J. D. Charles, *Virtue amid Vice: The Catalog of Virtues in 2 Peter 1*, JSNTSup 150 (Sheffield: Sheffield Academic Press, 1997); P. S. Zaas, 'Catalogues and Context: 1 Corinthians 5 and 6', *NTS* 34 (1988), pp. 622–629.

4. It is worth pointing out that we do not lack study of the individual Greek terms used for the virtues.

5. Schrage's characterization of a major stream of NT scholarship: W. Schrage, 'The Formal Ethical Interpretation of Pauline Paraenesis', in Brian S. Rosner (ed.), *Understanding Paul's Ethics: Twentieth Century Approaches* (Grand Rapids: Eerdmans, 1995), p. 301.

lists.[6] Perhaps the general conviction that the New Testament writers were considerably indebted to the Greco-Roman moral tradition for the specific content of their ethical teaching[7] has also diminished the value of virtue lists in the eyes of some.[8] Attention to the 'concrete ethics' of New Testament texts with any assumption of their relevance for today is readily dismissed as naive and anachronistic.[9] Wolfgang Schrage is one who is passionately committed to the importance of concrete ethical injunctions.[10] Yet in his *Ethics of the New Testament* one looks in vain for attention to more than a fraction of the specific items in the lists and clusters of qualities to be found in the New Testament.

It is important of course not to overmake the point. We do have significant study of the individual Greek terms used for the virtues. Despite the overinvestment in the lexical value of individual words, the entries in the *Theological Dictionary of the New Testament*[11] are still of considerable value. A little more recent, but not in the same detail, is the *Exegetical Dictionary of the New*

---

6. Surely standing behind Betz's insistence that items listed as the fruit of the Spirit 'do not represent qualities of personal behavior which a man can elect, cultivate, and appropriate as part of his character. Nor are they "good deeds" in the sense of Jewish ethics: they do not come from or constitute a code of law which must be obeyed and which can be transgressed' (H. D. Betz, *Galatians* [Philadelphia: Fortress, 1979], p. 286).

7. 'Modern scholars have shown that already the earliest Christian writers [i.e. those of the NT and the apostolic fathers] . . . were considerably indebted to . . . the Greco-Roman moral tradition' (A. J. Malherbe, *Moral Exhortation, A Greco-Roman Sourcebook*, LEC [Philadelphia: Westminster, 1986], p. 11).

8. The relative neglect of the study of Pauline ethics (though some catch up in this area is in progress) has made its own contribution to the neglect of the virtue and vice lists. See Rosner, *Understanding Paul's Ethics*, pp. 1–2. D. G. Horrell, *Solidarity and Difference: A Contemporary Reading of Paul's Ethics* (London: T. & T. Clark, 2005), pp. 7–10, though wanting to moderate Rosner's claim, is in basic agreement.

9. See e.g. Horrell, *Solidarity and Difference*, p. 3: 'Paul's ethics are not studied here with a view to setting out his convictions concerning what are sometimes referred to as his "concrete ethics" . . . Attempts to do this, at least when the underlying goal is to commend the same convictions today, often represent a naïve and anachronistic approach.'

10. W. Schrage, *The Ethics of the New Testament*, tr. David E. Green (Edinburgh: T. & T. Clark, 1988 [German original 1982]), p. 10.

11. Ed. G. Kittel and G. Friedrich, tr. G. W. Bromiley, 10 vols. (Grand Rapids: Eerdmans, 1964–76).

Testament;[12] and C. Spicq's *Theological Lexicon of the New Testament* should also be mentioned.[13]

Preachers' inhibitions

The state of the scholarship means that preachers are not as well resourced for preaching with a New Testament ethical focus as they might be. But this also probably means that in their theological and ministerial training they have not been encouraged in this direction. There are also, however, some additional inhibitions in relation to ethical preaching that can be identified and addressed.

Everybody wants their preaching to be gospel focused, grace focused and Jesus focused. And so they should. But with short sermons this often means that getting down to anything concrete or detailed can be too much of a challenge. Gospel preaching can be quite effective at encouraging people to aspire to the good *as they already understand it*, but it generally contributes little to the actual understanding of the good.

A number of things conspire against any widespread recognition of the need for teaching about the content of the good. One of these is the exaltation of conscience. Respecting the conscience of others is a virtue that can trace its pedigree at least back to Romans 14:10–23 and 1 Corinthians 10:23–30. But conscience as a source of knowledge about what is good has less secure credentials. In biblical terms conscience is an organ, operating both individually and corporately, for recognizing how a possible or actual deed is to be evaluated in connection with existing moral convictions, whether these are inchoate or articulate. Conscience works with the raw material of existing moral convictions; it does not create these convictions. The way that our ethical sensibilities seem so self-evident to us provides some initial plausibility for the idea that these are coming from our conscience, but the question of where these convictions have come from needs to be seen as dealing with quite another matter. Family background, education, social development and life experience all clearly contribute to the development of moral convictions. Peer influence, media and the classroom all play key roles here. But as Christians we are heirs to an important biblical conviction about where moral conviction should come from. In some shape or form God tells us how we are

---

12. Ed. H. Balz and G. Schneider, 3 vols. (ET Grand Rapids: Eerdmans, 1990–93).

13. Tr. and ed. J. D. Ernest, 3 vols. (Peabody, Mass.: Hendrickson, 1994).

to live. It is a matter of revelation, not a place for human autonomy. Certainly our consciences must be obeyed, but our consciences also need instructing.

A lot of preaching, perhaps unconsciously, works with the assumption that the relevant information base is already known by the listeners. Something generational is often involved here: for middle-aged and elderly people today, something more than a passing acquaintance with Christianity was part of their education and cultural formation; but creeping secularism means this is not true for those who are younger. If the knowledge base is there, the goal of the sermon can be activation and application. These are vital and deserve an honoured place among the preacher's aims, but if the knowledge base is very limited, activation and application will be correspondingly thin. The point here applies to Christian ethics as to other aspects of the Christian faith. Disciplined Bible reading is no longer engaged in by many. The pressures and patterns of life today mean that fewer people than ever manage anything more than a single Sunday service, if that. Many church people get their only Christian input from the Sunday sermon. What does not surface there can play no role in the formation of such Christian people. Are Christian consciences being instructed?

It is God who needs to convict people of their sin. But it is all too easy to get the implications of this quite wrong. It cannot mean that sin should never be labelled as sin. The prophetic consciousness so prominent in the Old Testament suggests that this cannot be the case, as does the caustic criticism Jesus was capable of, and the way Paul dealt with aberrant practices in his churches. Jesus' 'judge not' must never be taken out of context and turned into 'Who am I to judge?' The judging of Matthew 7:1 is condemnation, not moral labelling, and it involves taking the moral high ground with no recognition of one's own need for God's mercy and forgiveness. One can, however, be too eager to make the moral teaching of the New Testament land on other individuals. We can learn a lot from the juxtaposition in Jesus of uncompromising affirmation of the most demanding standards of goodness (e.g. Matt. 5:17–48) with a reputation for being 'a friend of tax collectors and sinners' (Matt. 11:19). With Jesus grace always comes first, but the discipleship to which he calls is, as well, full of demand. God is the one who ultimately convicts people of sin, but he does not do so in a vacuum. Moral teaching, moral suasion and moral labelling are all a proper part of the picture. It cannot be just a matter of leaving it all to the Holy Spirit.

Teaching about the content of the good involves a critical stance towards the bad; the more so, the more concrete the level. When 90% of couples have lived together before marriage or instead of marriage, and when 50% of today's children have their parents separated by the time the children are 16, advocating sexual continence before marriage and commending the lifelong nature of the marriage commitment sounds like direct criticism of the behaviour of many of those one looks upon in the congregation. And who wants to be negative? Who wants to generate a conflict situation? Who wants to discomfort those who have at least made the effort to come?

We have a natural desire to emphasize the common ground between ourselves and the wider community. Nothing wrong with that: it builds bridges; it offers its own quiet apologetic. But when the moral content of Christian preaching is largely restricted to secularly approved causes, such as concern for the poor and the claims of the environment, a serious emasculation and even a denaturing of the Christian message results.

Why it matters more than ever

There are, then, a good number of obstacles to overcome before we are ready for a robust preaching of the ethics of the New Testament. If the scholarship does not discourage us, then there are a good range of more immediate difficulties to be negotiated. More is at stake if we fail to do so, however, than has been the case for a very long time.

Britain has been making the journey from being a Christian country, to being a nominally Christian country, to being a post-Christian country. And it has been making the journey from Enlightenment modernism to post-modernism. Other countries with a strong Christian heritage offer versions of the same. This is oversimplification and it does no justice to the fractured and plural state of modern culture, but it will do for our present purposes. During the long period of Christendom, however defective in actuality the understanding and practice of Christian ethics was in the communities of Christendom, it was the ethics of Christianity as broadly understood that people were either living up to or falling away from. The church was the conscience of the community and the conscience of the nation. In this context the church could actualize and apply, refresh and offer correctives against the backdrop of the values held within Christendom. Not only has this backdrop largely disappeared, in important areas the values agenda of the present culture formers is sharply opposed to Christian views. A strong values input is coming from the educational elite, the media and the peers of our young people. The Christian church has never been immune from the seepage in of secular or other kinds of values. But we become a total walkover when we remain silent while the voices that surround us are, variously, strident, subtle, pervasive, plausible and persistent.

In the early church, Christian leaders had to induct their converts into a manner of life that stood over against the pagan environment and to a lesser degree over against the Jewish environment. Now again we can no longer take anything for granted. We need to mark out, explain, defend and watch over our patch.

Kinds of ethical material

Various kinds of ethical material can be identified in the New Testament. The most immediately obvious as ethical material belongs at both ends of a spectrum. I mean, on the one hand, lists and clusters of virtues or vices scattered through the New Testament, and, on the other hand, texts in which a matter of ethics is discussed at some length. But just as important will be value systems that implicitly undergird New Testament documents or parts of documents and narrative exemplary material. Limitations of space mean that I will only take up one kind of material here for further discussion.

Ethical terms in lists and clusters

Many virtue words turn up in lists and clusters across the New Testament. If we start from the fruit-of-the-Spirit list of virtues in Galatians 5:22–23 and create a chain by finding other lists and clusters that include at least one item from our starting list, and then do the same in relation to the new terms added, and so on, an impressive list of ethical terms is built up. By my count 261 different terms turn up, or if we bundle together cognate words – where the uses are reasonably convergent – the number of different items reduces to 182.

Why an interest in a set created in this manner? In individual lists and clusters in some cases the choice of terms will have been somewhat arbitrary (the things that came to mind in the moment), somewhat influenced by the individuality of the particular writer (some things will be dearer to the heart of one person than another) and somewhat related to the larger historical and/or literary context of the specific writing. But it is also likely that the different texts are also drawing upon a more or less shared – even if never fully articulated – pool of values,[14] and that there may be a measure of hierarchy

---

14. W. A. Meeks, *The Origins of Early Christian Morality: The First Two Centuries* (London:

in these values. In the nature of things there can be no direct access to this underlying shared set of values, if it exists. But the more comprehensively the procedure adopted here catches up the New Testament texts that contain clusters of values, the more likely it is that a substantial set of shared values lies behind the texts; and the more clearly an overall hierarchy of values emerges by counting up the frequency of different values vocabulary, the more likely it is that a hierarchy of values exists that at least most of the New Testament writers had signed up to. In fact nearly all the clustered uses of vocabulary for positively evaluated attitudes and actions has been caught up by the procedure adopted; the same result would have emerged had I started from any other New Testament list of valued qualities.[15]

One would not want to discount any of the virtues identified in New Testament lists and clusters, but for the purposes of preaching there is clearly a value in majoring on what the New Testament itself majors on.

So what kind of hierarchy emerges? Two word groups stand out as well ahead of all the others: faith and love.

The faith/faithfulness words, *pistis* and cognate terms, are most common. But since this word group is used with quite a range of senses – ranging from trust to commitment to reliability to belief in the content of Christian belief – various things are being affirmed and encouraged by the use of this vocabulary, and perhaps we should share out the frequency between them. In favour, however, of keeping the uses together is (1) the degree to which scholarly judgment about the force of different uses can be quite divergent in certain cases; and (2) the likelihood of some sort of perceived interconnection

----

Yale University, 1993), p. 4, suggests that 'morality names a dimension of life, a pervasive and, often, only partly conscious set of value-laden dispositions, inclinations, attitudes and habits'. I am suggesting that the lists and clusters, when pooled together, offer some kind of index, however rough and ready, to the typical morality of early Christians.

15. With the exception of 1 Pet. 3:8, which has no overlap of terms with any of the other NT virtue lists (though the virtues themselves are not at all out of line). Otherwise, all of the virtue lists identified in Seeberg's classic study have been swept up in the procedure adopted: A. Seeberg, *Der Katechismus der Urchristenheit*, repr. (Munich: Kaiser, 1966 [1903]); the section 'Die Sittenlehre: Die Existenz und der Inhalt "der Wege"' (pp. 1–22) can be found in translation as 'Moral Teaching: The Existence and Contents of "the Ways"', in Brian S. Rosner (ed.), *Understanding Paul's Ethics: Twentieth-Century Approaches* (Grand Rapids: Eerdmans; Carlisle: Paternoster, 1995), pp. 155–175.

between various of the meanings, such that there is already likely to be at points an original lack of precision about the intended sense.

Next in frequency come the love words, *agapē* and its cognate verb. To love is to have a high regard for, to set a great value upon another. In these texts 'love' is predominantly love towards others, but love for God and just possibly the awareness of God's love for oneself are also to be found. As suggested above for faith, it is likely that there is an interconnectedness of these various ways in which love is thought of: it is the discovery of God's love that awakens love in return and enables love of others.

Next down, as first of the 'second tier', come the righteousness words, *dikaiosynē* and its cognates. In our texts the word group is almost always used in relation to the doing of what is right and not in relation to one's standing with God. The notion of the right involved here spans from that in 'justice' to that in 'what is fitting or appropriate'.

Next comes *pneuma*, 'spirit', with its related adjective, followed fairly closely by the *agathos*, 'good', *ergon*, 'work', *alētheia*, 'truth', and *proseuchē*, 'prayer', word groups.

Pneuma is mostly used of the Holy Spirit. In the virtue clusters it has in mind the enabling role of the Spirit. A qualitative difference of behaviour and attitude is expected in people who have opened themselves to the working of the Spirit of God. But *pneuma* is also used of the human spirit. In the virtue clusters no sharp distinction is drawn between the human spirit and the divine, presumably because the human spirit is the sphere of operation of the divine Spirit. The presence of 'goodness' words can be no surprise in anyone's list of positive qualities. The predominant use is in relation to a good version of some act or quality. With *ergon*, most of the time there is a qualifier indicating the positive quality of the work. Its use, with or without a qualifier, points to the element of activism in the life of faith that is being encouraged. The prominence of *alētheia* marks the claim upon truth and the importance of truth for the early Christian community, as it does a profound desire for the authentic. *Proseuchē*, 'prayer', is not common in the larger clusters, but as a vital ingredient of the Christian life it turns up frequently in smaller clusters.[16]

There is a bit of a drop down now to the next tier. Here come – in descending frequency and in each case with its cognates – *hagios*, 'holy', *eirēnē*, 'peace', *hypomonē*, 'steadfastness', *sophia*, 'wisdom', *phobos*, 'fear', and *elpis*, 'hope'.

With the holy word group the focus is on dedication to God and freedom

---

16. Actually most of the uses of this root are found outside the clusters, and are therefore not counted here.

from contamination from the world, but with the God link still clearly in sight. The peace word group is used of the inner satisfaction of being at peace with God, but as well, and perhaps even at the same time, of being an active agent of peace. Peace in the political realm is not in view, but peace in connection with the wider community – as for example in Acts 9:31 – reaches in that direction. The realms involved are those of the inner life, personal relationships and community harmony. The frequency of the *hypomonē* word group is striking. The word can just mean patience, but in our texts a sense of persevering in the face of difficulty is clear. Standing out against opposition is part of this. Difficulty endured and delayed gratification are important elements in the early Christian ethic. I defer consideration of wisdom to later below, where I link it with *logos*. The *phobos* word group covers both the fear of God and the submissive reverence due to one's superiors. Finally, the hope words are oriented towards a confidently expected future; they pick up on one aspect of the faith word group.

Though one should be wary of investing too much in the significance of the specific order of frequency, a striking set of high-ranking virtues emerges. Faith/faithfulness and love are at the top. Righteousness is also prominent, with engagement with the Spirit, goodness, activism, dealing in truth and prayerfulness not far behind. With some drop down a next tier is provided by holiness, peace, steadfastness, wisdom, fear and hope. This is a strikingly religious set of virtues. In the abstract it is not a distinctly Christian set of virtues, but the actual outworking of them in a Christian context would be quite distinctly Christian.

There may however be a better way of ranking the virtues. The virtues that turn up in the New Testament lists or clusters can be linked into natural sets of virtues. Such linking is an imprecise science, but it offers the possibility of providing a more balanced picture of the significance of the ethics involved. Despite necessary caveats, creating the clusters is of considerable importance for the overall profiling of the virtuous life; and in most cases the linkages can be confidently made. And once we create sets of virtues a reconsideration of the rankings is called for.

Here I can report only the impact on ranking, and comment on distinctives in what emerges. Linking knowledge, wisdom, teaching and profession of faith words to *logos* propels this to the top of the list. Christianity is a message-dominated faith in which words matter profoundly; it is the message that is understood as the primary vehicle for carrying the religious reality into the life of the believer: made 'wise unto salvation' (2 Tim. 3:15 AV). For the early Christians this did not involve either the philosopher's focus on rationality or polemic against non-rational modes of communication. It is founded on a conviction that God had spoken in word and deed in Jesus Christ, and that a subsequent nexus of communication had a vital role to play in the fulfilment of the divine purpose. Faith/faithfulness keeps its place in the top rank, but linking related virtues causes love to come down to the second tier, where it keeps close company with goodness and activism. Slightly below come prayer and *dynamis*, 'power', which subsumes Spirit, and *charis*, 'grace'. Next are righteousness and steadfastness. In relation to the initial listing, fear drops down to a lower level, and joy, abundance (marking the exuberant or inspired dimension of Christian living) and humility come into the list. Otherwise there is some change of order, but nothing that would count as statistically significant. The order is steadfastness, holiness, joy, abundance, peace and humility.

We have a robustly religious and even Christian set of virtues here. For some in the set *Christian* is more immediately the case than for others. But even with virtues likely to be more widely signed up to there will be a distinctive Christian outworking if we stay close to the New Testament context. The virtue lists and clusters are, I suggest, a fruitful field to plough in, material that transcends the culture of the day.

A parallel exercise for the vices would, I suggest, be equally illuminating. One asymmetry that I have become aware of in some preliminary probing is that on the vice side there is a greater tendency to list concrete activities. The contrast is evident immediately in the list of works of the flesh in Galatians 5:19–21, where the list begins with 'sexual immorality, impurity and debauchery'.

Preaching on ethics

We come finally to the preaching task as such.

The Pauline pattern of rooting ethics in theology, marked by the way the practical and ethical material comes towards the end of the letters, will serve us well in our preaching of ethics. Both motivation for and the meaning of ethical behaviour depend upon the bigger framework within which the concrete ethics is set. Jesus differed with his Pharisaic opponents not so much over the content of the good – although at times he differed here as well – as over how that vision of goodness was to be brought to bear on people's lives. Context is everything. Christian ethical challenge expresses the claim of Jesus to be concretely Lord over our lives. Railing against the evils of people 'out there' is hardly something that calls to mind the spirit of Jesus. Becoming what we should be catches something of the soteriological and eschatological framework within which the challenge of Christian ethics should be set.

A pastoral perspective is always called for as well. If we are going to preach ethics, we are messing very concretely with people's lives. We cannot afford in preaching simply to say things because they are true. The question of how this truth will land must always be before our eyes. Non-judgmental kindness marked Jesus' engagement with the broken and the needy, but he was extremely severe and demanding at times with the self-assured. Preaching ethics should come out of an informed knowledge of and pastoral relationship with those to whom we preach. May it not be said of us that we 'load people down with burdens they can hardly carry, and . . . will not lift one finger to help them' (Luke 11:46).

Cultural sensitivity is important, if we are to preach ethics from an ancient set of writings into our contemporary situation. What God has given us in the directives of Scripture is not something abstracted from its cultures of original reception. Things always have their meaning in context, and we need to discern not only what is being said, but also what is being achieved by its being said, or said in this way. Ephesians 5:21–33 illustrates this point well. The basic outline for the list of relationships here comes from the wider cultural framework (the so-called household code). This is, however, not untouched by the new reality introduced in Christ. Christianity is a religion of mutual submission, not one of dominance and submission. The text sets out to infuse these old patterns with a new spirit. First it is all set into a new framework of mutual submission. Secondly, even as he is reinforcing the call upon wives to be submissive he is introducing a fresh image of what kind of person one is being submissive to. The church is subject to Christ as the one who is its Saviour. Something quite similar is going to be demanded of the Christian men to whom this submission is due. The specific form suggested for a man's submission to his wife is sacrificial love, designed to have in mind for his wife all the goals Christ has for the church in his self-sacrificing love for her. Ephesians 5 is doing something against the background of the culture of the day, and it is important to see this; however, we need to be sensitive not only to the cultural context of our texts, but also to the cultural context into which we are to speak. How would Ephesians 5 have been written, if it wanted to make its points against the background of twenty-first-century Western culture? Cultural translation is no simple matter. It is beset with the danger of loss on the one side and of confusion of an ancient cultural setting for the substance of the message on the other.

Given the increasing cultural distance between church and society our preaching of New Testament ethics needs to include an apologetic element. What lacks plausibility is unlikely to be seriously attended to. We can think here of theological apologetics and of pragmatic apologetics. Theological apologetics might involve a defence of why it is appropriate for God to direct human behaviour. Pragmatic apologetics will involve showing how aspects of Christian ethics make good practical sense for the individual and for the community. From time to time things come to public awareness that place in question the status quo; these are opportunities.

Differences of ethical understanding can divide Christians and split churches. Balanced ethical preaching needs to emphasize both the pluralism of Romans 14 – 15 and the uncompromising insistence of 1 Corinthians 5; freedom and discipline both have their place.

The goal of ethical preaching must finally be more about practice than about understanding; motivation for doing is more important than sophistication of articulation. Knowing how to connect the fine biblical sentiments with the realities on the ground that surround us is a vital kind of practical wisdom that must be cultivated.

Finally, ethical preaching will need to manifest humility. In a wider cultural context allergic to all forms of certainty, which wants to give a place to all options, it takes bravery or foolishness to speak out with confidence about how people should live. I believe we are called to do so, but we must not claim to know more than we do know and we must not claim for ourselves the last word in interpretative authority. In some matters there is an appropriate tentativeness. In some matters there is a place for recognizing plurality of Christian understanding. Core certainties should not be confused with any need for a rigid total package. In our rapidly changing times we need to find our way forward together in relation to challenges that have not come our way before.

14. PREACHING HOPE AND JUDGMENT

Stephen Travis

'I believe in Jesus Christ . . . [who] will come to judge the living and the dead . . . [and in] the resurrection of the body, and the life everlasting.' In various places I have asked people how often they have heard anyone preaching on these great themes. Even where the Apostles' Creed is regularly used in worship, the usual answer is, 'Hardly at all, except for a few words of comfort at a funeral.'

Of course, in some churches there is thoughtful and exciting preaching on these topics. But why such hesitation elsewhere? We may suggest a number of causes, some in the Western culture that surrounds us, and some that arise within ourselves.

Challenges from our culture

First, in a world where God for many is a distant memory there are no absolutes, no judge standing over us to whom we are ultimately accountable. People think of themselves as autonomous, free to act as they choose. If you don't believe in traffic wardens, you won't expect to find a parking ticket on your windscreen! Add to this a scepticism about survival beyond death, and the feeling grows that judgment is meaningless, an archaic idea best confined to medieval cathedrals.

Secondly, many assume that the account scientists give of the origin and end of the universe is the only story to be told. A theological account is dismissed as mere fantasy. To speak of the future coming of Christ smacks to them of a 'supernatural' or 'interventionist' theology that makes no sense within their world view. They refuse to entertain the possibility that there may be complementary stories that express reality from different perspectives. A kiss can be described in purely material terms, but any lover would protest that this explains only a small part of the truth. Similarly, prominent scientists who are Christians are able to hold together their scientific understanding of the world's future and their Christian hope of the world's ultimate transformation.[1]

Challenges from within ourselves

Preachers may be diffident about preaching on judgment out of a reaction to the sometimes unbalanced approach of previous generations. God was sometimes portrayed as the worst kind of nineteenth-century headmaster, devoid of compassion and eager to punish children severely for the slightest misdemeanour.

Some preachers may lack confidence in the biblical message itself, asking themselves, 'Can I really believe that God will raise the dead to life in a transformed universe? If I tell people we must all face judgment from God, will they think I am just weird? How "literal" or "metaphorical" is the Bible's language about the future? How can I answer the questions that people ask when topics such as the second coming of Christ and divine judgment come up? Among evangelicals there are conflicting views about such matters as the millennium and the nature of hell, so what chance have I got of making it all clear to others or even to myself? Am I at heart a universalist?'

Yet if we duck the challenge of preaching on themes so central to biblical faith we are, as Paul might say, 'of all people most to be pitied' (1 Cor. 15:19). Through prayerful study and discussion we must grapple with what we believe and why we believe it.[2]

---

1. See e.g. J. Polkinghorne, *The God of Hope and the End of the World* (London: SPCK, 2002); J. Polkinghorne and M. Welker (eds.), *The End of the World and the Ends of God* (Harrisburg: Trinity Press International, 2000); D. Wilkinson, *Christian Eschatology and the Physical Universe* (London: T. & T. Clark, 2010).

2. The last section includes some of the additional books that have helped me in this process.

Strategies for preaching

Eschatology, the doctrine of the 'last things', is not a ragbag of miscellaneous topics. It is about the climax of God's purpose for the world, and the different elements in it find their unity in Christ himself. It is rooted in the Old Testament, as Paul insisted in Acts 26:6: 'because of my hope in what God has promised our ancestors . . . I am on trial today' (Acts 26:6). Christ's final coming will mark the completion of what he began in Bethlehem, Galilee and Jerusalem. Judgment is essentially an assessment of human beings in the light of their response to Christ. Resurrection is the destiny of all who are united with the risen Christ. And the resurrection of human beings is only part of the renewal of the universe, of which Christ, in harmony with God the Father, is Creator, Sustainer and Lord (Col. 1:15–20). So our essential purpose in preaching will be to do as follows:

- *To teach these great truths*, sometimes by expounding a passage focusing on some of these key elements, sometimes by unravelling the muddles and answering the questions in people's minds.
- *To inspire action.* Often in the teaching of Jesus and Paul a doctrine is affirmed as a motive for action, while the main focus is on appeal to active response. Jesus' parables often work like this. And we find Paul responding to a doctrinal question about death and the future coming of Christ (1 Thess. 4:13–18), before portraying the lifestyle that should flow from the truth he has explained (5:1–11).
- *To stir the imagination.* A credal statement can summarize the essence of a doctrine, but an image, a parable, a story will fix it in the heart and mind. Think of the images Jesus used to speak of the kingdom of God, or the portrayal of the new heavens and new earth in Revelation 21 – 22. Learn from writers like C. S. Lewis who appeal to people's imagination as well as to their more rational selves.[3]
- Where a lectionary is used or a biblical book is worked through in a series of sermons, use the opportunities this presents to face – rather than skirt round – the more controversial issues. Particularly where the congregation is of various theological hues this enables the preacher to explore, for example, the theme of judgment without

---

3. See e.g. C. S. Lewis, *The Great Divorce* (London: Geoffrey Bles, 1946); T. Hart, 'Eschatology and Imagination', in S. Holmes and R. Rook (eds.), *What Are We Waiting For?* (Milton Keynes: Paternoster, 2008), pp. 127–137.

being accused of deliberately choosing the theme in order to 'get at them'!

We come now in more detail to our two great topics.

Preaching hope

The key themes

On several issues there are significantly different traditions of interpretation. I cannot deal with them here in detail, but comment on some briefly before coming to the main themes.[4]

First is the issue of eschatological language, and where we stand on the 'literal–figurative' spectrum. For example, when we say 'Christ will come,' how do we envisage that? Some have seen such language as pure mythology, or as referring simply to Christ's 'coming to us spiritually' in our own experience. Others, taking it quite literally, describe the event in precise detail, as though they have already seen the official film of it. It seems to me important not to assert too little about Christ's coming – it is a real event in which he will be revealed to the world and will transform it. But we must also not assert too much. Eschatological language is *imaginative* language – the only language we have to describe events beyond our present experience. As Tom Wright says:

> All our language about the future . . . is like a set of signposts pointing into a bright mist. The signpost doesn't provide a photograph of what we will find when we arrive, but a true indication of the direction we should be travelling in.[5]

Secondly, Wright and others have given prominence to the view that in Mark 13:26 (and parallels) 'the Son of man coming in clouds' refers not to Jesus' final coming but to the judgment on Israel in the destruction of Jerusalem (AD 70).[6] If this is correct – and the issue remains controversial – it

---

4. I have expressed my own perspective on these issues in *Christ Will Come Again*, rev. ed. (Toronto: Clements, 2004).
5. N. T. Wright, *Surprised by Hope* (London: SPCK, 2007), p. 118. See further G. B. Caird, *The Language and Imagery of the Bible* (London: Duckworth, 1980).
6. N. T. Wright, *Jesus and the Victory of God* (London: SPCK; Minneapolis: Fortress, 1996), pp. 360–365. For discussion see C. C. Newman (ed.), *Jesus and the Restoration*

takes away one passage commonly used in preaching on the second coming.[7] Difference of opinion is nothing strange in biblical interpretation, and preachers must aim at integrity in preaching by reaching their own conclusions about the meaning of a text.

Thirdly, there are important differences of interpretation between distinctive traditions within evangelicalism. The Dispensationalist perspective (more widespread in the USA than elsewhere), with its distinctive view on how 'the last days' will unfold, is very different from the view of other evangelicals.[8] Once again, preachers must interpret with integrity in the light of their own tradition, occasionally looking over the hedge to consider what they might learn from others.

Taking the final coming of Christ as the focus of hope, I suggest that we should focus mainly on the following features.

Who will come?

The Christ who will come is not an unknown figure but one whose character we know from his first coming (see Heb. 9:28). In Revelation 5 the Lion is also the Lamb, whose suffering love we have seen and experienced. Therefore we anticipate his coming not merely with apprehension but with love and eagerness.

For what purpose will Christ come?

The main aspects of this event are as follows.

1. The completion of Christ's work begun in his earthly life. The essential continuity between his first and final comings must be affirmed, despite all the contrasts between them.

2. The judgment of all humanity (see discussion below).

3. The arrival of the 'new heaven and new earth', in which the whole cosmos will attain its full potential, evil and suffering will be over, and God's people in their resurrected bodies will live for ever in his presence (Rom. 8:18–25; Rev.

---

of Israel: A Critical Assessment of N. T. Wright's Jesus and the Victory of God (Carlisle: Paternoster; Downers Grove: InterVarsity Press, 1999).

7. But it is important to stress that on the basis of numerous other texts Wright does affirm belief in Christ's final coming: Wright, *Surprised by Hope*, pp. 129–149.

8. The Dispensationalist view is famously expounded in fictional form in the sixteen books of the 'Left Behind' series by Tim LaHaye and Jerry Jenkins (Wheaton: Tyndale House, 1995–). For a concise critique see C. C. Hill, *In God's Time: The Bible and the Future* (Grand Rapids: Eerdmans, 2002), pp. 199–209.

21:4). The New Testament does not speak of 'the end of the world' but of the new creation in which 'heaven' (the realm of God) and 'earth' (the created order) are no longer at odds with each other. And just as the earthly body of Jesus was transformed into his risen body, so the present world order will not be destroyed and replaced by the new creation, but transformed into it.

4. The resurrection of God's people (1 Cor. 15:35–57). In an era when many Christians have only a vague hope of the survival of the spirit or a hazily defined heaven, it cannot be overstressed that the distinctive language of the New Testament is that of 'resurrection'. This means nothing less than the renewal of the whole person in a bodily form suitable for the new creation. Notice Paul's magnificent contrasts between earthly life and resurrection life (1 Cor. 15:42–44). His reference there to a 'spiritual body' does not mean something *less* tangible than our earthy bodies, but a real body animated by God's Spirit.[9]

There is of course a tension between biblical texts affirming that when we die we go to be 'with Christ' (e.g. Phil. 1:23) and those that speak of a future resurrection of all together at Christ's final coming (e.g. Phil. 3:20–21). This may imply an 'intermediate state' in Christ's presence, while we await the simultaneous re-embodying of all together when Christ comes. Or it could suggest that at death we pass beyond time as it is currently experienced, so that we 'immediately' come to the resurrection and the new creation. But the important thing here is that our ultimate destiny is not individual communion with God, but a rich *communal* life in a renewed universe filled with God's presence.[10]

When will he come?

The significance of this question is often distorted by those who use the 'signs of the times' in passages such as Matthew 24, or numbers in the book of Daniel, to calculate the timing of Christ's coming. This has been attempted unsuccessfully for centuries. Most recently Harold Camping calculated that the 'rapture' (a key event in the Dispensationalist scheme) would occur on 21 May 2011. When it did not happen he admitted he had made a mathematical miscalculation, and it would in fact be on 21 October 2011!

Yet we cannot ignore the New Testament emphasis on 'soon' (Mark 13:28–30; Rev. 1:1; 22:20) and 'sudden' (Mark 13:32–37; 1 Thess. 5:2–3). Despite this

---

9. Wright, *Surprised by Hope*, pp. 167–168, and see the whole of ch. 10.
10. A. C. Thiselton, *Life After Death: A New Approach to the Last Things* (London: SPCK; Grand Rapids: Eerdmans, 2012).

language, there is no evidence that first-century Christians expected Christ's coming within a specific time frame and then were disappointed when it failed to occur. This suggests that the language of imminence expressed the vividness of the hope and the certainty of God's intentions rather than offering a timetable. It motivated Christians to focus on their response to the hope.

How then should we live in the light of this hope?
Rather than answering speculative questions about what the future entails, Jesus spoke constantly of the implications for life now. When asked, '[A]re only a few people going to be saved?' he responded, 'Make every effort to enter through the narrow door' (Luke 13:23–24). Most of his parables are not so much descriptions of God's kingdom as exhortations to grasp its implications and live accordingly. It is treasure – and it takes everything you have to be part of it (Matt. 13:44–46). Since the time of its arrival is unknown the appropriate reaction is not to speculate about a date but to get on with the tasks of service (Mark 13:32–37).

Paul of course has much to say about attitudes formed in us by our hope in Christ. Despite the devastation caused by the death of those we love, we find comfort in God's promise, unlike those 'who have no hope' (1 Thess. 4:13). The apostle who has himself faced the prospect of death and has endured all kinds of suffering has learned the secret of being content in every situation, and is set free to think about others more than about himself (Phil. 1:19–26; 4:12–13). All our values are reshaped by the prospect of resurrection.

1 Corinthians 15:58 draws further implications. Because we anticipate bodily resurrection, what we do with our bodies in the present matters. Everything we do in Christian service makes a difference – for ever. And because the destiny of this world is not to be discarded but to be renewed, and because the resurrection has already happened in Jesus' case and the power of resurrection is at work in the world, this applies equally to what we may do in the arts and sciences, in working for justice, relieving poverty, caring for the environment and campaigning for peace. Though some Christians believe that such actions are a diversion from our real task of evangelism and church building, they are all part of building for God's kingdom.[11]

Preaching the biblical hope
Below I illustrate ways in which we might preach on the Christian hope.
1. Where many have quite vague ideas about the ultimate purposes of

---

11. Wright, *Surprised by Hope*, pp. 168–169, 204–205.

God or the nature of life after death, there is great value in sermons whose main function is to *teach central truths* such as those I have just outlined. New Testament letters often teach truths the intended readers need to understand more clearly so that their lives may more fully reflect the intention of God. So a sermon drawing out key points of, for example, 1 Thessalonians 4:13 – 5:11 or 1 Corinthians 15 would be an authentic re-enactment of that process. Like Paul in those passages, we can root the sermon in the current confusion and can include some practical implications of the hope as well as an exposition of the great truths.[12] In an age when many churchgoers hear little of the future life except at funerals – when they are least able to reflect thoughtfully on the theme – I find that people welcome preaching that explores questions such as the following:

- What is the evidence on which we base our hope of resurrection?
- Why 'resurrection' rather than 'immortality'?
- When will resurrection happen – when we die or when Christ comes again?
- What will life be like in God's new world?

2. When we come to *the practical implications of our beliefs*, there are many passages that connect the content of hope with the way we live. Examples in New Testament letters are Colossians 3:1–11; 1 Peter 1:13–16; 2:11–12; 2 Peter 1:3–11; 1 John 3:1–3. And of course this is characteristic of Jesus' teaching, especially through parables, as illustrated earlier.[13] But I want to emphasize here the importance of connecting our hope for God's new world with our engagement with this world, as described in connection with 1 Corinthians 15:58 in the previous section. That is an essential part of the church's mission. The church *as community* is the 'foretaste', the 'firstfruits' (Jas 1:18), the pilot plant in which God's goal of bringing 'all things in heaven and on earth' together under Christ (Eph. 1:10) is already being accomplished. It is not simply a 'mission-shaped church' but the embodiment of an eschatology-shaped mission.[14]

---

12. One way to connect with popular confusion about life beyond death is through the ways it is treated in some significant films. For a fascinating exploration of contemporary views of death and beyond expressed in film see C. Deacy, *Screening the Afterlife: Theology, Eschatology, and Film* (Oxford: Routledge, 2011).

13. See chapter 3 of this book.

14. See N. T. Wright on 'Eschatology-Shaped Church' <http://www.

Preaching judgment

Despite the difficulties, our culture is not entirely hostile to the idea of judgment. Some of the most popular television shows are contests in which people compete, and the less competent are gradually eliminated. In education and in the workplace, assessment is part of life. And when a child molester is convicted or a brutal tyrant captured, the popular press produces headlines such as 'Let him rot in hell'. The longing for justice is never far beneath the surface. And what if there were no ultimate judgment by God? The fact that God judges us means that our actions, our choices, our character matter to him. He invests all our lives with ultimate significance. *If there is no judgment, nothing matters*: God does not care, and our significance as humans is diminished.

In Scripture God's judgment is directed on the one hand at nations and systems (e.g. Babylon in Isa. 13, Israel in Amos and Hosea, Jerusalem in Luke 21:2–24, Roman politics and economics in Revelation), and on the other hand at individuals. Judgment of individuals mostly takes place at the final judgment associated with Christ's final coming. Since this is the main focus of judgment language in the New Testament it is what we will concentrate on here. But in the light of Old Testament perspectives it is certainly worth reflecting on whether we discern God's hand of judgment in events such as the fall of the Soviet Union, the uprisings in the Arab world and the world economic crises.

The key themes
Two biblical images of judgment
Biblical writers both express and justify the prospect of divine judgment in two main ways, as follows.

1. The image of the final judgment at which all are assessed and our ultimate destinies determined. The judge is variously identified as God or Christ (cf. Rom. 14:10 with 2 Cor. 5:10; also John 5:22–23, 27–30). The conviction underlying this image is that the Creator has the right to judge his creatures, and is in the right in the way he does it. 'Will not the Judge of all the earth do right?' (Gen. 18:25). His judgment is 'based on truth', is 'righteous' and without 'favouritism' (Rom. 2:2, 5, 11).

2. Images emphasizing the intrinsic link between human choices or actions and their consequences: the outcome is inherent in the deed. We find this in

---

fulcrum-anglican.org.uk/page.cfm?ID=297>, accessed 27 June 2012. Wright, *Surprised by Hope*, ch. 14, is full of biblical material expressing this perspective, which could form the basis of many invigorating sermons.

the image of the two ways – the narrow road leads to life and the wide road leads to destruction (Matt. 7:13–14). The outcome is not so much an externally imposed reward or punishment as the inevitable destination of the road chosen. The way judgment works, according to John 3:19–20, is that those who 'love darkness' bring judgment upon themselves by refusing to turn to the light of Christ. In Romans 1:18–32 Paul portrays the 'wrath of God' as the outworking of human refusal to live as the Creator intended. Three times Paul says that because of this refusal 'God gave them over . . .' (vv. 24, 26, 28). People abandon God; therefore he allows them to experience the consequences of their own choice.[15] In this sense God's judgment means that we get what we want.

The criterion of judgment

Consistently the New Testament teaches that we are judged 'according to what [we] have done' (e.g. Matt. 16:27; Rom. 2:6–11; Rev. 22:12). But alongside this we find Jesus asserting that our destiny is determined by whether we identify with him and his message (Matt. 10:32–33) or believe in him (John 3:18). Though these perspectives – judgment according to deeds and according to trust in Jesus – may seem confusing, they are not contradictory. To be 'saved' or 'justified' through faith in Jesus means to be brought into a right relationship with God, within which one experiences God's power at work. Like any gift, it is ours only if we receive and use it. The only kind of faith Paul approves is the faith that shows its reality by the fruit it produces – 'faith expressing itself through love' (Gal. 5:6). At the final judgment our deeds will be the evidence, or otherwise, of the genuineness of our trust in Christ.

The outcome of judgment

The final judgment will mean division between those who are revealed to belong truly to Christ and those who are not (Matt. 10:32–33; 25:31–46; Rom. 2:6–11). It will underline the self-judgment that people have chosen during the present life by their seeking or rejecting a relationship with God through Christ. Those who are condemned will be excluded 'from the presence of the Lord' (2 Thess. 1:9), while those who are in Christ 'will be with the Lord for

---

15. See e.g. J. D. G. Dunn, *Romans 1–8*, WBC (Dallas: Word, 1988), pp. 65, 73–76; S. H. Travis, *Christ and the Judgement of God* (Milton Keynes: Paternoster; Peabody: Hendrickson, 2009), pp. 60–62. The NT's expressions of intrinsic judgment are a major theme of my book.

ever' (1 Thess. 4:17; cf. the imagery of 'come' and 'depart from me' in Matt. 25:34, 41).

What form does exclusion from God's presence take? We come here to the difficult question of the nature of hell. Many take Jesus' references to 'unquenchable fire', 'the darkness outside', 'Gehenna', 'eternal punishment' and imagery elsewhere such as Revelation's 'lake of fire' as an indication that the destiny of those condemned is everlasting conscious torment. Others suggest that the imagery of 'destruction' – Paul's normal way of speaking about the same issue – suggests 'annihilation', whereby those cut off from the presence of God are not held in conscious punishment but simply cease to be.[16] Though this is an important debate, it risks downplaying the real focus of the New Testament – that those without Christ will be *cut off from him.* Compared with that tragedy, the question as to whether or not they continue in conscious existence is far less significant.

Will God bring all people into his presence?

An increasingly popular view is that God will ultimately forgive and accept all humanity into his eternal presence – either because in his love he simply decrees that this will be so, or because he will give people after death repeated opportunities to repent until they freely choose to respond in love to God's unfailing love. What sensitive Christian would not find this view attractive? And we must remember that we are not dealing here with a theoretical question, but with the destinies of people we know and love.

Rob Bell has attempted to show sensitivity to such issues in *Love Wins,*[17] and has been vilified by many for embracing universalism (as this view is known). Careful reading of the book will show that, though he explores universalism and the motives underlying it (ch. 4), he does not affirm it. His style is not always to give answers but to provoke thought, to raise questions and challenge old stereotypes that have become too comfortable. Does he not have a precedent for this in Jesus himself? So, while he sometimes leaves himself open to the criticism of being unclear or misleading, we can be thankful when

---

16. A classic presentation of the case for annihilation is E. A. Fudge, *The Fire that Consumes: The Biblical Case for Conditional Immortality* (Carlisle: Paternoster, 1994). A recent defence of 'eternal torment' is C. W. Morgan and R. A. Peterson (eds.), *Hell Under Fire* (Grand Rapids: Zondervan, 2004).

17. R. Bell, *Love Wins: At the Heart of Life's Big Questions* (New York: HarperCollins, 2011).

his sensitivity to people's real questions provokes deep thought about these issues.

Paradoxically, however, universalism fails to convince because it distorts the nature of love, which, by definition, never forces itself on its object. God's love for humanity implies that he gives us genuine freedom to accept or reject his love. The real possibility of condemnation cannot be denied except by denying the reality of human freedom and responsibility. If it is objected that for anyone to be in 'hell' would be a defeat for God, we should consider C. S. Lewis's reply:

> What you call defeat, I call miracle: for to make things which are not Itself and thus to be, in a sense, capable of being resisted by its own handiwork, is the most astounding and unimaginable of all the feats we attribute to the Deity.[18]

There are many questions for which we have no definitive answer. What about those who have never heard the gospel? Or those who have encountered only a confused Christian witness? What about those who die in childhood? But with confidence we can say that God is not arbitrary or unjust. He understands our hearts, and the circumstances in which we live and react to his love. Sometimes we have to hand over to him the questions that trouble us, the people we are concerned for, and entrust them to his holy love. And Jesus himself warned that the judgment would bring surprises (Matt. 25:31–46).

Judgment for Christians

In Greek as in English 'to judge', as well as meaning 'to condemn' may also refer to an assessment or discrimination without necessarily implying a negative outcome. No one escapes that final appraisal. '[W]e must all appear before the judgment seat of Christ' (2 Cor. 5:10). For those who are found faithful there is a welcome into God's eternal presence. Sometimes there is talk of 'reward' (e.g. Matt. 5:12; 1 Cor. 3:15). But no text that uses this word specifies whether it means anything over and above salvation itself, so it is unwise to speculate about 'degrees of reward' as has sometimes been done. Perhaps the 'reward' is equivalent to 'praise from God' (1 Cor. 4:5), or the joy of seeing that one's service to God lasts into eternity (1 Cor. 3:5–15; 15:58; 1 Thess. 2:19–20). Therefore we make it our aim 'to please . . . God, who tests our hearts' (1 Thess. 2:4).

---

18. C. S. Lewis, *The Problem of Pain* (London: Fontana, 1957), p. 115.

Preaching the judgment of God

For Jesus and the New Testament writers judgment is not the last word: it is followed by good news and the invitation to turn to Christ. No preaching, therefore, should focus relentlessly on judgment to the exclusion of the promise of grace.

1. An evangelistic message will have good reason to warn of the danger of facing judgment, but not at the expense of a positive portrayal of Jesus as Saviour. Hell is not God's *intended* destiny for any human being. It is a negative realm, the *absence* of everything God wants human experience to be. Hence the gospel imagery of 'the darkness outside', the closed door, the road to destruction, being 'lost' rather than 'found', 'dead' rather than 'alive'. Those vivid gospel images – and sometimes images we create ourselves – are likely to communicate more effectively than the more abstract language of theological discussion.

2. An apologetic sermon could respond to questions that are often in people's minds:

- Is God a cosmic sadist? An answer could show that the biblical God is not a sadistic headmaster who delights in punishment, but the God of love who wants people to live fulfilled, wholesome and generous lives and to find peace with him through the self-giving of Jesus Christ. The Bible does not portray hell as a torture chamber set up for God's pleasure, but as the absence of all that gives meaning to human existence. It is a terrible thing to be without God.
- Is God unfair to human beings? No, for we bring judgment on ourselves. To use Jesus' images – if we do not respond to the light, we stay in darkness. If we will not come to the feast, we stay hungry. No one can make their children love them. If they could, it would not be love.
- What about those who have never heard of Christ or for other reasons cannot thoughtfully consider the Christian message? The God made known in Jesus is just and all-knowing and will treat them in the light of this.
- If addressed mainly to Christians, a final section might offer guidance on the hard question of friends and family who are not believers – love, pray, offer the problem to God, who loves them even more than we do. If addressed to a wider audience, the final section would express the good news and invite a response – perhaps using the vivid imagery and personal challenge of John 3:16–21.

3. A passage such as Luke 3:7–20 offers the opportunity to express the bad news – the coming judgment on human sin (v. 7), the far-reaching nature of real repentance (vv. 8–14) – and the good news of the promise of a Saviour (vv. 8–18). (And if we get some flak for proclaiming this robust message, we are in good company: vv. 19–20!)

4. The three parables of Matthew 25 – each of which has an element of judgment and separation – could be seen as challenging us to live in the light of Christ's coming as Judge and Saviour, asking, 'What are you doing with Jesus' challenge to be right with God?' (vv. 1–13); 'What are you doing with the good news entrusted to you?' (vv. 14–30); 'What are you doing about the poor and despised, in whom Jesus himself confronts you?' (vv. 31–46).

Conclusion

Beside the rickety pulpit in the thirteenth-century church of St Ursanne, Switzerland, is a notice: 'It is dangerous to enter this pulpit.' To preach on hope and judgment certainly entails hazards and challenges. Yet the themes themselves provide not only the content but also the motivation for preaching: 'In the presence of God and of Christ Jesus, who will judge the living and the dead, and in view of his appearing and his kingdom . . . Preach the word' (2 Tim. 4:1–2).

Further reading

Other helpful books not cited in the text are as follows:

BAUCKHAM, R., and HART, T., *Hope Against Hope: Christian Eschatology in Contemporary Context* (London: Darton Longman & Todd, 1999).

EVANGELICAL ALLIANCE COMMISSION ON UNITY AND TRUTH AMONG EVANGELICALS, *The Nature of Hell* (London: Evangelical Alliance, 2000).

PARRY, R. A., and PARTRIDGE, C. H. (eds.), *Universal Salvation? The Current Debate* (Carlisle: Paternoster, 2003).

THE HERMENEUTICS OF RELATIONSHIP:
THEOLOGICAL UNDERSTANDING FOR NEW
TESTAMENT PREACHING

William Olhausen

Introduction

Most of the other chapters in this book deal with the particular challenges and
opportunities of preaching the different parts of the New Testament and they
address some of the important interpretation issues raised by the genre or the
author under discussion. The purpose of this chapter is to take a step back
and explore more generally what is involved in attempting to understand the
New Testament and to reflect on how we then prepare for communicating
this revelation through our preaching ministry.

What is hermeneutics and what does it tell us?

Hermeneutics is the theory and practice of understanding. Traditionally, it
was concerned with the problem of understanding ancient texts, especially the
biblical texts.[1] Two intellectual preoccupations have shaped the hermeneutic

---

1. The scope of hermeneutic theorizing has now extended to all forms of
   communication, including real-time speech situations. Indeed modern linguistics,
   with its emphasis on synchronic speech, has provided rich data and modelling that

agenda: history's effects on human consciousness and the nature of language. In terms of history, the hermeneutic tradition recognizes its importance for understanding the human condition: to be human is to live at a particular point in history within a given tradition. In its more extreme form (Marxism for instance), this emphasis on the relationship between history and human identity results in a version of historical determinism. The second intellectual interest is with language. The turn to language was based on a simple philosophical critique of rationalism. What is reason if not the capacity to speak? And, if that is the case, language mediates the workings of the human mind. Answers to the big questions of being (ontology) and of knowledge (epistemology) were now to be found in the study of language because language is the lens through which we see the world.[2] Once language becomes the privileged gateway of human thought and experience it is a short step to a fully developed doctrine of linguistic relativity. In other words, the way the world is depends to a greater or lesser extent on a person's language. Not only are the authors of the New Testament removed from us in time and space, but they are removed from us in the language that mediated their world.

Taken together, history and language are at the heart of the hermeneutic challenge, to which a range of responses have been made. At one extreme are those who suggest that the problem is more apparent than real and so any gap in understanding is minimal. At the other end of the spectrum are those who claim that meaning is ultimately a chimera within a never-ending excess of symbols, which themselves exist within an arbitrary linguistic system. The first response is hermeneutically naive and the second does not take account of a sufficiently informed understanding of the way language works. Somewhere between these two extremes is space to explore the possibility, and indeed the responsibility, of reaching understanding. Through a process of careful listening in which the resources of exegesis and hermeneutics are brought to bear, our aim should be to reach a point where the horizon of the past meets the reader's own present horizon.[3]

---

can help us in making sense of texts by extending our understanding of the ways people use language. Given the foundational importance of communication to human beings it will come as no surprise to learn that hermeneutics has become a multidisciplinary project.

2. In its more extreme version, language becomes a sort of virtual world in which we are hermetically sealed off from the world.

3. Gadamer referred to this as a 'fusion of horizons' (Hans-Georg Gadamer, tr.

The value of developing a relational hermeneutic

The linguistic turn in hermeneutics is indicative of the interest shown in language in the wider world of philosophy and the social sciences. In particular, attention has turned to the way people use language in everyday life. As Joel Green has rightly noted, an emphasis on 'language in use' 'provides a potentially fruitful way for navigating between apparently competing modes of interpretation that focus on either the history behind the text, the world of the text, or the reading community in front of the text'.[4] Attention to language in use puts the focus on relationships both in the text and within the world of the preacher.[5] This contextual sensitivity to linguistic meaning has raised the profile of social science for hermeneutics. Stephen Barton explains why: 'social sciences focus attention on "synchronic" relations, that is, on the way meaning is generated by social actors related to one another by a complex web of culturally determined social systems and patterns of communication'.[6] As we will see, a relational hermeneutic is particularly helpful for the sort of understanding required of New Testament preachers. But first, we need to get a flavour for how a 'language in use' approach helps to elucidate the two horizons.

A relational hermeneutic in action
When we sit down to read the biblical texts, it is easy to assume that we are engaged in a private conversation and to forget that the life of the text as well as our own life is made up of a complex of different relational pressures. Texts and people are the product of relationships. Our language, the way we speak, is similarly determined in large part by these relationships and by our

---

J. Weinsheimer and D. G. Marshall, *Truth and Method*, 2nd rev. ed. [New York: Continuum, 2003]).

4. Joel B. Green, 'Discourse Analysis and New Testament Interpretation', in Joel B. Green (ed.), *Hearing the New Testament: Strategies for Interpretation*, 2nd ed. (Grand Rapids: Eerdmans, 2010), p. 218.

5. Gricean pragmatics remains seminal for relational pragmatics and so for relational hermeneutics. See Penelope Brown and Stephen C. Levinson, *Politeness Theory: Some Universals in Language Usage* (Cambridge: Cambridge University Press, 1987).

6. Stephen C. Barton, 'Historical Criticism and Social Scientific Perspectives in New Testament Study', in Green, *Hearing the New Testament*, p. 42. See pp. 42–50 for discussion of strengths and pitfalls of social scientific approaches to NT interpretation.

own history. Therefore, the preacher preparing a sermon, like the theologian or philosopher, can easily slip into two closely related errors of thinking. First, what has been called the 'occasionalist illusion' is when we forget that instances of language arise out of a given context of use or 'field'.[7] Whilst there is an overlap of linguistic meaning between these various contexts, there are also important differences in the way power, social and cultural factors affect the choices we make in social interaction. Consider the workplace for instance. Professional life tends to have its own conventions, rituals and expectations. Sport is another example of a social field in which there are ways of speaking and relating to each other. It is very difficult to isolate the meaning of a stretch of language or text outside its particular field or language game. Even the language used by the preacher will reflect the concerns of a given church community and also betray the preacher's own network of relations. The congregation for their part will be hearing the preacher's language through their own experience and knowledge of the world. Preaching, as with communication in general, is intrinsically relational.

The second related error, sometimes called the 'subjectivist illusion', is to forget our history. This means that much about how we feel or behave in any given situation is at a pre-conscious or pre-rational level and so we are unable to reflect fully on the relationship that exists between our history and the language we generate as historical beings. Hermeneutics can therefore help the preacher appreciate the ways in which we are conditioned by our history: the place where we have grown up, the rituals, values and practices of our home life, our education and our professional work. The name given to capture the historical identity or profile of a person is 'habitus'.[8] One leading anthropologist has described the habitus as 'the active presence of the whole past of which it is the product'.[9] Elsewhere he puts it like this: 'The body is in the social world but the social world is within the body.'[10] It is worth noting

---

7. Ken Turner introduces Bourdieu's important notions of 'fields' and the 'habitus' with reference to the Modernist fallacies of 'occasionalism' and 'subjectivism' (Ken Turner, '$W_x = D(S,H) + P(H,S) + R_x$': Notes Towards an Investigation', *Revue de Sémantique et Pragmatique* 13 [2003], pp. 47–67).

8. See Bourdieu's discussion of the habitus in Pierre Bourdieu, *In Other Words*, tr. Matthew Adamson (Cambridge: Polity, 1990), p. 131. See also idem, *Distinction: A Social Critique of the Judgment of Taste* (London: Routledge, 2004), p. 80; and idem, tr. R. Nice, *The Logic of Practice* (Cambridge: Polity, 1990), p. 56.

9. Bourdieu, *Logic of Practice*, p. 56.

10. Ibid., p. 190.

in this context that the history of a text's interpretation is a very important element not just in the self-understanding of the Christian church but also in the way certain biblical texts are read. Consider the importance of Augustine, Luther, Calvin or Barth for the Protestant church. Such is their influence that it is very difficult to imagine ourselves in a world of Christian understanding without them.

A more fine-grained understanding of the relational nature of the way meaning is generated will assist the preacher both in attending to the horizon of the New Testament texts and in interpreting their own horizon.[11] It will encourage a greater appreciation for the way human behaviour, including both positive and destructive patterns of behaviour, can be systemically embedded not just in the life of an individual but also in the life of a community or an institution. This perspective is especially important where there is a tendency for preaching to be directed at the individual rather than also addressing the church body and/or particular groupings in the church. Finally, the preacher will be more appreciative of the miraculous nature of new birth and the need for a pastoral strategy that fully appreciates the need for whole-life discipleship.

The need for a relational hermeneutic that is properly theological

Communicative action, the things people do with language, reflects both the relational and historic nature of human identity. However, there are a number of branches to hermeneutics, each with its own sources and interests.[12] Theological hermeneutics is concerned with understanding God or, at the very least, understanding what other people have understood by 'God'. Preaching certainly demands theological understanding but, most

---

11. The opening chapter of Calvin's *Institutes* is especially helpful in making the point that understanding of self and understanding of God are interrelated (John Calvin, *Institutes of the Christian Religion*, ed. J. T. McNeill, tr. and indexed F. L. Battles, 2 vols. [Philadelphia: Westminster, 1960], pp. 35–39). See also D. A. Carson, 'Preaching that Understands the World', in Christopher Green and David Jackman (eds.), *When God's Voice Is Heard: Essays on Preaching Presented to Dick Lucas* (Leicester: Inter-Varsity Press, 1995), pp. 145–160.

12. These include juridical hermeneutics, literary hermeneutics, the appropriation of hermeneutics in critical theory and, of course, theological hermeneutics. Hermeneutics also has an important role to play in the philosophy of science.

importantly, preaching has to do with communication from God: hearing God's Word. Accordingly, the question becomes 'What sort of understanding does the preacher need in order to hear the Word of God in the texts of the New Testament and, in turn, to communicate this same Word to the people of God?'

A theological hermeneutic must take account of Scripture's hermeneutic

If the preacher is to be faithful to the pages of the New Testament, then Old Testament and New Testament must be taken as one continual story of God's dealings with a world created and redeemed in love through the Word made flesh.[13] This approach is not well received in the majority of university biblical studies departments but it is faithful to the Christian tradition and is further warranted by a hermeneutic principle: listening to the text on its own terms. In allowing us to see behind the curtain, the biblical drama identifies the breakdown in relationship between God and human beings as the primary obstacle to reaching understanding. This theme, which is a consistent thread through the Old Testament and into the Gospels, bears witness to humanity's unfaithfulness to God's Word in the successive stories of the Fall, Israel's covenant unfaithfulness and, finally, Israel's rejection of her Messiah.

In hermeneutic terms, the biblical story explains that the 'gap' in understanding has been or is being bridged in two ways: first, the noetic effect of sin on our ability to respond faithfully to God's Word is, within God's providence, overcome by the revelatory agency of the Spirit, who now points us to Christ. Secondly, the presence of the Spirit in the life of the church bridges the historical distance between our horizon and the horizon of the New Testament age. We are therefore not just related to the events of the New Testament within a tradition across time but are related to these events by the Spirit's presence through and in time. To borrow Gadamer's phrase, the Spirit is the one who enables us to fuse the horizons. The whole sweep of the biblical drama provides some rich resources for a theological account of the hermeneutic problem and, in doing so, begins to provide the sort of theological hermeneutic needed for preaching the New Testament.

We move now from the big picture to a particular passage in the New Testament. How is the gospel communicated to a pagan world in the 'now' of God's favour and the 'not yet' of sin and brokenness?

---

13. For an excellent overview of the biblical story see Craig G. Bartholomew and Michael W. Goheen, *The Drama of Scripture: Finding Our Place in the Biblical Story* (Grand Rapids: Baker Academic, 2004).

Paul and the art of Christian communication

When looking for New Testament assistance in preaching, it is natural to learn from Paul. He was, after all, a witness to the resurrection, a missionary, pastor and theologian. His letters are among the earliest expressions of communicating the content and implications of the gospel. 1 Corinthians represents a particularly fruitful case study as it concerns a church community that, in many ways, reflects the sorts of issues the pastor still faces: factionalism, counterfeit spirituality, syncretism, immorality; and all this within a context of cultural and religious pluralism. The passage under consideration is 1 Corinthians 1 – 4, especially 1:18 – 2:16. It is sometimes referred to as Paul's 'message of the cross', a phrase taken from 1:18, which captures well the theological emphasis needed for a church community characterized by 'jealousy', 'strife' and 'divisions' (3:3).

The first thing to notice is that Paul's teaching is prompted by a specific pastoral problem. In 1:11 Paul explains that he has heard reports from Chloe's people about some sort of division within the church community. New Testament preaching requires not only a detailed understanding of the gospel together with a detailed understanding of the human condition; it also requires the wisdom to make the connection in real time. To put it another way, the preacher needs to consider the symptoms, make a diagnosis and administer the right medicine. This will involve using words that make sense within the congregation's experience. In other words, they must at least be clear what the medicine is for, even if they choose not to take it. The hermeneutic principle in play is relevance, another relational buzzword.[14]

Secondly, Paul's reference to the cross reminds us that the faith to which the New Testament bears witness also rests on the brute facts of history. Paul would simply not have understood the idea that matters of faith might somehow be separated from history. His teaching, in keeping with the rest of the New Testament, makes no space for a 'spiritualization' of the gospel nor for that matter can it be reduced to a version of existentialism. Language and history go together within a world that exists in relationship to and with

---

14. Taken from Gricean pragmatics, the notion of 'relevance' has been turned into a cognitive-linguistic theory in its own right. See Dan Sperber and Deirdre Wilson, *Relevance: Communication and Cognition* (Oxford: Blackwell, 1986). More recently, Stephen Pattemore has drawn on Relevance Theory for his work on Revelation (Stephen Pattemore, *The People of God in the Apocalypse: Discourse, Structure and Exegesis* [Cambridge: Cambridge University Press, 2008]).

God. The hermeneutic principle is again relational, this time with the world: meaning is dependent on things in the physical world and this too is encoded within language itself – it is part of the grammar, or logic, of Christian faith.

Thirdly, Paul's understanding of the cross is dependent on revelation.[15] We have already seen that biblical theology tells a consistent story of how sinful humanity is dependent on God's grace in order to hear and respond to his communication with us. Now again we are reminded that the cross is a word that transcends human wisdom and estimations of power. But how does revelation work? If we limit ourselves to this extended discourse, there are a number of things involved. First, Paul proclaimed the testimony about God (2:1); secondly, the cross was at the heart of this testimony; thirdly, Paul's preaching was not particularly impressive by human standards; and, finally, revelation is dependent on the Spirit's agency. The *apodeixis* of verse 4 is a demonstration or proof of God's power.[16] Whatever our particular theology of signs and wonders, in the New Testament records revelation is often accompanied by experientially dramatic episodes. It does not need to be normative but it is one of the ways in which the Spirit bears witness to the truth. If we read on, we see that the experience of the Spirit is also accompanied by the noetic effects of the Spirit's agency. Consequently, Paul speaks of a secret wisdom made known by the Spirit (2:10–11). Indeed the Spirit mediates the very mind of Christ (2:16). In this context John Stott's exhortation to preachers is worth hearing:

> Only Jesus Christ by his Holy Spirit can open blind eyes and deaf ears, make the lame walk and the dumb speak, prick the conscience, enlighten the mind, fire the heart, move the will, give life to the dead and rescue slaves from Satanic bondage . . . Therefore, our greatest need as preachers is to be 'clothed with power from on high' (Luke 24:49).[17]

The hermeneutic principle arising from the communication of revelation is again relational. This time the relational component of meaning is speaking

---

15. See also Paul's autobiographical remarks in Gal. 1:11–12.

16. The sequence of events narrated here in 1 Cor. 2:1–5 might lend support to Longenecker's reading of Gal. 3:3–5. Longenecker suggests that Gal. 3:4 be read as a positive experience linked to the Galatians' reception of the Spirit (Richard N. Longenecker, *Galatians*, WBC [Dallas: Word, 1990], pp. 103–105).

17. Stott also refers us to 1 Pet. 1:12 and 1 Thess. 1:5 (John R. W. Stott, *I Believe in Preaching* [London: Hodder & Stoughton, 1982], p. 329).

truthfully about God's salvation for the world and the presence of the Spirit. The Spirit is a participant in the preaching event to the extent that the testimony is relationally faithful, that is, true.

Fourthly, Paul's discourse takes authority seriously. This authority can be understood under two headings: institutional authority and scriptural authority. By institutional authority I mean the authority that belonged to Paul on account of his apostolic vocation (1 Cor. 1:1) and his pastoral role in the life of the church, not least as the founding pastor (1 Cor. 3:10). Whilst Paul's apostolic vocation was unique to him, the preacher today also ministers out of a vocation and is accountable to the institution of a church structure. Institutions impose their own dynamic on the meaning of Christian discourse. Despite opposition, Paul's confidence was not in himself but in the one who had called him and in the work to which he was called. This sort of confidence is completely consistent with humility. Again, the hermeneutic principle can be understood as relational. This time we see how the preacher's institutional status has an important bearing on the sermon. Institutional meaning is dependent on institutional agreement. This is why our doctrine of the church (ecclesiology) is so important and why there is so much confusion for all concerned when parts of a church depart from the received 'mind of the church'.[18]

Paul also appeals to the authority of the Scriptures (1:19, 31; 2:9, 16). There is not the space to develop the importance of the Scriptures for Paul and the other writers of the New Testament or to comment in any detail on how they were used. It is enough to iterate the need for a coherent Christocentric biblical theology. The Old Testament then becomes an essential resource for filling out Christian meaning, defending Christian revelation and telling the Christian story from creation to new creation.[19] The hermeneutic principle is the value set on history and the biblical tradition as a source of knowledge and wisdom.

---

18. Paul's comments in 1 Cor. 4:6, taken together with 4:17, represent valuable comments for any ecclesiology.

19. Paul's appeal to earlier traditions of Scripture has been understood to function in three related ways: intertextually, rhetorically and as narrative. For details see Steve Moyise, *Paul and Scripture: Studying the New Testament Use of the Old Testament* (Grand Rapids: Baker Academic, 2010), pp. 111–125. See also Thiselton's valuable discussion of the ways in which Paul cites the OT (Anthony C. Thiselton, *The First Epistle to the Corinthians*, NIGTC [Grand Rapids: Eerdmans; Carlisle: Paternoster, 2000], p. 161).

Finally, Paul employs a variety of moods in his writing. The great social anthropologist Erving Goffman talks about speakers changing their 'footing'. Each time speakers shift the topic, mood or tense of their speech it not only affects their status in the conversation (however slightly) but it also has a bearing on the way in which the listener responds.[20] So, for instance, Paul uses declarative speech, moves from 'I' to 'we', asks rhetorical questions, quotes authoritative sources, narrates shared experiences, and so on. In New Testament studies this sort of phenomenon is looked at under the topic of rhetoric. The hermeneutic insight lies in the dynamic nature of communicative action and the complexity of a speech situation that moves far beyond the rudimentary theories of communication that simply posit a speaker and a hearer (or a 'sender' and a 'receiver').[21] When it comes to preaching, the idea of a conversation is much nearer the reality than monologue or even dialogue. Having considered aspects of Paul's discourse, we need to see how and in what way this teaching was backed up by the character of his life.

Grace, wisdom and love in Paul's theology of the cross: Christlike character as part of a theological hermeneutic

The hermeneutic tradition insists that intellect is not a sufficient resource for reaching understanding. We also need to cultivate empathy: empathy for a text or for other people. A theological hermeneutic will also insist on the need for empathy with God. But what does empathy look like? 1 Corinthians 4 concludes the section dealing with the reports brought by Chloe's people in which Paul has drawn heavily on a theology of the cross. It is a difficult passage but it continues to give some valuable insights into Paul's character, insights that demonstrate a range of essential practices for a theological hermeneutic beneficial to the task of preaching. Most importantly of all, Paul understood his life to be a participation 'in Christ' (4:17). Paul's character reflects this inti-

---

20. Erving Goffman, *Forms of Talk* (Philadelphia: University of Pennsylvania, 1981), p. 133.

21. Searlean speech-act theory makes this mistake. For example see Dascal's critique of the monological tendencies in speech-act theory (Marcelo Dascal, 'Speech Act Theory and Gricean Pragmatics: Some Differences of Detail that Make a Difference', in S. L. Tsohatzidis [ed.], *Foundations of Speech Act Theory: Philosophical and Linguistic Perspectives* [London: Routledge, 1994], pp. 323–334).

mate relationship so that his very anthropology becomes Christlike.[22] I want to draw attention to just three benefits of this relationship. First, Paul, who himself had an experience and knowledge of grace, insists that grace is the starting point for all of us (1 Cor. 4:7).[23] Grace reminds us that we stand on level ground with the rest of humanity and so it fosters gratitude towards God and generosity towards others. Preaching is premised on grace and, indeed, has grace as its subject matter.

Secondly, being 'in Christ' inevitably involves a sharing in his sufferings. For instance, in 1 Corinthians 4:9 Paul describes his own suffering in terms that reflect the cross. The hermeneutic pay off here is wisdom. In ways that are perhaps unfathomable for us to comprehend, sharing in Christ's suffering yields the sort of wisdom found nowhere else, which is precisely the sort of wisdom that authentic and mature New Testament preaching demands. The cross provides a vantage point from where we can best see and evaluate the world, enabling us to pass righteous judgment on human culture in its entirety. This critical function is possible because the cross tells us most clearly about God's love and truth and, at the same time, it tells us most clearly about the human condition and the world's need. Wisdom is the biblical equivalent of the hermeneutic interest in 'judgment', and sound judgments are no doubt the fruit of wisdom. Another fruit of cruciform wisdom is humility, and humility teaches us to cultivate dependence on God.[24] Prayer too as an expression of dependence is an essential practice of theological hermeneutics.

Thirdly, as well as grace and wisdom the preacher must cultivate a ministry exercised in love. This involves the preacher in acknowledging his or her position of power. Social scientists have made us painfully aware of the nature of power, and especially the abuse of power, in and through institutions. In this respect the preacher is vulnerable. Paul's bruising relationship with Corinth might have left him unable to sustain an appropriate pastoral relationship with the church. However, such was the depth of his understanding of Christ's love revealed in the cross that he was able to be a loving parent to Timothy (4:17) and also a concerned parent to the wayward church (4:14). Whilst paternal language may be out of place now, in chapter 13 of the letter Paul sets out perhaps the most powerful definition of love found in all of literature. And,

---

22. This communion with Christ may be another way of seeing how the hermeneutic gap of language and history is resolved.

23. For Paul, 'grace' is often shorthand for the gospel. See e.g. Rom. 3:24; 1 Cor. 1:4; 2 Cor. 5:17 – 6:1; Gal. 2:20–21.

24. In this context Phil. 2:1–5 is especially relevant.

of course, the character and quality of the love described by Paul entails the whole fruit of the Spirit. Paul's example sets before us a trinitarian pattern: a life lived in and for Christ in the power of the Spirit to the glory of God the Father.

Conclusion

Having identified history and language to be the central concerns of hermeneutics, we saw how communicative meaning between people is not only affected by their history but is also disciplined, to a large extent, by a whole series of relational concerns reflected in the way people use language. Whilst the relational quality of understanding is also a central theme of the biblical story, the relationship in view is between human beings and God. The resources needed to overcome the 'gap' in understanding the divine Word are found, after Pentecost, in a revelation of God's grace in Christ. In the light of hermeneutic concerns, a discussion of Paul's word of the cross identified a number of elements in his discourse that are indicative of faithful New Testament preaching.

16. THE ROLE OF EXEGESIS AND BIBLICAL TEXTS IN PREACHING THE NEW TESTAMENT: ENGAGING WITH THE 'NEW HOMILETIC'

Helge Stadelmann

Homiletical theory has been fluctuating between text orientation and listener orientation for almost a hundred years. When the influence of Barthian theology and homiletics became dominant in German-speaking Europe from the 1920s onwards, text orientation prevailed for about four decades. Preaching was understood to be the proclamation of God's Word, occurring in the process of the faithful exposition of a biblical text whenever God willed to speak through it to the hearts of the listeners.[1]

In the course of the so-called empirical turn of homiletics since the late 1960s, the centre of gravity moved from the biblical text to the contemporary context: preaching now no longer meant in the first place expounding a text and applying it to the listeners, but conducting a conversation with the listeners about their lives on the basis of an idea that might have been derived from a biblical text or from other sources.[2] The main focus moved

---

1. K. Barth, 'Das Wort Gottes als Aufgabe der Theologie', *Christliche Welt* 36 (1922), pp. 858–872; *Homiletik: Wesen und Vorbereitung der Predigt* (Zürich: TVZ, 1966 [orig. 1933]).

2. D. Rössler, 'Das Problem der Homiletik', *Theologia Practica* 1 (1966), pp. 14–28; E. Lange, *Predigen als Beruf*, ed. R. Schloz (Munich: Chr. Kaiser, 1982), pp. 58, 65; G. Otto, *Predigt als rhetorische Aufgabe* (Neukirchen-Vluyn: Neukirchener, 1987),

from the question of 'what' to preach (formerly: the biblical text applied in Christ-centred perspective) to questions such as 'how', to 'whom', 'in what situation' and 'for what purpose' to preach.[3] The modalities and recipients of the sermon became prominent. In addition, in the course of reader- or listener-oriented hermeneutics the sense-generating capacity was translocated from the text to the reader (i.e. the preacher as exegete), and then from the preacher and his sermon to the creative listeners, whose listening product did not necessarily need to coincide with the original meaning of the sermon or the biblical text.[4] Underlying these changes were hermeneutical developments that no longer differentiated between the *meaning* of a text, determined by the original intention of the author as expressed in the signs of the text within a given context, and its varying *significance* for different people (even sometimes for its author at later points of time!), resulting in quite diverse *applications* in changing circumstances.[5] Rather – as part of the postmodern paradigm – 'meaning' was now seen as something changing in ever-new encounters between a text and its different readers. These developments tended to undermine the importance of the biblical text and thorough exegesis for contemporary preaching, placing increasing emphasis on aspects of communication and reception.[6]

Even so, even as late as in the mid-1980s, European Protestant theology was – from a North American perspective – characterized as not allowing enough listener orientation in homiletics. As Fred Craddock put it:

---

pp. 16, 50; M. Nicol, *Grundwissen Praktische Theologie* (Stuttgart: Kohlhammer, 2000), p. 87.

3. E. Lange, 'Zur Theorie und Praxis der Predigtarbeit', in E. Lange, P. Krusche and D. Rössler (eds.), *Zur Theorie und Praxis der Predigtarbeit: Predigtstudien. Beiheft 1* (Stuttgart: Kreuz, 1968), pp. 44–45.

4. G. M. Martin, 'Predigt als "offenes Kunstwerk". Zum Dialog zwischen Homiletik und Rezeptionsästhetik', *EvT* 44 (1984), pp. 46–58.

5. One of the most prominent advocates of this differentiation between meaning and significance being E. D. Hirsch, *Validity in Interpretation* (New Haven: Yale, 1967), p. 8: '*Meaning* is that which is represented by a text; it is what the author meant by his use of a particular sign sequence; it is what the signs represent. *Significance*, on the other hand, names a relationship between that meaning and a person, or a conception, or a situation, or indeed anything imaginable' (his italics); cf. e.g. pp. 140–144.

6. Of course, there have been attempts to re-emphasize the role of the biblical text for Christian preaching; e.g. H. Hirschler, *Biblisch Predigen* (Hannover: Lutherisches Verlagshaus, 1988).

The Protestant tradition as it continues to prevail in Europe, although with some modifications here and there, not only places preaching at the center of the church . . . but also warns against allowing the listeners too large a place in the sermon. In America, that tradition has undergone a great deal of change . . . The American pulpit has sought in many ways to make the congregation more ingredient to preaching.[7]

Since the early 1970s Craddock has been one of the most influential figures in the rise of the so-called New Homiletic, which set the trend for the next decades.[8]

Of course, text orientation and listener orientation, theological content and skilful presentation need not be mutually exclusive! But while half a century ago the relativizing effects of radical historical-critical hermeneutics tended to discourage the preaching of biblical texts,[9] today occasionally it is homiletical theory that assigns a minor role to the biblical text in sermon preparation.

---

7. Fred B. Craddock, *Preaching* (Nashville: Abingdon, 1985), p. 39.

8. Influential proponents of the New Homiletic are Fred B. Craddock, *As One Without Authority*, 4th rev. ed. (St. Louis, Mo.: Chalice, 2001); *Preaching*; Eugene L. Lowry, *The Homiletical Plot: The Sermon as Narrative Art Form*, expanded ed. (Louisville: Westminster John Knox, 2001); *The Sermon: Dancing the Edge of Mystery* (Nashville: Abingdon, 1997); David Buttrick, *Homiletic: Moves and Structures* (Philadelphia: Fortress; London: SCM, 1987); Thomas G. Long, *The Witness of Preaching*, 2nd ed. (Louisville: Westminster John Knox, 2005); *Preaching and the Literary Forms of the Bible* (Philadelphia: Fortress, 1989); Richard Lischer, *The Preacher King: Martin Luther King Jr. and the Word that Moved America* (Oxford: Oxford University Press, 1995); Lucy A. Rose, *Sharing the Word: Preaching in the Roundtable Church* (Louisville: Westminster John Knox, 1997); Mike Graves, *The Sermon as Symphony: Preaching the Literary Forms of the New Testament* (Valley Forge: Judson, 1997); Jana Childers, *Performing the Word: Preaching as Theatre* (Nashville: Abingdon, 1998); James W. Thompson, *Preaching Like Paul: Homiletical Wisdom for Today* (Louisville: Westminster John Knox, 2001); Ronald J. Allen, *Preaching: An Essential Guide* (Nashville: Abingdon, 2002); Paul S. Wilson, *Preaching and Homiletical Theory* (St. Louis, Mo.: Chalice, 2004).

9. In the late 1960s Rudolf Bohren complained about the discrepancy between students' pathos in exegetical seminars and their lameness in the pulpit: 'After he has buried the text by means of historical criticism he is supposed to awaken it again existentially. No wonder that the preacher becomes desperate here, and in many cases will either leave preaching or the method' (R. Bohren, *Dem Worte folgen* [Munich: Siebenstern, 1969], pp. 65–66 [my tr.]; cf. ibid., p. 73).

Within the New Homiletic some disparity can be felt between highly creative proposals concerning the form and presentation of the sermon and a certain reluctance concerning the role of text and exegesis in their preparation and substance. Certainly, this varies from proponent to proponent. But a volume on 'Preaching the New Testament' is well advised to take a closer look at this subject.

The uneven balance between text and listener in the homiletics of Fred Craddock

The New Homiletic started out as a post-1968 movement envisioning the preacher 'as one without authority'.[10] Fred Craddock, initiator of this new approach to homiletics, was convinced that emancipated modern people would only accept and trust a preacher who no longer proclaimed eternal truths from the pulpit derived deductively from a holy text. Instead, he must start inductively, with the situation of the audience, being attentive to their insights, involving them in a mental dialogue, and enabling them to come up with their own results – with the consequence that the sermon is not completed by the mouth of the preacher, but by the ear of the listener.[11]

Starting with the listeners and their situation and ending with the listeners and their new hearing of an ancient text became typical for the New Homiletic. It is no accident that in elaborating on the twin tasks of interpreting the listeners and interpreting the biblical text as prerequisites of the sermon, Craddock starts with the listeners and their contexts.[12] To be sure, any efficient preacher preparing for the pulpit has to gain a detailed knowledge of his listeners, no matter what his homiletical theory is. But to begin with the listeners entails the dangers of (1) reflecting on them in too general a way, and (2) then viewing the text from the outset too one-sidedly from the perspective of those supposed listener concerns. On the other hand, starting with the biblical text and exegeting it to uncover its originally intended meaning gives the text a chance to speak first – and then the preacher can look in depth at where his topic coincides with real-life situations, questions and concerns of the members of a congregation.

---

10. Thus the programme and title of the ground-breaking book by Craddock, *As One Without Authority*.

11. Ibid., pp. 5–6, 14–15, 17, 26–27, 44–55, 104.

12. Craddock, *Preaching*, pp. 84–98, 125.

As interpreter of the text the pastor is advised by Craddock to follow normal procedures:[13] repeated reading of the selected text, solving textual problems, ascertaining that the text selected is a thematic unit, examining it in its different (historical, literary, theological) contexts. In this exegetical procedure Craddock follows a certain hermeneutical middle position: the exegete should not disregard the writer's intention, but rather be sensitive to it; on the other hand, the author's intention should not be the sole canon of interpretation, since texts contain a surplus of meaning, not being exhausted by any prior understanding, or even by the original intention.[14] Here the emancipation of the reader from the text begins. The interpreter is advised to enter a 'process of withdrawing from the text and recovering [his] distance from it',[15] deciding whether he wants to side with the text in its canonical end-form or with previous levels, whether he wants to side with the author or not, and finally deciding on how in short statements to formulate in his own words what the text is saying and doing. This last element seems like good advice: even if an interpreter sticks more strictly to the authorial intention of the canonical end-form of the text than Craddock does, he still would want (1) to formulate its message (what the text is saying), and (2) to consider – even adhere to – what the text is doing (i.e. whether it is narrating, explaining, informing, celebrating, etc.).

If Craddock's advice for exegesis already contains a reader-oriented subjective element, his next interpretative step on the way towards the sermon deepens that. The interpreter's task now is to negotiate, to go back and forth, between the listeners and the text in order to narrow the gulf between them.[16] In this process 'new hearings' of the canonical text are thought to be possible, because the canon is closed only historically; theologically it is deemed still to be open. What others would call 'progressive revelation' within the canon is seen by Craddock as ever new interpretation by the people of God; correspondingly, preachers today are invited to come up with new interpretations of Scripture within their congregations.[17] Such interpretation for Craddock is always the particular understanding of a text for someone somewhere.[18] Meaning thus becomes particular and subjective in this type of hermeneutics,

---

13. Ibid., pp. 99–124.
14. Ibid., p. 115.
15. Ibid., p. 117 (cf. pp. 117–124).
16. Ibid., pp. 125–150.
17. Ibid., pp. 128–129.
18. Ibid., p. 136.

and homiletics becomes postmodern. The balance between the text and the reader or listener tips towards the latter.[19]

This tendency continues into the actual sermon. Though Craddock developed his homiletics as a New Testament professor, the exposition of holy texts was not his first concern.[20] 'Expository or biblical preaching has been found guilty of archaism, sacrificing the present to the past.'[21] Rather than starting deductively with an authoritative text and a thesis broken down into sermonic 'points', moving from exposition to application, the sermon should move inductively from experience to deliberation to truth emerging in the conscience of the listener.[22] Now if this were only a strategy trying to win a post-1968 generation for the gospel, with the goal of leading them into the Scriptures,

---

19. As a NT scholar Fred Craddock had taken over the 'New Hermeneutic' of his day. During a sabbatical at Tübingen he encountered Gerhard Ebeling and Ernst Fuchs and their hermeneutical approach, and was heavily influenced by them. See Dawn Ottoni-Wilhelm, 'New Hermeneutic, New Homiletic, and New Directions', in Alexander Deeg and Martin Nicol (eds.), *Bibelwort und Kanzelsprache: Homiletik und Hermeneutik im Dialog* (Leipzig: EVA, 2010), pp. 51–52; cf. Scott M. Gibson, 'Critique of the New Homiletic: Examining the Link Between the New Homiletic and the New Hermeneutic', in Haddon Robinson and Craig B. Larson (eds.), *The Art and Craft of Biblical Preaching* (Grand Rapids: Zondervan, 2005), pp. 476–477. Drawing on this kerygma theology, Craddock tends to emphasize the revelatory quality of the spoken Word of God over against the written Word: he sees an inherent danger in the latter becoming a paper pope (*As One Without Authority*, pp. 32–33, 35–36).

20. This seems to be true even though Craddock surely calls for preachers to have regular study times. In his book *Preaching* he has an excellent chapter on 'The Life of Study' of the pastor (pp. 69–83). Studying does not take the pastor away from his pastoral duties; rather, it is part of his pastoral work. The pastor mentally takes his flock with him into his study room. Here 'in small time slots' he will certainly read brief journal articles and check biblical references and lexical articles (p. 78). But his regular reading will be good literature: novels, short stories, poetry, because it 'enlarges one's capacities as a creative human being and has a cumulative effect on one's vocabulary, use of the language, and powers of imagination' (p. 79). As part of his study time the pastor should also attend workshops and seminars to address his weaknesses as well as his strengths. The cumulative fruit of his studies will result in creative ideas for the pulpit and enhance all aspects of his pastoral life.

21. Craddock, *As One Without Authority*, p. 17.

22. Ibid., pp. 44–45; cf. p. 100.

Craddock's approach would seem to be analogous to the apostle Paul's strategy of proclaiming the gospel to the heathen of his day, starting with their experience of nature or religion, but finally leading them to the gospel message and its scriptural basis (Acts 14:15–17; 17:22–31). But this seems not to be the case. Even though Craddock once remarks in passing that 'the Scriptures are normative in the life of the church' (as the historical canonical document), and that 'Sermons not informed and inspired by Scripture are objects dislodged, orphans in the world, without mother and father',[23] the biblical text does not seem to play the predominant role for him in the sermon. Certainly, he views the text as the ground out of which the unifying idea of a sermon emerges.[24] Biblical texts are seen as examples of former proclamation when in specific situations the church, led by the Spirit of God, came to certain conclusions – which should be an example for the church today.[25] But the decisive point for Craddock is that *sermons* should achieve today what the *text* achieved then – no matter whether they actually interact with the text or loosely walk alongside the text, or whether a reference to some text is just implied by the preacher.[26] Craddock does not clearly specify where and how biblical texts might have their place in an inductive sermon.[27] However directly or indirectly Bible texts may be used, they are thought to serve as catalysts in given situations to bring about fresh experiences of the occurrence of God's Word:

> In this encounter with the text, the Word of God is not simply the content of the
> tradition, nor an application of that content to present issues, but rather the Word

---

23. Craddock, *Preaching*, p. 27.

24. Craddock, *As One Without Authority*, pp. 80–85.

25. Ibid., pp. 96–101.

26. Craddock, *Preaching*, p. 28.

27. In the 2001 reprint of his book *As One Without Authority* Fred Craddock added four appendices with sample sermons (pp. 131–156). To each of them a Bible passage is assigned: Rom. 11:33–36; Mark 4:34–41; Luke 1:26–38; Mark 16:8. But these texts never actually become visible in the sermon. The central idea obviously derives from the text, but beyond that many stories are told which represent analogies to or embellishments of the (hidden) text. One looks in vain for anything like an exposition of the Scriptures. In the end the preacher has planted a religious thought worthy to think about – but based on the evidence of his nicely told stories. For the listener the convincing source of authority, ultimately, is the persuasively narrating preacher – not the Scriptures that remain hidden in the background. In such an approach is the preacher really 'one without authority'?

of God is the address of God to the hearer who sits before the text open to its becoming Word of God. Most importantly, God's Word is *God's Word* to the reader/ listener, not a word about God gleaned from the documents.[28]

What is emphasized is not so much the God who has spoken once for all (Heb. 1:1–2), but the God who is brought to speech by the interpreting preacher and the creatively receptive listener.

The junior role of the biblical text in Eugene Lowry's homiletical theory

Let us now consider the drama approach to homiletics as developed by Eugene L. Lowry. With his books *The Homiletical Plot* and *The Sermon: Dancing the Edge of Mystery* he has become one of the main exponents of the New Homiletic.[29] His valuable insight is that in an age in which the perception habits of people are moulded from childhood onwards by stories told on television and in films (somewhat lesser also by literature and theatre), preaching has to detect anew the importance of story. He therefore suggests regarding the sermon as a narrative art form, giving it the shape of a plot.

As a plot the sermon has to move 'from *itch* to *scratch*, from issue to answer, from conflict to resolution, from ambiguity to closure born of the gospel',[30] just as a film would do. The sermon plot normally follows a four-step sequence: (1) *Upsetting the equilibrium of the audience*: awake the consciousness of an existing problem in the hearers ('Oops!'). (2) *Analysing the discrepancy*: thicken the plot by deepening the problem, asking for reasons and causes till you have explored the problem to the bottom line ('Ugh!').[31] (3) *Disclosing the clue to resolution*: present the sudden shift ('Aha!' [cause] and 'Whee!' [effect]). (4) *Experiencing the gospel*: anticipate the future, made possible by the good news ('Yeah!').[32] Homiletically of utmost importance for

---

28. Craddock, *As One Without Authority*, p. 92 (his italics).
29. Eugene L. Lowry, *The Homiletical Plot: The Sermon as Narrative Art Form* (Atlanta: John Knox, 1980; expanded ed., Louisville: Westminster John Knox, 2001); *The Sermon: Dancing the Edge of Mystery* (Nashville: Abingdon, 1997).
30. Lowry, *Homiletical Plot*, p. 118 (his italics).
31. This step might take up most of the sermon; ibid., p. 39.
32. Thus in Lowry, *Sermon* (1997), pp. 74–89, and in the new expanded edition of the *Homiletical Plot* (2001), pp. 118–121. In the original 1980 edition of the *Homiletical*

Lowry is that the solution to the problem(s) raised is never given in the early parts of the sermon, but only towards its end. According to Lowry many traditional sermons are guilty of presenting the solution too soon, in the introduction, by announcing the answer in the form of a homiletical idea or a preview of the 'points' that will be unfolded in the course of the sermon,[33] a procedure he sees as detrimental to any dramatic tension-and-suspense pattern.

Unquestionably, the plot format can enhance relevant preaching. It avoids premature, easy answers, makes listeners think, keeps their attention and lets them experience biblical solutions as existentially relevant answers. On the other hand, what does the plot structure do to the biblical text? The danger is that it superimposes a 'one-fit-for-all' scheme on any text. It 'is the homiletical bind being moved from problem to solution, from itch to scratch, that shapes the form of the sermon, not the biblical, historical, doctrinal, or ethical content', Lowry decrees.[34] Only if the text is a biblical narrative or parable should the plot structure not be superimposed on the text, for narrative texts are supposed to have their own plot structure and can be preached accordingly.[35] One consequence of imposing the plot scheme on every text is that there remains little opportunity to expound the text in the sermon. The text serves as a springboard towards the area in which to look for concrete problems bothering people. But then – in parts 1 and 2 of the plot – the 'conflict' and 'complication' are developed inductively in dialogue with real life. When finally the 'sudden shift' is announced and the 'resolution' is offered, the end of the sermon is in sight. The unfolding of the resolution has to be short, since there is 'not much time left in the sermon. We are at least three-fourths through – perhaps with only a few sentences left'.[36] Indeed, 'it is quite possible that the text may not appear in the sermon as preached until quite late . . . In such a case the preacher may want to suspend the text while hunting for something to unlock the way for the sudden shift and good news.'[37]

No wonder that exegesis plays a rather limited role in the preparation of

---

Plot, pp. 53–79, Lowry uses a five-step structure of the plot with step 4 *Experiencing the gospel* ('Whee!') and step 5 *Anticipating the consequences* ('Yeah!').

33. Lowry, *Homiletical Plot*, pp. 21, 35–36, *passim*.

34. Ibid., p. 24.

35. Ibid., pp. 105–115.

36. Lowry, *Sermon* (1997), p. 86.

37. Ibid., p. 112.

such (rhetorically perhaps enthralling) sermons. Lowry suggests three stages for sermon preparation.[38]

1. The first stage starts with 'immersing oneself in the text' – a promising announcement at first sight! But what is meant by this immersion is a repeated creative-meditative reading and pondering of the text with a view to thinking where it might touch life in an area that really itches. In that area the prospective preacher then looks for further meaning, poses critical questions to the text, and asks whether things might not be totally different. He should let his mind loose, allowing himself the freedom of creative associations and even risky thoughts. The text has just been the runway for a take-off into further ideas.

2. In the second stage the prospective preacher returns to the text, creatively identifying important issues, images and incidents there, and pondering how they might find a place in the sermon. Only at the end of this creative play of mind should a certain exegetical control be exercised, in two steps: first, the preacher is now asked to do his own 'exegesis' as 'scholar in residence', that is, as 'the expert in knowing how a particular passage and a particular congregation might relate to each other'.[39] Secondly, he is now allowed to consult external experts by referring to their commentaries. Not earlier, for commentaries – Lowry explains, quoting Craddock – tend to 'intrude themselves between the text and the preacher and begin explaining everything. Such an attitude never lets the homiletical mind loose'![40] Serious exegetical work exploring the intended meaning of the text is minimalized in the preacher's study. Sermon preparation should instead be imagined 'as a kind of improvisational jazz piece'.[41]

3. In the third and final stage the sermon is shaped: the focus – or central 'itch' – is decided upon. Certain elements out of the text are chosen to be touched on in the plot structure of the sermon. An idea has to be developed on what the 'sudden shift' might look like and which aspect of the good news could be utilized for it. The complete plot structure of the sermon will be designed. In the end the preacher will have developed a clear idea of what should happen the following Sunday as a result of his sermon: namely, the redemptory 'scratch' from God's hand bringing relief, understanding, enlightenment and divine encounter to the people. The junior role is assigned to the

---

38. Ibid., pp. 90–114.
39. Ibid., p. 105.
40. Ibid., p. 104.
41. Ibid., p. 105.

biblical text and its exegesis in the creative or dramatic construction of the plotted sermon.

This is surprising, for it is Lowry's explicit intention that in the end 'the Word' will have been proclaimed! What word? According to Lowry, 'proclamation of the Word' is an event that can only be hoped for – while 'preaching' can be designed and done by a human. Preaching is a 'task term'; proclaiming the Word, an 'achievement term'. For Lowry, the Word of God is not something in the biblical text (as the classical dogma of biblical inspiration suggests); nor is it something occurring by the supernatural intervention of God during the faithful and Christocentric exposition of the Bible (as Barthian theology suggests).[42] Rather, it is supposed to occur whenever the plot captures the listeners: when people are touched by the gospel during the act of dramatic preaching. Then the 'Word' has been proclaimed.[43] The plot structure, mounting tension followed by sudden relief among the listeners, is meant to be the instrument of such evocation. Whether such evocation of a divine touch will actually be achieved in the course of the sermon is not at human disposal. The task can only be dramatic preaching.

In Lowry's view, biblical 'literalists' are not very interested in homiletical acts of evocation. Rather, they just repeat what they 'believe God said – and that's the end of the matter. Mystery no more; it is swallowed up by absolute knowledge.'[44] They 'leave the dance at the edge of mystery and . . . plod along the road of truth'.[45] But according to Lowry, divine truth is not something given in the biblical text, ready to be preached. Truth can be experienced personally only in special events of evocation. Propositional divine truth uttered in sermons does not exist.[46] Again, even from this perspective it is no wonder that compared to the dramaturgical and analytical skills demanded of the prospective preacher exegesis plays a minor role in sermon preparation! The 'Word' to be proclaimed is not necessarily what the biblical text intended to say. The 'Word' rather is the result of a creative process instigated by a meeting of the text and the creative reflections of the preacher in his study, where he

---

42. K. Barth, *Homiletik: Wesen und Vorbereitung der Predigt* (Zürich: TVZ, 1966), pp. 58–71; 'Das Wort Gottes als Aufgabe der Theologie', *Christliche Welt* 36 (1922), pp. 858–872; 'Menschenwort und Gotteswort in der christlichen Predigt', *Zwischen den Zeiten* 3 (1925), pp. 119–140.

43. Lowry, *Sermon* (1997), pp. 37–38.

44. Ibid., p. 41.

45. Ibid., p. 42.

46. Ibid., pp. 44–46.

ponders the text in the light of his congregation as well as the congregation in the light of his text, and then performs his findings in a dramatic plot that (hopefully) grasps his hearers and evokes in them the mysterious encounter with the ineffable. The 'Word' then is a revelatory mystical experience, brought about – God willing – by a well-planned and plotted performance.

Perspectives opened by the New Homiletic for biblically based preaching

The communicative horizons opened up by the New Homiletic do not necessarily need to be seen as an alternative to thorough exegesis of the meaning and form of a biblical text in preparation for preaching and its recognizable use as the basis for the message of a sermon. Aspects of the approaches of Jana Childers and Thomas G. Long assure that these elements can indeed be integrated.

The example of Jana Childers
Jana Childers, one of the main proponents of the New Homiletic, has not brought the exegetical and communicative components together in her otherwise most helpful book *Performing the Word*,[47] but she has opened the door for this.

Her main aim is to learn from actors to achieve a lively homiletic. In her view too much contemporary preaching lacks passion and does not sound like the preacher believes what he is preaching. Too often sermon texts are read from the pulpit – making them 'devotional literature' instead of preaching occurring.[48] An Aristotelian lecture style prevails. But preaching should be an event in which a message is expressed authentically. In this regard Childers is convinced that preachers can learn considerably from professional actors.

Actors give their 'voice and body to a message, idea, or experience that needs one'.[49] In order to be able to do this, the preacher – like any serious actor – has to train mainly his voice, but also his body language to convey every possible nuance genuinely. For this the preacher – like actors – has to

---

47. J. Childers, *Performing the Word: Preaching as Theatre* (Nashville: Abingdon, 1998).

48. Ibid., p. 20. Childers's critique is supported by empirical persuasion research: listeners attribute credibility to orators who succeed to demonstrate persuasion while speaking; cf. J. Knape, *Was ist Rhetorik?* (Stuttgart: Reclam, 2000), pp. 74–75.

49. Ibid., p. 49.

observe real life meticulously and to internalize how joy, love, fear, grief, and so on, are expressed naturally. Whenever the Bible speaks of such realities that need a dedicated person to communicate them to the people, a preacher should know how to lend his body to the biblical text in order to express all the aspects it contains factually and emotionally in an authentic way.

According to Childers, only 'a faithful interpreter', who has understood the text and knows how to express its contents with integrity, can bring to life what it wants to say.[50] Unfortunately, Childers does not take the opportunity here to elaborate in any detail on what the contribution of exegesis to the task of the preacher would be at this point. Only in passing does she mention exegesis, and fails to make explicit how an exact understanding of a text, the formulation of its message in view of the listeners, and its lively performance could practically culminate in the sermon. Rather, she recommends experimenting with the text and in this way trying to find a convincing expression of what it might have meant.[51] Exegesis seems not to be the special area of her expertise. On the other hand, she draws helpful insights from what actors do, as containing possible clues for the integration of text and performance. Actors, in fact, spend hours in the pursuit of understanding and internalizing a text that they eventually have to act out. In doing likewise, the preacher (like a good artist) becomes an 'unselfish performer', entering 'into a profound partnership with the text'.[52] Childers even sees the sermon as the incarnational result of the synthesis of text and performer – a synthesis, though, in which the integrity of both is preserved.[53]

Here the preacher or performer seems to be on a par with his text. Subordinating oneself to the text is not recommended by Childers. The preacher's loyalty to the text stops at the point where he would need to sacrifice his identity.[54] That the preacher might have to preach the biblical Word even to himself – against his preconceived attitudes, practices and desires – is not the view of her still mildly emancipatory hermeneutics. Imagine an actress: if she cannot identify with a text, she will probably decline the role. But an actress would not step on stage or before the camera and change the text, say, of Shakespeare, or the script. Perhaps preachers, who could not identify with the message of the biblical text as it stands, should also consider declining

---

50. Ibid., p. 78.
51. Ibid., pp. 79–80.
52. Ibid., p. 95.
53. Ibid., p. 53; cf. pp. 97, 100.
54. Ibid., p. 97.

their pulpit role rather than voicing their disagreement or reinterpreting the text to the point of changing its meaning. On the other hand, preachers could learn from actors to indeed be a fully identified 'unselfish performer', having entered 'into a profound partnership' with their text.

Jana Childers urges preachers to learn from the dedication, discipline and esteem of texts and people observable among actors in the theatre.[55] With a comparable attitude and art, preaching might truly become a lively event for those gathering around the Word. If the Word of God, as the unique word the church has to proclaim, is performed faithfully and passionately, why should it not be able to gain a hearing in an age shaped by television and cinema? Perhaps though it should be emphasized more articulately than Jana Childers does that the church must be clear on *what* to perform, and not just on improving *how* it performs. Mere plotting and acting would not do in competition with the multitude of events on offer in our time.

The example of Thomas G. Long

One of the more balanced proponents of the New Homiletic is Thomas G. Long, though even his hermeneutics shows a certain listener-oriented bias. In the late 1980s he enriched the homiletical scene with his important books *The Witness of Preaching* and *Preaching and the Literary Forms of the Bible*.[56]

Long envisions the preacher as a witness to the gospel:

> Bearing witness to the gospel means engaging in serious and responsible biblical preaching. Preaching is biblical whenever the preacher allows a text from the Bible to serve as the leading force in shaping the content and purpose of the sermon . . . Biblical preaching is the *normative* form of Christian preaching.[57]

Even though sermons may vary, at times taking either a more pastoral or a more prophetic tone, Long insists that we 'constantly guard against our inevitable tendency to silence the full witness of Scripture'.[58] For him it is not the communication habits of our society that are the benchmark for the pulpit, but the biblical contents. He is convinced that

---

55. Ibid., pp. 99–120.
56. Thomas G. Long, *The Witness of Preaching*, 2nd ed. (Louisville: Westminster John Knox, 2005); *Preaching and the Literary Forms of the Bible* (Philadelphia: Fortress, 1989).
57. Long, *Witness*, p. 52 (his italics); cf. p. 67.
58. Ibid., p. 244.

the shallowness of communication in our time generates a hunger for an urgent and important word. If our sermons begin to imitate the flashy, superficial style of the media, we relinquish the great opportunity we have been given to speak that word.[59]

In order to accomplish this goal Long instructs the preacher first to get involved in detailed 'exegesis for preaching'.[60] In the end the preacher should be able to state 'what the text says' (its message) as well as 'what the text does' (its intention).[61] He should also heed how the text says what it says, by paying attention to the literary forms of biblical texts.[62]

The problem is that Long follows a special 'exegetical method for preaching', building on listener-oriented hermeneutics. To be sure, on the one hand he opposes an allegedly 'pastoral' approach that takes its reference point from the existing human condition, by turning to the Bible only to draw affirmation from there. Instead, preaching means

to tell the story of the Bible so clearly that it calls into question and ultimately redefines what we think we know of reality and what we call wisdom in the first place. The Bible becomes the key to unlock the true nature of life, not vice versa.[63]

On the other hand, the 'preacher goes to the biblical text *from* the congregation, *on behalf* of the congregation, and, in important ways, *with* the congregation'.[64] This results in a different type of 'exegesis' than that of a biblical scholar or

---

59. Ibid., p. 239.

60. See his outline of this, ibid., p. 70; explicated, pp. 69–98.

61. Ibid., pp. 106–108. This double aspect is peculiar not only to the New Homiletic, but also to newer forms of expository preaching; e.g. Charles B. Bugg, 'Back to the Bible: Toward a New Description of Expository Preaching', *RevExp* 90 (1993), p. 416; and H. Stadelmann, *Evangelikale Predigtlehre*, 2nd ed. (Witten: R. Brockhaus, 2008), pp. 65–77, 153–154.

62. Long, *Literary Forms*, pp. 41–126. Here Long considers in detail the use of psalms, proverbs, narratives, parables and epistles in sermons, always asking the four questions 'What is the genre of the text?', 'What is the rhetorical function of this genre?', 'What literary devices does this genre use to achieve its rhetorical effect?' and 'How may the sermon, in a new setting, say and do what the text says and does in its setting?'

63. Long, *Witness*, p. 36.

64. Ibid., p. 101 (his italics).

commentaries.[65] The latter are there for critical historical analysis, gathering 'data *about* the Bible'; while 'exegesis for preaching' in the first place has to do with attentive listening, hearing 'the living word that comes *through* the Bible'.[66] According to Long, the preacher approaching his text with his congregation in mind first has to listen attentively to the text[67] – confronting it with any critical questions, viewing it from all possible imagined perspectives (of the different people involved in the story: from the angle of men, women, children, rich, poor, feminists, homosexuals, unchurched, Buddhists, etc.), thinking it through with the different members of the congregation in mind – in order 'to hear in that text a specific word for us', whoever this 'us' might happen to be.[68] Steps of historical, literary and theological analysis, as well as a look into commentaries are done only afterwards, to check finally whether the interpretation can be maintained for today.[69]

Basic to this approach is one conviction: 'A biblical text can potentially yield many meanings, and the next time we go to the same biblical text we may well hear a very different claim than we heard this time.'[70] Long just wants to grasp 'a portion of the text's impact for no sermon can exhaust the possibilities for meaning present in a biblical text'.[71] In this postmodern approach 'exegesis' becomes something rather subjective. Why not instead differentiate between the originally or historically intended 'meaning' of a text – to be detected by sound exegesis – and the multifaceted 'significances'

---

65. Ibid., pp. 69, 84, 105–106.

66. Ibid., p. 88 (his italics).

67. Ibid., pp. 81–88.

68. Ibid., p. 69. Similarly, Long, *Literary Forms*, p. 34: 'Preaching does not involve determining what the text *used* to mean . . . Preaching involves a contemporary interpreter closely attending to a text, discerning the claim that text makes upon the current life of the community of faith, and announcing that discovery in the sermon' (his italics).

69. Long, *Witness*, pp. 84, 88–96.

70. Ibid., p. 100. According to Long, 'meaning erupts in the interaction between text and interpreter' (*Literary Forms*, p. 34). In this hermeneutic – quite common today – the *intentio operis* (the meaning rendered possible by the work) is set free from the *intentio auctoris* (the meaning intended by the author). To 'put something in writing is to set it free from the particular set of circumstances that were present at the time of its writing and to invite other readers in other circumstances to find new meaning there' (*Literary Forms*, p. 35).

71. Long, *Literary Forms*, p. 33.

and applications of that text for different people in different places and times, thereby strictly making the former the criterion for the legitimacy of the latter?[72]

For Long the process of subjective interpretation does not end here. It is not only the preacher-exegete who changes meaning, by detecting new interpretations of a text, but the hearers may also change the meaning of what they hear when listening to the sermon:

> In short, the hearer is a co-creator of the sermon. Preachers may be passing out eggs, but hearers are making omelettes, and a sermon preached to seventy-five people is actually transformed by them into seventy-five more or less related sermons.[73]

Certainly, Long's emphasis on preaching biblically and his claim to prepare for sermons exegetically are to be welcomed. His emphatic consideration of the listeners is indispensable too. But it would be a decisive step forward if the subjective and multifaceted interpretations of preachers and listeners were not too readily called the 'Word of the Lord'. A better alternative is to have the witness of preaching inalienably linked to the faithful testimony of what biblical texts actually intended to say – speaking the message in such a way that its claim can be heard in diverse situations today as the Word from God.

© Helge Stadelmann, 2013

---

72. See n. 5 above (Hirsch, *Validity in Interpretation*).
73. Long, *Witness*, p. 170.

17. PREACHING THE GOSPEL FROM THE GOSPELS

Paul Weston

Introduction

One of my formative memories as a student is of listening to a series of 'expositions' on the latter chapters of Luke's Gospel by a young and upcoming New Testament scholar called Tom Wright. They opened my mind in a fresh way to the potential and power of 'gospel' exposition: not just as a teaching vehicle for believers, but as a set of stories that opened up the meaning of life for non-believers as well. I began to realize that my student experience of preaching hitherto had been rather narrowly focused. 'Teaching' was the exposition of the text of Scripture for believers; whereas 'evangelistic' preaching was intended for non-believers; and nearly always turned out to be a 'thematic' treatment of the 'gospel'. This tended to draw together different texts from Scripture in support of a three- or four-point 'summary' of the good news (filled out with stories and illustrations of course), which usually began theologically with God as Creator, moved on to describe our rebellion as sinners from his purposes, and culminated in the good news of the cross and the offer of forgiveness.

Although the styles of evangelistic preaching this approach produces continue to be blessed, in my own evangelistic ministry I have come to favour a more 'narratival' approach; starting from particular gospel stories and moving 'out' from them to the wider story, rather than starting with a big doctrinal framework and working 'in'. I have come to believe that the most effective form of evangelistic preaching is one that invites listeners to enter into the imaginative framework of the gospel stories themselves: enabling the words of Jesus to interpret themselves within the framework of each story, and – in the process – inviting listeners into a new way of seeing the world.

Rediscovering the gospel narratives as *narratives of the gospel*

This approach seems to make best sense of the gospel narratives as we have them, and indicates that an integral part of their purpose is not just to disciple believers but to 'evangelize' non-believers.[1] They are not simply stories that help to 'illustrate' the gospel found later in the more 'doctrinal' parts of the New Testament. No, these stories are *themselves* the substance of good news about Jesus that transforms.[2]

The writer of the fourth Gospel is the most articulate in this respect, writing that his collection of Jesus' stories is written down 'so that you may come to believe that Jesus is the Messiah, the Son of God, and that through believing you may have life in his name' (20:31).[3] This climactic statement occurs directly after the post-resurrection incident in the upper room and

---

1. Precise distinctions between the activities of 'teaching' and 'evangelizing' are difficult to establish from the NT evidence. Jesus is frequently described as 'teaching' (*didaskein*) and 'evangelizing' (*evangelizein* or *keryssein*) in his proclamation of the kingdom without enough detail to differentiate these activities exactly (e.g. Matt. 4:23; 9:35; Luke 20:1). In relation to Matthew's usage see the discussion in U. Luz, *Matthew 1–7: A Commentary*, Hermeneia (Minneapolis: Fortress, 2007), pp. 168–169. The same applies to Luke's portrayal of Paul (Acts 5:42; 28:31). The gospel material assumes an evangelistic and teaching aspect all the way through. This is supported by the multilayered portrayal of the disciples' 'conversion'; see John Drane, *Faith in a Changing Culture: Creating Churches for the Next Century* (London: Marshall Pickering, 1997), pp. 91–104.

2. See the opening to Mark's Gospel: 'The beginning of the good news of Jesus Christ, the Son of God' (1:1).

3. For a wider discussion of this verse, and whether it refers to an initial or ongoing faith, see D. A. Carson, *The Gospel According to John*, PNTC (Leicester: Inter-Varsity Press, 1991), pp. 87–95, who argues that it is primarily evangelistic. Unless stated otherwise, all Bible quotations in this chapter are from the NRSV.

centres on 'doubting Thomas' (20:24–29). Thomas's presumption (a very 'modern' one) is that '[u]nless I see the mark of the nails in his hands, and put my finger in the mark of the nails and my hand in his side, I will not believe' (v. 25).

When Jesus appears a week later and Thomas is granted divine insight that Jesus is indeed 'Lord and God' (v. 28), Jesus responds with a *question*, 'Have you believed because you have seen me?, and then a *statement*, 'Blessed are those who have *not* seen and yet have come to believe' (v. 29). The question points up the potential problem for the disciples in their missionary task, that faith must surely somehow be related to actually seeing Jesus *in the flesh*. But the statement transcends this limitation, and opens up the possibility of a saving faith now no longer dependent upon seeing him in person. In the summary verse that follows (v. 31) John says, in effect, that his intention in writing the Gospel is precisely to make this new kind of 'seeing' possible for future generations. For in the retelling of his gospel stories Jesus will continue to be both seen and heard, and may be *met* in faith and trust, even though Jesus himself has physically departed. In theological terms, therefore, not only do these stories proclaim Jesus 'descriptively', but – more importantly – they 'reimage' him in a way that makes him truly 'present' across the ages, enabling hearers and readers in future generations both to see Jesus and to respond to him.

How then do the gospel stories 'preach' the good news? And how do they enable our contemporaries to meet Jesus today?

They tell the story of Jesus

At one level, this is of course a rather obvious point, but it is surprising how often 'themes' are lifted from the Gospels and preached on without much reference to the story of Jesus, as if it is the theme that is more important than the person around whom they gain their meaning. Many of the stories in the Gospels are stories told *by* Jesus of course, but they function as part of the more basic story told by the Evangelists *about* Jesus. As C. F. D. Moule put it many years ago, 'the Synoptic Gospels represent primarily the recognition that a vital element in evangelism is the plain story of what happened in the ministry of Jesus'.[4] Each of the Evangelists does this in particular ways, highlighting the aspects of Jesus' identity and mission that were evidently significant for their intended audiences, but this should not overshadow the

---

4. C. F. D. Moule, *The Phenomenon of the New Testament: An Inquiry into the Implications of Certain Features of the New Testament* (London: SCM, 1967), p. 113.

basic underlying storyline. They are *about* Jesus, and therefore preaching from the Gospels, as Don Carson puts it, 'is above all an exercise in the exposition and application of Christology'.[5]

In an age in which biblical literacy continues to be on the wane, and there is an almost complete ignorance of Jesus' words and deeds amongst unbelievers, my experience is that many are often surprised and amazed that Jesus actually said or did the things recorded of him. Now – as then – these stories bring us face to face with Jesus, and our preaching must reflect this in its emphasis and focus. We are called to preach Jesus.

They tell the story of Jesus in story forms

In preaching Jesus, we also need to pay close attention to the persuasive power of the story forms by which the Jesus story is communicated. Robert Gundry alludes to this when he describes the 'evangelistic mode' of Mark's Gospel as 'apologetic but narratival'.[6] As noted above, some preachers tend to ignore the narrative structure of the Gospels by using the stories in merely illustrative ways in the service of more 'structured' or 'propositional' sermon forms. But whereas arguments and propositions tend usually to be more cerebral – and even confrontational – activities, stories take their hearers on a journey, enabling them to associate with, differ from or simply listen in to the different 'actors' in the narrative. And of course the gospel stories are crafted to enable hearers to do this supremely in relation to Jesus himself. The reason for their effectiveness is that they enable not just 'descriptive' appreciation but 'participative' encounter. Put more generally, they enable us to enter for a while into another world; to see things from new and different perspectives; to be given time to weigh the merits of this new way of seeing – sometimes even by a momentary but voluntary suspension of disbelief. The gospel stories say in effect, 'Why not try seeing things *this* way.'[7] And good preaching will help hearers to do this.

Perhaps it is Walter Brueggemann who has done most to help us to see the narratives of the Bible as an invitation to reimagine life in this alternative frame of reference. He argues that biblical exposition cannot be

---

5. Carson, *John*, p. 102.

6. R. H. Gundry, *Mark: A Commentary on His Apology for the Cross* (Grand Rapids: Eerdmans, 1993), p. 1050.

7. See the discussion of 'story' in N. T. Wright, *The New Testament and the People of God: Christian Origins and the Question of God* (London: SPCK, 1992), pp. 69–80 (his italics).

a 'scientific enterprise designed to recover the past as historical criticism has attempted' but is, rather, an 'artistic preoccupation that is designed to generate alternative futures'.[8] The aim of its proclamation is therefore 'an altered perception of world, neighbor, and self, and an authorization to live differently in that world'.[9] Though Brueggemann's main focus is the Old Testament, one could make the same point about the gospel stories. They are designed to reorient perceptions in the light of who Jesus is revealed to be.

They paint pictures of the kingdom

I remember in my teenage years being intrigued by the question 'What did the hearers described in the Gospels understand Jesus' message to be about?' After all, there are comparatively few explicit references to the cross or resurrection in the early ministry of Jesus, and yet right from the outset of his ministry he called people to respond fully to the presence of the kingdom. 'The time is fulfilled, and the kingdom of God has come near'; he says (Mark 1:15), 'repent, and believe in the good news'. So what is the good news in these stories?

The answer to this must revolve around the Evangelists' overwhelming portrayal of Jesus as 'King' and 'Lord'. They answer the question 'Who is truly King in God's world?' They show him at work in his world, overthrowing would-be pretenders to this title, restoring the ruptured harmony of God's creation, inviting reconciliation between Creator and creature through faith and repentance. But the kingdom – though visibly present in and around Jesus – is yet to arrive in all its fullness. The collected miracle stories, exorcisms and healing miracles therefore help to demonstrate by word and action what this kingdom is about, but they also *anticipate* its fuller life. They act rather like 'cinema trailers', showing us enough about the soon-to-be-released blockbuster to make us want to go and see it. So the actions, as well as the words of Jesus (especially in the parables), dangle possibilities in front of the hearer. And the Evangelists themselves seem content not to complete the picture in every detail, or to tie up all the loose ends in the argument, but rather to direct our attention to Jesus as the focus of all that they point forward to in faith and expectation.

---

8. W. Brueggemann, *Redescribing Reality: What We Do When We Read the Bible* (London: SCM, 2009), p. xx.

9. W. Brueggemann, *Biblical Perspectives on Evangelism: Living in a Three-Storied Universe* (Nashville: Abingdon, 1993), p. 129.

Gospel narratives and preaching skills

What then are the skills we need as preachers if we are to do justice to these gospel texts?

Learn to tell stories well

If our sermons are to reflect the fact that the Gospels evangelize by telling stories, then preachers more at home with an introduction, three points and a conclusion will need to work at the *art* of storytelling. These are not necessarily new skills, but ones that may need to be rediscovered, nourished and developed. Learning to paint a picture with an economy of words, or to imagine the unspoken thoughts going on in a dialogue, or to evoke the likely feelings and reactions of onlookers in a scene, involves different, though complementary, skills to the more formal disciplines of word study and exegesis.

These skills will help us not just to craft more engaging 'narratival' sermons, but will serve to enable a greater identification between the original story audiences and their contemporary counterparts. But we do not start from scratch, for human beings have always been 'narratival beings'. As Alasdair MacIntyre puts it, 'we dream in narrative, daydream in narrative, remember, anticipate, hope, despair, believe, doubt, plan, revise, criticise, construct, gossip, learn, hate and love by narrative'.[10] But more than this, we habitually construe the 'meaning' of our lives in terms of the narratives we inhabit. As the American sociologist Christian Smith writes, 'People ... most fundamentally understand what reality is, who they are, and how they ought to live by locating themselves within the larger narratives that they hear and tell, which constitute what is real and significant for them.'[11]

By paying attention therefore both to the narrative world of the gospel stories, and our contemporary 'stories', the preacher's task is one of invitation; as Trevor Hart puts it,

> to step into the [biblical] narrative and consider the world from within it, to see whether it does not make more sense than other alternative stories told about it. This is ... essentially an appeal to the imagination, an invitation to construe the

---

10. Alasdair MacIntyre, *After Virtue: A Study in Moral Theology*, 2nd ed. (London: Duckworth, 1985), p. 211, quoting words of Barbara Hardy.

11. Christian Smith, *Moral, Believing Animals: Human Personhood and Culture* (New York: Oxford University Press, 2003), p. 119.

world differently, to entertain the possibility that things are other than we have
hitherto supposed.[12]

To preach the gospel stories demands not just rhetorical skills, therefore,
but a wider cultivation of the arts of imaginative listening and telling. But it is
worth the effort, for story forms connect deeply with universal human emotions and aspirations. They 'travel'.

Invite listeners on a 'journey'

Good preaching on the gospel stories will frequently allow their structure
and flow to dictate the resulting 'form' and 'feel' of the sermon. They will
not always anticipate the denouement ahead of time, but allow for a sense
of 'journeying'. This will often call for exploratory forms of communication, such as thinking aloud alongside people, rather than preaching *to* them.
For example, the recorded conversations between Jesus and the 'rich young
ruler' in Mark 10 or the 'woman at the well' in John 4 are presented in the
form of interrogative 'journeys', with each stage of the conversation leading
either towards some form of descriptive statement as in Mark 10:22, where
we are told that the rich man 'was shocked and went away grieving, for he
had many possessions', or to a verbal conclusion as in John 4:26, where
Jesus says to her, 'I, the one speaking to you – I am he' (NIV). Of course
we know the outcome ahead of time, and we may therefore be tempted to
preach this as the main point of the sermon – with the story as illustration
– but the narratives themselves are crafted in a way that invites the hearer
to think alongside each participant, with the conclusion as yet unsettled.
It is left 'open', inviting both dialogue and our own participation in the
outcome.

So an effective sermon on either of these passages might develop the
unfolding conversational interplay between Jesus and his original hearers,
and intersperse this with its implications for contemporary hearers. My own
experience is that this requires the skill of 'conversational' preaching, taking
hearers with me into the story, and accompanying them through it. I try to
look with them at the questions the story raises, explore the implications of
what is being done and said, and help them to associate with the characters in
the narrative. And by doing so, of course, I want most of all to help them to
respond appropriately to the person of Jesus.

---

12. Trevor Hart, *Faith Thinking: The Dynamics of Christian Theology* (London: SPCK,
    1995), p. 153.

Create connections

This 'conversational' preaching requires what John Stott described as 'double-listening': that ability to identify the points of intersection between the story being narrated in the Gospels and the issues that face us in the contemporary world. This is intrinsic to the apologetic enterprise, no matter what kind of preaching we are engaged in, but to think about it from a narratival point of view highlights particular features.

A first point of contact between the gospel stories and our story is 'topical'. The Gospels deal consistently with issues, questions, dilemmas and emotions consistent with our own. Moreover, these concerns are often highlighted because they are the starting point for many of the stories themselves.[13] They may be 'aspirational' ('[W]hat must I do to inherit eternal life?', Mark 10:17), 'interpersonal' ('[W]ho is my neighbour?', Luke 10:29) or 'material' ('Teacher, tell my brother to divide the family inheritance with me,' Luke 12:13). But they are the 'stuff' of life in every age, and allow the preacher to open up the promise and the challenge of the good news. Preachers need to work hard at identifying what these are, and to describe as part of the sermon *how* these biblical themes 'connect' with contemporary questions and aspirations, so that the gospel stories can go on being places of engagement and encounter.

A second point of contact is at the level of our 'value commitments'. One of the ways in which we associate with a character in a story is by asking questions such as 'What would *I* have done in those circumstances?' or 'What do *I* think about that?' We usually do this subconsciously, but our responses to these instincts are nonetheless profound. The questions the gospel narratives raise for us function precisely at this kind of level. Do my 'value commitments' – subconscious or otherwise – bear scrutiny in the light of *this* story?

A final point of contact is the very humanity of Jesus. Fyodor Dostoevsky wrote, for example, 'I believe there is no one lovelier, deeper, more sympathetic and more perfect than Jesus.' It is of course a fundamental theological truth that God became human in the person of Jesus, and that the incarnation is God's ultimate 'point of contact'. But this should inspire us to preach the life of Jesus as one who shows us what real humanity looks like, the 'blueprint' for human living, human life as it was intended to be. Yet he also points us beyond ourselves. There is often a powerful sense of identification

---

13. As Walter Hollenweger put it, 'the starting point of Jesus' evangelism is mostly . . . a question, or the concrete situation of the people around him. . . . It starts from a situation' (*Evangelism Today: Good News or Bone of Contention?* [Belfast: Christian Journals, 1976], pp. 80, 82).

in preaching about Jesus, but a yearning too. There is something 'other' about him. As the author of Hebrews says, though he was one who 'in every respect has been tested as we are', yet he was 'without sin' (Heb. 4:15). The wonder of preaching Jesus is that it is through his intimate identification with our humanity that he transcends it as the divine image, bringing transformation and making ultimate sense of it through forgiveness, reconciliation and recreation.

Gospel narratives and sermon strategies

What then of sermon construction? How does one go about preparing a sermon from the Gospels?

What I have discussed so far suggests that it involves the bringing together of a number of elements, both imaginative and exegetical. As with other preaching genres, there is no fixed 'form', but there are a number of guidelines to consider.

Ask the 'plot' questions

One way of approaching these stories is to think of them as involving three 'plots'. First, there is the *biographical* plot, which sets the individual narrative in the larger chronological storyline of Jesus' life and ministry. Locating individual stories within this larger framework is often significant in discovering their deeper meanings.[14] Secondly, there is the *narrative* plot of the story form itself. One of the enduring insights of the older 'form' critics was that the stories of the Gospels were handed down to us by a process that had already shaped and moulded them for the purposes of communication. This insight can encourage the preacher by providing an already-crafted structure, which holds together the essential elements of the story. These will include an 'introduction' (a question/situation/setting), a 'development' (which may create a tension or raise further questions) and a conclusion (often framed in the words of Jesus himself, or significant words *about* him), which may either resolve the tension and invite a response, or else resolve the tension whilst raising further questions.[15] Finally, there is the *theological* plot of the gospel

---

14. Note e.g. the central 'hinge' in Mark's Gospel at 8:27–29 (Peter's confession at Caesarea Philippi), which begins to establish what *kind* of Messiah Jesus will be, and therefore introduces the paradigm for what it will mean to follow him (esp. in 8:31 – 10:45).

15. As an example of the latter see the range of questions raised at the end of the storm-stilling episode in Mark 4: two on the lips of Jesus ('Why are you afraid?

writer. By this, I refer to the aims and purposes of the gospel writer in writing and arranging the material in the way he has, in order to bring out the significance of the stories for life and faith.

An example of these three elements in operation is Matthew's portrayal of the resurrection (27:57 – 28:20). Its place in the *biographical* plot is climactic, both bringing Matthew's story to a close, whilst at the same time heralding something dramatically new in the life of Jesus and the community of faith. The account is composed of five individual stories, each with its own *narrative* plot (Matt. 27:57–61, 62–66; 28:1–10, 11–15, 16–20). Each of these could be considered separately, but by looking at their arrangement within the wider framework of the resurrection story as a whole, we may discern something of Matthew's *theological* plot, and therefore his purposes in writing.

For example, the 'great commission' (28:16–20; which is usually preached without regard to its context) is actually closely related to the preceding section (vv. 11–15) and contrasts two kinds of 'preaching': the preaching of the guards who, having gone to the highest authority in the land are told what to say on the basis of *falsehood*, and the preaching of the disciples who, having been commissioned by the highest authority in the universe, are told what to say on the basis of the *truth*.

The resurrection itself (28:1–10) is the centrepiece of the whole, with the other stories 'fanning' out from either side of it.[16] These surrounding stories present in effect an alternating point and counterpoint about 'friends' and 'enemies' of the truth, and serve to emphasize the theological centrality of the resurrection itself, and the division it causes:

Joseph as 'friend' (27:57–61)
   Guards as 'enemies' (27:62–66)
      RESURRECTION (28:1–10)
   Guards as 'enemies' (28:11–15)
Disciples as 'friends' (28:16–20)[17]

Have you still no faith?', v. 40), and one from the disciples ('Who then is this, that even the wind and the sea obey him?', v. 41). In setting the story in this framework, with its concluding questions, Mark's aim in telling it is already signalled.

16. See the parallel discussion in R. T. France, *Matthew*, TNTC (Leicester: Inter-Varsity Press, 1985), pp. 402–406.

17. Matthew's selection of these materials lends support to this pattern. Whatever the connection between the other elements and the existing traditions, both 27:62–66 and 28:11–15 are peculiar to Matthew.

This, in turn, is part of Matthew's overall *theological* plot, worked out in the relationship between the fledgling messianic community and those arrayed in opposition to it.

How might we preach this? There are of course many ways of doing so, but the theme of the resurrection triumph of the gospel of Jesus in spite of its opponents is powerful evangelistically as well as pastorally. In the original context it is developed in relation to the 'powers' allied against it (note the implied humour in 28:2: emphatic in response to the nervy emphasis on 'securing' the tomb in 27:64–66). In contemporary terms the equivalent 'powers' that stand against the gospel and the faith we place in them (not least for equivalent forms of misplaced 'security') are legion, and could be developed in a number of ways at personal, corporate and political levels.

Ask how Jesus is pictured, and what response is called for
As noted earlier, it is appropriate and useful to note how the gospel stories reveal different aspects of Jesus' 'kingship' or 'lordship'. Luke, for example, clearly signals that the exorcism stories demonstrate the fact that the kingdom has now arrived ('if it is by the finger of God that I cast out the demons, then the kingdom of God has come to you', Luke 11:20). Or again, the nature miracles reflect the renewing of the original work of creation, putting it back in harmony with its creator.[18] And of course, both these strands of material anticipate and herald the ultimate 'power encounter', which will find its climax at the crucifixion (e.g. Mark 3:27 in the context of vv. 21–29).[19]

In the light of this, two points arise. First, it immediately raises the question of whether one should always preach explicitly about the cross in gospel sermons. On the one hand, the answer is 'not necessarily'. Paul's sermon at Athens, for example, does not include any reference to the crucifixion of Jesus, or the benefits of his death, and yet Luke portrays it as an evangelistic success. For amongst the responses recorded, some named individuals 'became believers' and joined up with Paul (Acts 17:34). On the other hand, one can say that the 'logic' of the cross (and resurrection too) can be said to underpin the entire gospel narrative (and of course takes up a disproportionate amount of space in the biographical 'plot').[20] Whether one refers to it or

---

18. See Mark 7:37, with its echo of Gen. 1:31 (see R. A. Guelich, *Mark 1 – 8:26*, WBC [Dallas: Word, 1997], p. 397).

19. See also e.g. John 12:31–32.

20. See e.g. Jesus' words in Luke 24:25–27 and 45–47 about the scriptural 'logic' of the passion. See also the discussion in Kenneth E. Bailey, *Poet and Peasant: A*

not is therefore once more dependent on context. For example, in a *series* of sermons from the Gospels, one would be less inclined to do so if the context does not suggest it than one would in a one-off sermon to which outsiders had been invited.

Secondly, and in more general terms, it is always helpful to ask how the Evangelist describes responses to the revelation of Jesus in a particular story, and what he intends us to learn from them. Are they positive or negative? Are they about faith or unbelief (and why)? Sometimes the intended outcome is stated as part of the story itself, and provides its 'punchline' (e.g. Mark 4:40; Luke 10:37; 15:6, 9, 32). At other times, it is suggested by the wider context, or personified by the actions of one of the characters (e.g. Mark 10:22; Luke 17:15–19). Either way, sermon preparation is helped when one recognizes the response expected by the Evangelist to the given revelation of Jesus.

To appeal or not to appeal: should we invite people to respond to gospel preaching?

It will be clear from the chapter so far that the gospel writers wrote their stories both to disciple believers as well as to draw outsiders to initial steps of faith in Jesus. Our own preaching of these stories should therefore envisage the same sorts of outcomes. But what else may we learn from the Gospels about gospel 'invitations'?

In the first place, it is clear that the gospel of the kingdom, which Jesus proclaims and embodies, is portrayed by the Evangelists as the announcement of a fact that demands a decisive response (Mark 1:15, 'the kingdom of God has come near; repent, and believe in the good news'). Everything has changed in the light of Jesus' coming, and to share in the proclamation of this fact implies that we should not be asking 'whether' to look for a response, but 'how' we should do so.

Secondly, it is also clear that the invitation to enter the kingdom is a rich combination of grace and freedom. Jesus himself appears to have held together the complementary truths about God's sovereignty and human responsibility without any sense of contradiction. This is beautifully demonstrated in Matthew 11 where, after Jesus has chastened the towns of Chorazin,

Literary Cultural Approach to the Parables in Luke (Grand Rapids: Eerdmans, 1976), pp. 188–190, about the atonement background to the parables in Luke 15.

Bethsaida and Capernaum for their lack of faith (vv. 20–23), he juxtaposes two wonderful statements. First, he says that 'All things have been handed over to me by my Father; and no one knows the Son except the Father, and no one knows the Father except the Son and anyone to whom the Son chooses to reveal him' (v. 27). It is only by the grace of God in Christ that we can respond to the good news. But then, in the very next verses, he issues an invitation: 'Come to me, all you that are weary and are carrying heavy burdens, and I will give you rest. Take my yoke upon you, and learn from me; for I am gentle and humble in heart, and you will find rest for your souls' (vv. 28–29). On the one hand, there is a committed conviction about the sovereignty of God in revealing his character to whomever he chooses: on the other (and seemingly based upon this conviction), an open invitation to all who sense their need.

Practically

Talk of 'response' in the context of gospel preaching immediately conjures up questions about 'evangelistic' appeals, and there are times, of course, when such calls to commitment are entirely appropriate. My own practice on these occasions – in line with the thrust of this chapter – has been to set them in a wider context. Our preaching should encourage our hearers (at whatever stage they are) to ask, 'Now that I know this about God, how should I be thinking and behaving?' I would nearly always include a prayer of commitment for those responding to Jesus for the first time, but I would also want to invite response at different levels for others too, followers as well as enquirers. However we do this, the following observations may be helpful.

First, many 'evangelistic' appeals tend to come across as separate 'sermons' (often based loosely on John 3:16!), which are tacked on to the end of a thematic talk, or one based on another gospel story entirely, but without any intrinsic connection to this material. By contrast, the gospel narratives make their appeal as a direct result of their content. Jesus' words to the lawyer following the 'good Samaritan' story is to '[g]o and do likewise' (Luke 10:37); or to the woman caught in adultery, 'Neither do I condemn you. Go your way, and from now on do not sin again' (John 8:11). In other words, the content of the 'appeal' is precisely a call to respond to the word of the gospel that has just been heard. So if a 'formal' prayer of response is used, make sure it reflects the concerns at the heart of the sermon, and make its words those of response to the appeal in the story.

Secondly, we tend to assume in the West that right thinking precedes right action, and that therefore repentance of mind will always precede obedience in action. But the gospel stories represent a more holistic view of discipleship in which this division is not nearly as clear-cut. In fact, some significant gospel stories demonstrate that right acting is the primary indicator of saving faith.[21] Sometimes therefore the 'appeal' of the gospel stories is a call to right action rather than simply a change of mind, though of course the two are integrally connected. Jesus' central appeal to 'repent and believe the good news' is not only communicated with rich variety, but is made concrete in a variety of ways too.

Conclusion

Leighton Ford wrote that gospel preaching is not 'theorizing about God', but 'the telling of a story – the old, old story of Jesus and His love'.[22] I hope that this chapter has either whetted or re-energized your appetite to preach the gospel stories. In preaching Jesus, may we and those who listen be enabled in the power of the Spirit both to encounter him and to respond to his call.

© Paul Weston, 2013

---

21. E.g. Zacchaeus in Luke 19:8; or see John 17:7, where Jesus tells the religious authorities that they will know his identity once they have started 'doing the will of my Father in heaven'.
22. Leighton Ford, *The Christian Persuader* (London: Hodder & Stoughton, 1967), p. 94.

INDEX OF SCRIPTURE REFERENCES